PRACTICING
shariah
Law

PRACTICING
Shariah
Law

Seven Strategies for Achieving Justice
in Shariah Courts

Hauwa Ibrahim

Defending Liberty
Pursuing Justice

Cover design by Bobbie Sanchez/ABA Publishing.

Page layout by Quadrum Solutions.

The materials contained herein represent the opinions of the authors and editors and should not be construed to be the views or opinions of the law firms or companies with whom such persons are in partnership with, associated with, or employed by, nor of the American Bar Association or the Center for Human Rights unless adopted pursuant to the bylaws of the Association.

Nothing contained in this book is to be considered as the rendering of legal advice, either generally or in connection with any specific issue or case; nor do these materials purport to explain or interpret any specific bond or policy, or any provisions thereof, issued by any particular franchise company, or to render franchise or other professional advice. Readers are responsible for obtaining advice from their own lawyers or other professionals. This book and any forms and agreements herein are intended for educational and informational purposes only.

Printed in the United States of America.

16 15 14 13 12 5 4 3 2 1

Library of Congress Cataloging-in-Publication Data

Ibrahim, Hauwa.

Practicing Shariah law / Hauwa Ibrahim.

p. cm.

ISBN 978-1-61438-675-9

1. Islamic courts—Nigeria, Northern. 2. Women (Islamic law)—Nigeria, Northern. 3. Criminal justice, Administration of (Islamic law)—Nigeria, Northern. 4. Islamic courts. I. Title.

KTA3474.I27 2012

340.5'9096695—dc23

2012028881

Discounts are available for books ordered in bulk. Special consideration is given to state bars, CLE programs, and other bar-related organizations. Inquire at Book Publishing, ABA Publishing, American Bar Association, 321 N. Clark Street, Chicago, Illinois 60654-7598.

Dedication

To Marie-Pierre Poulain, for believing in me.

To Eric Lankton, for taking the first steps with me.

To José Ramón Sánchez, for pushing the process to the finish line.

To Nico (Abubakar) and Silvio (Mahmoud)
Dionisotti, for enduring an absentee mother.

اَللّٰهُ لَآ إِلٰهَ إِلَّا هُوَ ٱلْحَىُّ ٱلْقَيُّومُ لَا تَأْخُذُهُ سِنَةٌ وَلَا نَوْمٌ لَهُۥ مَا فِى ٱلسَّمٰوٰتِ وَمَا فِى ٱلْأَرْضِ مَن ذَا ٱلَّذِى يَشْفَعُ عِندَهُۥٓ إِلَّا بِإِذْنِهِۦ يَعْلَمُ مَا بَيْنَ أَيْدِيهِمْ وَمَا خَلْفَهُمْ وَلَا يُحِيطُونَ بِشَىْءٍ مِّنْ عِلْمِهِۦٓ إِلَّا بِمَا شَآءَ وَسِعَ كُرْسِيُّهُ ٱلسَّمٰوٰتِ وَٱلْأَرْضَ وَلَا يَـُٔودُهُۥ حِفْظُهُمَا وَهُوَ ٱلْعَلِىُّ ٱلْعَظِيمُ ﴿٢٥٥﴾

Allah—there is no deity except Him, the Ever-Living, the Sustainer of [all] existence. Neither drowsiness overtakes Him nor sleep. To Him belongs whatever is in the heavens and whatever is on the earth. Who is it that can intercede with Him except by His permission? He knows what is [presently] before them and what will be after them, and they encompass not a thing of His knowledge except for what He wills. His Kursi extends over the heavens and the earth, and their preservation tires Him not. And He is the Most High, the Most Great.

—Qur'an 2:255

Table of Contents

About the Author

HAUWA IBRAHIM IS ENTERING her fifth year at Harvard University. Prior to joining Harvard Divinity School Ibrahim were a Radcliffe Fellow and a jointly appointed Fellow to the Human Rights Program and the Islamic Legal Studies Program.

Hauwa Ibrahim was born in a rural village Hinnah, in Gombe State of Northern Nigeria where she was ingrained with values that have strengthened her life's journey and resolve. Moving from a more simple village life that included household chores such as water and firewood portage, evolving to a State supported girls education, Hauwa eventually trained as an attorney with the goal of contributing to justice for those who may not have its access. Working as a lead attorney with a team devoted to the cause of human rights for women in Nigeria, she has won a number of precedent-setting cases before Islamic Shariah courts. While a Radcliffe fellow, Ibrahim adopted an interdisciplinary approach to delve into the theoretical foundations of Shariah law and examine how they have influenced legal practice, which has, in turn, affected the human rights of women. Her approach has been to honor and respect the law, and always work within it, taking personal responsibility for the long-term consequences of the outcomes. For her work, she has been honored with awards such as the European Parliament 2005 Sakharov Prize for Freedom of Thought, which honors individuals or organizations for their efforts on behalf of human rights and freedoms. She was the first sub-Saharan African woman to be awarded this prize as well as the Cavaliere Award, the highest Human Rights Award from the Italian Government. In addition, Hauwa Ibrahim has been awarded Honorary Doctorate of Philosophy degrees at: Carl von Ossietzky University, Oldenburg, Germany, and Godwin University College Honorary Doctorate in Human Letters, CT, USA. She has been appointed as a visiting professor in colleges and universities in Europe and the USA:

Visiting Professor
    Harvard University, Visiting Lecturer
    Saint Louis University School of Law,
    Stonehill College
    University of Pennsylvania School of Law
    Carl von Ossietzky University, Oldenburg, Germany
    College of William and Mary
    World Fellow at Yale University

Acknowledgments

SEVERAL RESIDENTIAL FELLOWSHIPS AT Harvard University provided both the intellectual community and the financial support to make this book possible. The book was conceived at the Radcliffe Institute for Advanced Study, benefited from time in the Islamic Legal Studies Program at Harvard Law School, and came to fruition thanks to a three-year residence in the Women's Studies in Religion Program at Harvard Divinity School. Research, editing, and publication were also supported by grants from the Social Science Research Council and from Patricia Cooper, Lynda Goldstein, and Ann Carter. I owe so much to Ann Braude, whose sincere belief in this project sustained me in moments of doubt. Her enthusiasm inspired me to reach ever further, and her wisdom taught me to grasp what I found. Her advocacy won the support of Dean William A. Graham, whose hospitality and generosity welcomed me into the community of Harvard Divinity School. Indeed, this book is the collective effort of many. I especially want to acknowledge Suzanne Karl for reading the first draft of the manuscript, which I was unable to read until she sorted it out; and the pillars of my professional life, Professor Roger Goldman and Giuseppe Bisconti, Dr. Kamari Clark, and Dr. Steven Funk who have inspired me in many ways. To my guardian angel, Carrie J. Hunter; to Caroline Riss, my first research assistant who taught me so much; to Alex McDonough; to Auntie Beverly Merklee; to all of the Colorado women for their support and encouragement; to Virgilio, to Berel Rodal, and to Peter Goldsmith, former attorney general of Great Britain. I am deeply grateful to the United States, its citizens, and its great learning environment that has made it possible to think and re-think, strategize and re-strategize, and make the impossible a reality—to know that we all have potential and we can pull that together and make something out of what may look like nothing. To Ambassador Howard Franklin Jeter and John Campbell, two USA Ambassadors to Nigeria who gave us listening ears. The amazing resources and staffs of Harvard libraries were a game changer. To Michael Arnold for conveying the Seven Strategies concept; to John Ciampa for reading and commenting on one of the drafts; to Kirk Betts who will forever be a soul mate; to my Uncle, Henry Musa Garba; to my brother-in-law, Alhaji Audu Magaji; to H. R. H.; to Alhaji Bashir Albasu; to Alh Inuwa Gombe, Mustapha Jokolo, to Prof. Ibrahim Mukoshy; to my American parents, Maureen and Harold, and my American sister, Barbara O. de Zalduondo; to my Lord, Honorable Chief Justice Mohammed Lawal Uwais (JSC) rtd, whose first reference of me opened countless opportunities in the USA; to Justice Umaru Kalgo (JSC) rtd, for being my inspiration; to Nimi Wariboko for his wisdom and foresight; to Baobab for Women's Human Rights, Development Exchange Center, and Bauchi for "opening up the field" for its fortunes; to the Nigerian Bar Association for grooming me; to Aunties Asma'u Joda and Hannatu Akilu; to Jennifer, Tom, my friend Max, and Ben and Nathalie Hillman; to Yamaltu Deba Emirate who appointed me *Sauraniya* (Queen); The Chief and people of Hinnah (my village) for allowing me the opportunity to pursue education; to my clients, who gave me the privilege to represent them in court and in prisons; to Lawyers Without Boarders; to France and Quebec, especially François Cantier; to very many others whom by their words of discouragement and dismissal of the first draft of the manuscript kindled a fire in me to get this book done. To my students at St. Louis University School of Law, 2006, who gave me my first teaching experience in the USA; to my students at Harvard

Divinity School, 2010, from whom I learned so much more than I taught; to the Center for the Studies of World Religions at Harvard University for giving me a very quiet space from which to work (January to June 2010). To my younger brother Alhaji Abubakar Ibrahim Ajiya, who has encouraged me, immensely. To my mother who may not understand what I am doing—twenty years ago she believed I had read enough for a lifetime, but marveled when I told her I was about to begin reading and writing—she is the source of my strength. To my sisters, Aishatu Magaji, Amina Ibrahim, Hadiza Ibrahim, Abbati Ibrahim, Safiya Ibrahim, and my extended families of the Baba Ajiya (Madigol) and Ali Biri. To Prof. Jacob Olupona; Jacob Rhoads; Kathleen Sullivan, former Director of the American Bar Association Liaison Office; American University; Washington College of Law, especially Dean Grossman, Cynthia, and my other professors; to Yale University; American Academy for International Law, which gave me my first experience of studies in the United States in 2000; to St. Louis University, especially Prof. Henry Odwer; Harvard University; Radcliffe Institute, which hosted me in 2008–2009, where the idea of this book began; to my beloved Dean Barbara Grosz. To Alice Speri and Jia Hui Lee, my research assistants at Radcliffe Institute. Special thanks as well to my dear editor Nancy Shoptaw and editor Karen Propp; Barbara Gyure; Mallam Abdulmalik Badamasy; and A. A. Machika, former Attorney General of Katsina State, whose Islamic scholarship and belief in the first draft kept the flame in me to continue writing. My sincere gratitude to our team at the American Bar Association, especially Wm. T. (Bill) Robinson III (ABA President 2011-2012), Tim Brandhorst, Richard G. Paszkiet, and Neal Cox. My heartfelt thank you to those who remain unnamed. Please know that you are counted among those who are deeply appreciated.

Foreword

IN THE NAME OF ALLAH, THE MOST Gracious, the Most Merciful, praise be to Allah, the Lord of the Worlds, and blessings and peace be upon the seal of the Prophets and Messengers, our Prophet Muhammad and upon his family and companions.

The subject of this book is the contour of Shari'ah law in Northern Nigeria. It is certainly not the Shari'ah per se but the practice of law in Shari'ah courts with seven strategies illustrating the goals as "their application is discussed within the legal contour of Shari'ah law in Northern Nigeria."

To begin with, this work is, no doubt, a pioneer work in Nigeria in the field of delivering justice in Shari'ah courts and in accordance with the modern, codified approach. There are a lot of works on justice delivery in Nigeria, and such work of the Federal Judiciary of Nigeria is well documented internationally. However, this work is completely different and important.

Hauwa Ibrahim invested a lot of hard work and was able to overcome a myriad of obstacles in compiling this highly sophisticated work with its mass of references, especially the scope of Islamic references. She has marvelously done a well-researched and thorough work on a highly volatile subject. Fortunately, having accumulated a good amount of experience as an attorney in Bauchi State of Nigeria coupled with her Islamic background and understanding of Islamic jurisprudence, our learned legal luminary happened to be well equipped to handle such cases of Shari'ah comfortably.

The nineteenth century witnessed the Islamic Revival Movement, which was led by the Islamic scholar Sheikh Usman bin Fodiyo with scholars such as Yakubun Bauchi, the illustrious son of Bauchi, one of the movement's lieutenants. This awareness of the settings will indeed be of great help in perceiving and understanding the later adoption of Shari'ah in the late 1990s.

The jihadists who founded the Caliphate established Islamic Educational Centres per excellence all over the Caliphate—Sokoto, Gwandu, Kano, Katsina, Katagum, Yola in Adamawa, Ilorin, Zazzau Bidda, Marua in Cameroon, and Sayi in the Republic of Niger, just to mention a few. They wrote books covering a wide spectrum ranging from Fiqh, polity, and medicine, to mathematics and astronomy. Everything was fully documented in prose and poetry and in several languages, such as Arabic, Fulfulde, and Hausa.

Islamic jurisprudence is divine as far as Muslims are concerned and is a complete way of life. Its sources of derivation are the Qur'an, the Hadeeth, etc., and any source based on secular acquired knowledge is acceptable with a proviso. The secular, acquired knowledge from the Islamic point of view includes the social, natural, and applied sciences, which are susceptible to ongoing growth and cross-cultural borrowings, as long as they maintain consistency with the Shari'ah as the source of values.

Hauwa Ibrahim has opened a new horizon for both judiciary and academic milieu. Albeit, we are fully aware that in the present century things have become very confusing and we have begun to see, almost universally, speculations even about the word "truth" and how true or relative it is. No doubt the Almighty Allah reserved some people, like Hauwa, to shed more light on ambivalent, hazy, or obscure perceptions as well as on the ambiguity that conceals even the difference that existed and the profound dichotomy between secularism and sacrosanctity. It is such scholarship that helps to overcome deep-seated challenges and show the way out of the predicament, all while correcting the anomalies and miscarriages of justice.

I am sincerely happy and grateful to the Almighty who granted me this opportunity not only to read this work and learn a lot about our legal system as well as its inadequacies, but also to have the honor to preface this great work. It is a treasure for our legal practitioners.

Professor Ibrahim Ahmad Mukoshy
Usmanu Danfodiyo University, May 2012

Map and Geographic Spread of Muslim Majority Countries and Nigeria[1]

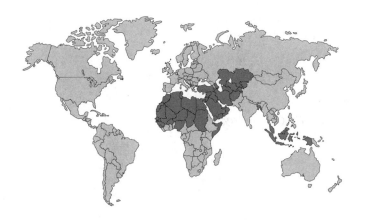

Countries with the Largest Muslim Populations (2009)

List of Countries by Muslim Population:

Indonesia: 202,867,000 (88.2%)

Pakistan: 174,082,000 (96.3%)

---

1.   Source: http://en.wikipedia.org/wiki/Muslim_world.

India: 160,945,000 (13.4%)

Bangladesh: 145,312,000 (89.6%)

Egypt: 78,513,000 (94.6%)

Nigeria: 78,056,000 (50.4%)

Iran: 73,777,000 (99.4%)

Turkey: 73,619,000 (98.0%)

Algeria: 34,199,000 (98.0 %)

Morocco: 31,993,000 (99.0%)

Iraq: 30,428,000 (99.0%)

Sudan: 30,121,000 (71.3%)

Afghanistan: 28,072,000 (99.7%)

Ethiopia: 28,063,000 (33.9%)

Uzbekistan: 26,469,000 (96.3%)

Saudi Arabia: 24,949,000 (97.0%)

Yemen: 23,363,000 (99.1%)

China: 21,667,000 (1.6%)

Syria: 20,196,000 (92.2%)

Malaysia: 16,581,000 (60.4%)

Russia: 16,482,000 (11.7%)

Niger: 15,075,000 (98.6%)

Map of Nigeria

This map was obtained from the government of Nigeria, National Population Commission, Abuja, Nigeria, August 2010.

Map of Northern Nigeria

This map indicates the Northern region of Nigeria. Source: http://www. waado.org/nigerdelta/maps/willink_commission/nigeria_northern.html.

Map of Nigeria

This map was obtained from the government of Nigeria, National Population Commission, Abuja, Nigeria, August 2010.

Preface

THE PURPOSE OF THIS BOOK IS TO provide insight into practicing law in Shariah courts. *Practicing Shariah Law: Seven Strategies for Achieving Justice in Shariah Courts* is about sharing questions that arise from being in the field and seeking justice under the law both legally and spiritually.

If the reader goes away with nothing more than understanding that the approach advocated in this book is to always respect Islam, the Shariah laws, the wisdom of local people and leaders, both temporal and spiritual, be they educated or not, and an appreciation of local and national laws, as well as the international treaties signed by a nation, *Practicing Shariah Law* will have fulfilled its mission.

Thus, it is essential to maintain the spirituality of Islam not to distort the intent or practices from texts as provided for in the Holy Qur'an and the Hadith, given its best context and meaning. Know that staying within the law is the best way to seek justice for your client.

For myself, it was a long journey and I am still on it. I have learned to hear the quiet still voice that is not my own, to listen to that which is over and above, and to seek for a deep sense of direction. Sometimes it takes time, but the clarity does come. I find myself reflecting upon my life as a child in the village of Hinnah; the dark dawn mornings when my mother would wake me for the purification and prayers; our father, and later, grandfather, leading these holy prayers. My life in my village was the foundation and mortar of my life today. Never forget where you come from—honor and deference carry us along on our journey.

Over the past years, the spiritual leaders of Nigeria have called for spirituality and moderation from believers. One such clear voice is the current Sultan of Sokoto, the spiritual leader of Africa's largest Muslim population, who advocates understanding religious texts in order to bridge gaps in both knowledge and practice, building a bridge of understanding amongst the religions in Nigeria and beyond. I cannot but say he is my inspiration.

Let appreciation for all, from the lowest and most desperate to the strongest leaders of nations, be our foremost asset in seeking justice for our clients. Let us not allow our educations to get in the way of receiving wisdom from those who are not literate. Trust that they have great knowledge and they too, for the most part, want to be a part of seeing that justice is delivered.

The Law is the noble pursuit of justice. Across time and space, the spirit and intent of the Law—informed by the divine essence of our collective being—has been the unfading light through the darkness and insecurity of history, steadily safeguarding man's hope for a better future. Our actions are an expression of experiences long gone and of experiences yet to come. Aware of the inequalities and injustices of the past, of those present in our own time, and of our responsibility to free ourselves from future wrongs, it is a duty owed to us and to others to labor for the fulfillment of the Law's potential. This is the hope and aim of this book.

While the temple of justice is a natural, transparent and all-inclusive space, the network of paths that lead to it is at times complicated and beset with many obstacles. The introduction of new Shariah in Northern Nigeria in 1999 set in place a delicate and flexible boundary between the rule of law and individual interpretations of the Law that are unjustifiably causing individual and social ills. Although the implementation of Shariah in Northern Nigeria presents many challenges, as well as broader issues that can cloud the spirit and radiance of the temple of justice, as lawyers we must be unwavering in our commitment to do what is right and seek to express in our actions the divinity of our humanity. In Shariah law, the Islamic notion of justice should not be altered or tampered with because of social and economic inequalities that may mute the concerns, aspirations, and fulfillment of natural capabilities of the less privileged of society.

The seven strategies described in this book are part of a dialogue for learning the terrain and how best to work around the disparities in the "new Shariah," exploring ethical issues drawn from various sources, including the Holy Qur'an, Hadith, and Sunnah. Although their application is discussed within the legal contour of Shariah law in Northern Nigeria, the strategies are not confined to any one framework of reference and may be a valued resource to many.

No opinion that I have expressed in this book is above argument or criticism. I am not an academic or a scholar of religion or a political philosopher. I am just a lawyer. What follows is a reflection of my experiences while defending clients in Shariah courts. As such, the reader will find no ideological allegiance that carries my voice forward except my unwavering commitment to justice and fairness for all human beings. It is a book written by a legal practitioner, sharing the strategies and resources that have served me well throughout my career. The multilayered composition of this book, weaving together Islamic law, national laws, international treatises, and religious texts is intent on providing lawyers all possible avenues for drafting a defense strategy that reflects the integrity of Shariah and upholds the values of the community.

A number of important academic works have been written about Shariah law. However, while such studies are often conclusive, this book aims to accommodate the changing nature of Shariah as it is applied in Northern Nigeria. Since their implementation and subsequent codification from 2000 to 2003, Shariah law codes have been regularly amended. This book reflects the latest of the amendments known to the author. However, the strategies and resources outlined in this book move past them and look toward the overarching ideal of justice and fairness, placing them in a space that sustains the functional character of the work. Take and infer from them what would be most useful according to circumstance.

This approach has allowed me to stress the need to be cognizant of the weight that unfamiliar sources often add to our own beliefs and views. This book does not shy away from citing both Islamic and non-Islamic sources and suggesting various interpretative strands that, in different ways, reflect the ideals of Shariah. As such, it is important to note—especially in my reading of religious texts—I claim no authority. Indeed, I am well aware of the different meanings and contradictions found in the Qur'an and other religious texts. But as noted by Asma Barlas, "while it may not be easy to say what would be the best meaning of every Ayah [verse] . . . it is reasonable to hold that the best meanings would recover justice."[2] Through the centuries, in all religious traditions, diverse opinions have arisen claiming the correct interpretation of religious sources. Notwithstanding the rich history of exegetical treatises, this work, written as a guide for lawyers seeking justice for their clients in Shariah courts, presents a reading of religious materials that stresses man's collective labor for justice and peace, evidence not only in our own time but in the lives and teachings of prophets whom we daily turn to for guidance.

My selective citation of Qur'anic verses may well lead to criticism of a disregard for an academic's approach to the texts. I hope the reader forgives my limited and imperfect understanding of Islamic history and theology and instead sees my references to and interpretation of religious materials as a point of departure for fruitful debate about how best to achieve justice and fairness. Islam stands for peace, truth, freedom, and human dignity. It falls to us to respect and protect that which informs people's lives while at

---

2.   Barlas, *"Believing Women" in Islam*, 16.

the same time safeguarding the principles that sustain the courage of the human heart and the empathy of the human mind.

I hope to improve this work over the course of time, and I welcome all responses and additional information that will refine what is presented herein. All that is good in this book comes from the Almighty, and all defects come from my own human weaknesses.

Hauwa Ibrahim
Colorado Scholar
Harvard University, Women's Studies in Religions Program, July 2012

Abbreviations List:

ACPRA: African Charter on Peoples' Rights (Ratification and Enforcement) Act

APC: Arewa People's Congress

CA: Court of Appeals

CBO: Community-based organization

CEDAW: Convention on the Elimination of all Forms of Discrimination Against Women

CEELI: Central European and Euro-Asia Law Initiative

COP: Commissioner of Police

EA: Evidence Act

EHRR: European Human Rights Report

ESCR: Economic, social, and cultural rights

FSC: Federal Supreme Court

HRC: Human Rights Committee

ICCPR: International Covenant on Civil and Political Rights

JCA: Justice of the Court of Appeal

JSC: Justice of the Supreme Court

LPA: Legal Practitioner's Act (of the Nigerian Bar Association)

LWB: Lawyers Without Borders

NGO: Nongovernmental organization

NNLR: Northern Nigeria Law Report

NWLR: Nigeria Weekly Law Report

OAU: Organization of African Unity

OIC: Organization of Islamic Countries

ICTY: International Criminal Tribunal for the former Yugoslavia

JP: Justice of the Peace

LFN: Laws of the Federation of Nigeria

PC: Penal Code

PLD: Palestinian Law Decision

SAN: Senior Advocate of Nigeria

SC: Supreme Court

SCA: Shariah Court of Appeal

SCR: Supreme Court Report

SPCL: Shariah Penal Code Law

SSSPC: Sokoto State Shariah Penal Code

SSSPCL: Sokoto State Shariah Penal Code Law

SSSCPCL: Sokoto State Shariah Criminal Procedure Code Law

UDHR: Universal Declaration of Human Rights

UIDHR: Universal Islamic Declaration of Human Rights

UN: United Nations

UNHRC: United Nations Human Rights Committee

WACA: West Africa Court of Appeal

WWHR: Women for Women's Human Rights

ZACC: Zuid Afrika Constitutional Court

ZSPCL: Zamfara State Penal Code Law

ZSSPCL: Zamfara State Shariah Penal Code Law

When we are able to fuse our horizon with the horizons of another person, we reach the high point of all inquiry. Here is where truth is to be found in its purest, waiting for its moment of disclosure, the moment when multiplicities of minds are agreed on what they see.

—Hans-Georg Gadamer

Introduction

As LAWYERS, WE SOMETIMES FIND ourselves confronted by situations where no clear law or prior precedents exist. Nowhere is this situation more prevalent than in regions of the world where local customs and secular legal code are overlaid with religious laws to form a complex—and controversial—matrix of legal theory and opinion. Such is the situation in Northern Nigeria, which is the focus of this work and where I practice law. Nevertheless, similarly complex situations exist elsewhere, and I am eager to derive and explain lessons from my experiences that will prove useful both in Northern Nigeria and far beyond. My objective in writing this book is to provide lawyers practicing law under Shariah with seven strategies that have served me well under difficult circumstances throughout my career; strategies that assure me I am doing everything in my capacity to ensure that the rights of the accused are protected.[3] Although each case consists

---

3.   The word Shariah literally means a way to the watering place or a path to seek felicity and salvation. Shariah is spelled several ways in the Shariah penal code laws of various states in Nigeria, as well as in books, articles, and other written materials. For the purpose of this book, the author is adopting the spelling of Shari'a, Sharia'h, Shariya, etc., as Shariah. It is defined as an institution that Allah سبحانه و تعالى ordained to guide the individual relationship to God, his fellow Muslims, his fellow men, and the rest of the universe. See Doi, *Shariah*, 2; and El-Nimr, "Women in Islam," 88.

of a unique set of specific details, this work intends to provide the reader with basic strategies—illustrated through examples from actual cases—that demonstrate how these fundamental principles can be applied.

The seven strategies summarized below are woven around understanding and learning how best to work within the local culture and legal context for any given case.

1. Understand the Dynamics: Develop discipline and an ability to decipher what is meant rather than what is said.

2. Pay Attention to Details and Look for a Creative Approach: Be on the lookout for pertinent information no matter how small the detail, and learn to use it creatively.

3. Be Focused and Stay Focused: In the middle of what may appear as cultural chaos and a deluge of information, it is essential for the lawyer to remain focused.

4. Be Firm yet Flexible: Know how and when to stand firm on the principles of law, while maintaining interpretive flexibility given the social norms and culture of the local people.

5. Play to Your Strength—The Law: To know the law thoroughly is the true strength of a legal practice. This includes relentless exploration of its possibilities both to achieve justice for clients and to ensure the bigger picture goal of victory for society.

6. Plan a Defense: Of utmost importance is knowledge and application of the rule of law, procedures, technicalities, and basic human rights protections.

7. Think Globally, Act Locally: Develop the ability to see far beyond the horizon, to think and strategize globally, within the law, while acting locally and immediately.

Although their application is discussed within the legal contour of Shariah law in Northern Nigeria, the seven strategies are universal for Shariah wherever it is in effect; the application is not confined to any one frame of reference. Nor are these strategies dependent on one another, but work together in helpful dialogue. In legal practice, these strategies can be the base and the buttresses that help build, sustain, and strengthen arguments before the court.

My own journey began as a prosecutor within the Ministry of Justice in the state of Bauchi, Nigeria, and lasted from February 1989 to October 1996. I opted out of the Ministry after reaching the rank of Principal State Counsel and founded Aries Law Firm, so that I could serve as defense counsel. From that point, my career in law came to be defined by the great professional challenges of representing primarily pro bono clients. In May of 1998 I moved to Abuja, the capital city of Nigeria, to continue my legal practice while also consulting on various United Nations projects and providing free advocacy services for indigent clients.

My first case under the codified Shariah criminal law in early 2000 began with a telephone call from Dr. Ayesha Imam, the Executive Director of Baobab, a women's rights nongovernmental organization (NGO) based in Lagos.[4] Dr. Imam asked me to assemble a legal team to defend a thirteen-year-old girl, Bariya Ibrahim Magazu, who had been tried and convicted for fornication (*zina*[5]). The conviction was made by the Tsafe Shariah court in Zamfara State in Northern Nigeria, which instituted Shariah in 2000. Baobab was prepared to assist and support a legal team to reverse the conviction. My role in the defense of Ms. Magazu, who was ultimately punished with a public flogging rather than death by stoning, and of other defendants like her earned me the headline, "Hauwa Ibrahim, the Lawyer for the Adulteress."[6]

In the past decade (2000–2008), I have been involved in the defense of more than one hundred cases (sixty of which involved women), both in courts

---

4.   Dr. Imam is one of the founding directors of Baobab for Women's Human Rights in Nigeria.

5.   The term *zina* is also referred to as "illegal" fornication. Under Section 4 of the Pakistan Offense of *zina* (enforcement of hudud) Ordinance, 1979, "a man and a woman are said to commit zina, if they willfully have sexual intercourse without being married to each other." Later the words *consensually* and *voluntarily* were added to *willfully*. See Hudood Ordinance, Council of Islamic Ideology, 1979, 2003: A Critical Report, Islamabad, Government of Pakistan, 5.

6.   *The Reporter* (Ethiopia), front page, Sept. 11, 2002.

and in prisons, under Shariah. These include the cases of Safiya Hussaini Tugar Tudu and Amina Lawal Kurami, both of whom were sentenced to death by stoning in Nigeria. Some of these cases made headlines around the world.[7] From these experiences, I have grown to appreciate how to practice law with a delicate balance of how to best defend women facing serious sentences by working within the framework of Shariah and maintaining the highest global standards of justice and the rule of law.

Though Shariah is now practiced in several countries, there are few resources for defense lawyers to reference that will help them plan their strategies. At times there are no books, precedents, written decisions, computers, or online legal resources—the sorts of resources that lawyers in many other legal systems have in abundance. I have learned through experience, and over the course of my career have developed strategies and materials that I hope will serve to fill this gap for lawyers who seek justice for their clients under Shariah. This book will be especially helpful to those lawyers/attorneys who are unaccustomed to practicing law in environments such as Northern Nigeria's Shariah courts, where there exist regional differences in the application of the law. I am hoping it will serve as a valuable guide for those dedicated to pursuing justice as a readily accessible yet powerful aid.

This book addresses both theoretical strategies and practical aspects for practicing law within Shariah courts—especially the challenge of protecting women's rights under the codified Shariah as it is practiced in Northern Nigeria. One can only imagine the loneliness, vulnerability, and helplessness of those we defend who are poor, voiceless, powerless, illiterate, and mostly uninformed about the legal system and their rights. The awareness of my own humble beginnings and the tremendous blessings I have enjoyed inspire and strengthen my commitment to represent and assist these marginalized people. While my personal hardships pale in comparison to those whom I

---

7.   Cooper, "Woman Awaits Stoning Appeal," *Anderson Cooper 360.*

have represented, I now embrace my clients with a greater understanding and compassion, and a deeper sense of calling.

Human rights and equal justice under the law apply to all of humanity. These are the foundations for healthy societies; yet, as is common knowledge, women in many communities around the globe are silenced, abused, and/or abandoned by the laws of men. The future of global peace, security, and freedom will depend on how societies, religions, and cultures give *all* human beings equal rights under the law. As I shall discuss in coming chapters, effective representation depends upon lawyers deepening their understanding and awareness of how laws have been construed within their local religious, political, historical, and cultural contexts. Where Shariah has been implemented in such a way that women are disproportionately and harshly punished, it is essential to deploy a rich array of strategies and resources that will protect their rights in the face of such unjust application of the law. That is the hope, spirit, and intent of this book.

CHAPTER ONE

Understand the Dynamics

In October 1999 the governor of Nigeria's state of Zamfara "launched" and caused the "criminal aspect of Shariah" to be codified into what was hitherto the Penal Code of Northern Nigeria.[8] Shariah would later be enacted into law by eleven other states in Northern Nigeria. The interpretations of the codified criminal Shariah would test many levels of Nigerian society—Muslim clerics (*Mallams*[9]), the courts and its processes, lawyers and judges, ministries of justice, and the police—as well as challenge many of the applications of due process and the rule of law.[10]

---

8.   Chukkul, "Penal Code," 158.

9.   This book contains foreign words whose origins are not always absolute. Most of the foreign words are in Hausa, a native language of Northern Nigeria where the author practiced law for more than twenty years. Many of the Hausa words are derivatives of Arabic, since this region of Nigeria is largely Muslim; however, some words derive from other African tribes. The book also makes good use of Latin words and phrases, since Latin has its roots in the foundation of law. English translations or definitions of foreign words are given either in the text or in footnotes.

10.   The term "codified" must be qualified in reference to the Shariah Penal Code of Northern Nigeria. During the British occupancy of Nigeria, from 1861–1960 (*Encyclopedia of African History*, Cambridge University Press, 1962), Britain built a legal system based on the traditional system of dispute adjudication, which incorporated some aspects of Shariah civil law. After Nigeria gained its independence in 1960, some Nigerian states began

When the Shariah Penal Code Law (SPCL) was introduced in Northern Nigeria, much of its population believed that this should not be questioned. Citizens should, as usual, rally around their leaders, applaud them, and allow the Shariah laws to be implemented. Later, when our legal team filed the first case in Shariah court, some members of the public reacted negatively, interpreting the filing as opposition to Shariah.[11] To avoid this perception, we had to be very clear about our intentions. Our defense of Shariah cases in courts had nothing to do with being for or against Shariah, but merely demonstrated our commitment to uphold the law, both Shariah and the Constitution of the Federal Republic of Nigeria, to ensure that justice was served for our clients.

To avoid the stigma of being perceived as "anti-Shariah," "anti-values," or "anti-society," the successful lawyer in Shariah trials will stay focused on the case and its particular merits—and conduct oneself according to the highest standards of legal practice. Moreover, when arguing cases in areas that have codified Shariah law, a nuanced understanding of the local historical, cultural, social, and political dynamics is required of counsel. Lawyers practicing under such circumstances will do well to fully comprehend why the members and/or leaders of the society sought the codification of Shariah criminal law.

Defense counsel must appreciate the interplay between the courts, villages, law enforcement authority, Muslim clerics, and the accused,

---

to further integrate Shariah civil law into their legal systems. In 1999, twelve northern states (discussed later in this chapter) incorporated the criminal aspect of Shariah law into their legal systems (which already contained civil aspects of Shariah law). To this author's knowledge, the criminal aspects of Shariah law (provided for in various Shariah penal code 2000–2002) had not been included in state legal systems prior to 1999. Shariah criminal codes were often similar to the Penal Code of Northern Nigeria (PC) with added provisions and altered punishments for certain offenses. In reference to the Shariah Penal Code of Northern Nigeria, the term "codified" denotes the addition of criminal aspects to the already existing civil provisions found in Shariah law.

11.   References to our "legal team" may include some of the following individuals: Mr. Yunus Ustaz Usman, Senior Advocate of Nigeria (SAN); Mrs. Omo-Osagie; Hurera A. Attah; A. M. Yawuri; Abdulkadir Idris; Mariam Imhanobe; Ramatu Umar; Ndidi Ekewe; Mallam Mustapha Husseini Ismail; Eniola Akinton; Linda Bala; and Hauwa Ibrahim.

and how they shape and affect the lives of individuals who are often impoverished and uneducated. They need to understand how Shariah applies to populations that include non-Muslims, and how the tenets of Shariah confirm, complement, or contradict the existing national legal framework as defined by a constitution and other national and international legal frameworks. The better equipped lawyers are to navigate the domain posed by the intersection of other legal codes and Shariah legal code, the more adept they are at winning justice for their clients in challenging and imperfect legal environments.

Overview: Islam, Shariah, and Nigeria

The Qur'an reveals to believers: " . . . this day, I have perfected your religion for you, completed My Favor upon you, and have chosen for you Islam as your religion" (5:3). It is important to note that Islam is not just one social category among many that inform people's personal and social lives. It is not only a set of moral instructions that Muslims must follow. Islam is a comprehensive way of life[12] concerned with individual rights, practices, and rules, but also with issues often associated with the state and governance.[13]

Therefore, Shariah "covers all aspects of human endeavor, economic, political, social, or theological and it's a complete way of life of a Muslim, from cradle to the grave."[14] This is to say that while the primary focus of both civil and common law is public behavior, Shariah is far broader; it is a guide for how Muslims should behave and interact within public and private society. Although Shariah in some societies in Northern Nigeria may not take precedence over civil and common law, Shariah sets forth Islam's rules for personal behavior, including prayer, fasting, hygiene, and diet, as well as for civil and criminal matters such as marriage, inheritance, contracts, and crime. These rules are derived from the Holy Qur'an, Hadith,

---

12. Ambali, *Practice of Muslim Family Law*, 1.
13. Esposito, *Oxford History of Islam*, 66; Lings, *Muhammad*, 108; see also Doi, *Cardinal Principles of Islam*, 190.
14. Bello, *Understanding Shariah in Nigeria*, 21.

Ijtihad, and more.[15] Literally translated as "the path to follow God's Law,"[16] Shariah law is thus generally viewed by Muslims as a vehicle to solve all problems, whether civil, criminal, or international. Many Muslims believe Shariah should regulate all public and private aspects of the lives of Islam's adherents.[17]

To begin to understand the reasons for the codification of the criminal aspect of Shariah in Nigeria and the repercussions of the codification of Shariah worldwide, it is helpful to look at Nigeria's history and economics, its ethnic and religious populations, and its internal political power structure. Also important is Nigeria's position as a leading African country and the eighth most populous country in the world. Occupying a landmass three times the size of the United Kingdom, Nigeria is Africa's most populous nation, and includes the continent's largest Muslim population of approximately 70 million people. While accurate counts of Nigeria's population are difficult to come by, its approximately 150 million citizens are estimated to be 40 percent Muslim, 35 percent Christian, and 25 percent nonreligious, or those practicing traditional African religions.[18] Nigeria has historically not applied the criminal aspect of Shariah law, as set forth in the Shariah penal codes prior to 2000.

Nigeria is divided into six geopolitical zones (the Northwest, the North Central, the Northeast, the Southwest, the South-south, and the Southeast). Each of the zones comprises six states, except for the Northwest

---

15.   The Holy Qur'an is the Islamic sacred book of which Muslims believe to be the last testament. See I. A. Ibrahim, *Guide to Understanding Islam*, 54. Hadith are the sayings, practices, lifestyle, and deeds of the prophet Muhammad ﷺ. *Ijtihad* are Islamic scholarly opinions based on the Qur'an and Sunnah. Other sources of rule include, for example, *qiyas*, where the offender is to be awarded punishment identical with his offense, and *Ijma*, which is consensus of the *mujtahids*, that is, the learned scholars who exercised disciplined efforts to arrive at certain judgments. See generally Kamali, *Shariah Law*.

16.   Ambali, *Practice of Muslim Family Law*, 2.

17.   Sidahmad, *Hudud*, 2; see also Caldarola, *Religions and Societies*, 11.

18.   The data provided in this section by some staff members of the population commission are generally accepted estimations. In addition, the data corresponds with the author's interviews with cross sections of Nigerians, July–August 2010, as well as other fieldwork. The Nigerian population commission, which is the statutory body for this information, indicated that the data was not officially available.

which numbers seven and the Southeast with five, for a total of thirty-six states.[19] A slight majority of these states are located in the Northern zones (nineteen states); the other largest zones are the Southwest (nine states) and the Southeast (six states).[20]

Provisions of the Penal Code Laws of Northern Nigeria appeared to serve the people well for nearly four decades; judgments were generally accepted without contention. Then in 1999, after a long period of military rule, Nigerians embraced civilian leadership and elected as president, Olusegun Obasanjo, a self-described born-again Christian from the Southwest region. Thirty-six governors, one for each Nigerian state, were also elected. Implementation of campaign promises made during the elections resulted in the introduction of criminal Shariah, shortly after the governor of Zamfara State took the oath of office.

The newly elected executive governor, Ahmed Sani (Yeriman Bakura), quickly delivered on his campaign promise to install the criminal aspect of Shariah law and launched what was dubbed "the new Shariah." Governor Sani had mobilized the large Muslim voting bloc in his state, in effect clinching the election by promising implementation of Shariah. He was the first leader in Nigeria's post-independence history to introduce capital punishment (such as death by stoning and crucifixion) into the Penal Code of Northern Nigeria,[21] a code derived from both secular and Shariah law that was enacted following Nigeria's independence from British rule on October 1, 1960. Almost immediately after the inauguration of Shariah, Area Courts (local courts whose jurisdictions were limited) became "Shariah Courts" with expanded jurisdiction to adjudicate criminal cases under the codified Shariah Penal Code Law of the state of Zamfara.

Other state governments, under pressure from their Muslim citizens, soon followed Zamfara's lead. As stated in *Thisday* newspaper:

---

19.   See Adams and Trost, *Handbook on World Families*, 25.
20.   States in the Northern zones implementing Shariah are Bauchi, Borno, Gombe, Jigawa, Kaduna, Kano, Katsina, Kebbi, Niger, Sokoto, Yobe, and Zamfara. However, there is question as to the full implementation of Shariah in Gombe.
21.   Zamfara State Shariah Penal Code Law, 2000, Sections 127(b) and 153(d).

Northern sources say that contrary to what the media would have us believe, pressure to institute Shariah has been a bottom-up phenomenon. The elite are said to be under a lot of pressure from the common people to give them Shariah. The man who speaks against the law, or opposes it in any form, becomes very unpopular; these same sources say that [President Shehu] Shagari, like many of the governors who would eventually join [Governor] Sani on the Shariah bandwagon, was initially lukewarm about the whole affair. And so with all the pressures, what does a wise man do? Just keep quiet and not comment at all. Is it any wonder why it seems so quiet on the Northern front?[22]

Despite their congruent interests, the codification of criminal Shariah in twelve states across Northern Nigeria has been far from uniform, resulting in different codifications of Shariah penal codes in each of the states. In retrospect, it seems there were no structured guidelines for the new legislation and the transition appears to have been undertaken in a hurried manner.[23] The state governments gave the impression that their main concern was demonstrating that the codified Shariah could be—indeed had been—established, rather than ensuring that fairness and respect for human rights and fundamental freedoms and justice would be maintained. Moreover, this "hurriedness" had an adverse effect on the training of judges, who went from handling mostly civil matters in Area Courts to handling cases with expanded criminal jurisdiction. Finally, many of the codes were so hastily drafted that they could be easily challenged in courts, and hence their effectiveness could be compromised.[24]

---

22. "Shariah and the Press in Nigeria: Islam Versus Western Christian Civilization," *Thisday*, (Lagos, Nigeria) March 26, 2000, 37. Note that Shehu Shagari was Nigerian President from 1979–1983.

23. Peters, *Reintroduction of Islamic Criminal Law*, 16.

24. See, for example, Zamfara State Sharia Penal Code Law, Section 63, which provides for basic criminal responsibility (i.e., *mens rea*), and Section 92 (offenses and

Rationale for the Introduction of the Codified Shariah

Several reasons have been offered for the 1999 codification of Shariah and its implementation in Northern Nigeria. Suggested rationales include the people's desire to create a fair and less corrupt society, a related attempt by the people to assert cultural self-determination in a fragmented and increasingly globalized world, and the successful utilization of legal reform by politicians as a tool to gain the support of the Muslim majority in the north.

A common rationale for the public's support of Shariah implementation in Northern Nigeria was its means to restore justice, peace, morality, and stability. Immorality was to be abolished by actions such as shutting down brothels and beer bars, insisting that bachelors and prostitutes get married, and combating corruption in the government. Public figures, including Muslim clerics, lawyers, and scholars advocated Shariah law in the sincere belief that it could be a powerful force to improve living conditions and restore justice to a corrupt society.

A related theory is that the codification of Shariah in the Nigerian legal system is principally the effort of "fundamentalist groups" that aim to reform what they see as the moral laxity of society and who impose their own understanding of Islamic values on the people.[25] Muslims often dismiss this view as the product of "Western" propaganda that distorts Shariah, portraying it outside of the religious and cultural contexts that give it meaning. Shariah, many Muslims contend, is a "complete way of life" that is in accord with justice and respects human life.[26] According to Professor Abdur Rahman Doi, Shariah originated from the direct commandment of Allah

---

punishment . . . with respect to blood money and *mens rea* is not necessary) of the same code that seems to state a contrary position. Also, the omission of proof of *zina* in most of the Shariah penal codes—most likely to avert the issues of constitutional conflict with respect to evidential proof—The Evidence Act is an instrument recognized by the Constitution of Nigeria and may only be amended by the National Assembly, which is yet to so amend.

25.   Sanusi, "Fundamentalist Groups," 79. Mr. Sanusi is currently the Central Bank Governor of Nigeria.

26.   Saiyidain, *Islam*, 27.

سبحانه و تعالى, but there is the provision or power given to man to interpret this divine commandment (i.e., by means of analogical deductions and through other processes). He further opined that the first source of Shariah is the Holy Qur'an.[27] Meanwhile, Nigerian Muslims have insisted that, indeed, Shariah is the way of life and that is what defines their being as Muslims.[28]

The danger of generalizations made by the "Western" media about the Muslim faith—to say little of some gross mischaracterization of Islamic beliefs—is that it often leads the most devout of Muslims to respond in ways that are equally misleading. In an attempt to differentiate their world from "the other" corrupt and dishonest cultures who are in a continued struggle with the teachings of Allah سبحانه و تعالى, some of the most devout Muslims may end up validating the "Western" media's challenges about Shariah by highlighting its most excessive punishments; for example, stoning, amputation, and flogging of Muslims, as penalties for Muslim offenders. Unfortunately, this view often trickles down to the people, who, at times, suffer deeply as a consequence of a few Muslims' misunderstanding of the meaning and just application of Shariah.

Although there are varied and contradictory opinions regarding the provisions, texts, and application of Shariah, it is important to remember that it is not uncommon to other religious texts. It has been suggested, however, that the codified Shariah may not be a matter of choice for practicing Nigerian Muslims. Shariah is integral to Islam, and therefore an inalienable part of a Muslim's life.[29] In accepting Islam, one accepts the responsibilities, the five pillars attached to it: professing the *kalman shahada* ("There is no God but Allah سبحانه و تعالى and Muhammad [صلى الله عليه وسلم] is his prophet"); praying five times daily; giving the *zakat* (tithe); fasting during the month of Ramadan; and making a pilgrimage to the holy land of Mecca if one

---

27. Doi, *Shariah*, 7.
28. Jega, *Identity Transformation*, 64.
29. Doi, *Shariah*, 84.

can afford it.[30] In the words of Ali Ahmad, a professor at Bayero University in Kano, Nigeria, a community cannot be said to be truly Muslim if it merely picks and chooses from among the various aspects of the Muslim faith, such as mixing monotheism with animistic religious traditions.[31] Islam requires that Muslims adhere to the provisions of Shariah.[32] The plain and solid foundation of Islamic belief should not be eclipsed by exegetical complexities that the codified Shariah may bring.

Salvation in Islam depends on all of the above pillars and articles of Islam as an entirety. It further means that the salvation that a Muslim longs for can be attained when he paves the way for the salvation of his fellow being, and for the entire human race.[33] In addition, some Muslims consider it a duty to establish an Islamic state because it is believed that in doing so one will help bring paradise within reach for those who aspire to it. These notions often transcend class, making the implementation of this law equally appealing to the elite and to the commoner. It is evident, though, that there is a vacuum in the governance structure in Nigeria that seems to exploit the weak and the impoverished. High unemployment, poverty, unequal distribution of wealth, corruption, and the inability of the state to deliver adequate social services represent serious problems for most Nigerians. Some political candidates, however, pledged to be capable of addressing these issues by promising that the codification of criminal Shariah would ensure a time of prosperity and rid the state of social ills. This has not yet been the case.

---

30.   The Arabic written here means, "May Allah bless and honor him and grant him peace." This phrase is uttered after hearing or saying the name of a prophet of Islam. *Kalman sha'adda, or La illah ha illallah, Mahammadan rasulil la, sallalahu allehu wasallam,* in Hausa means, "There is no God but Allah سبحانه و تعالى, and Muhammad (ﷺ) is his prophet."

31.   Islam is not severable; it is all or nothing: Muslims cannot pick and choose doctrines to obey (Qur'an 5:3; 13:36). See Philips, *Fundamentals of Tawheed,* 17; see also Vatikiotis, *Political Change in Southeast Asia,* 156; and Rippin, *Muslims,* 104.

32.   Zafar, *Law and Practice of Islamic Hudoods,* 64.

33.   Al-Faruqi, *Social and Natural Sciences,* 45.

Assenting Voices

Proponents of Islamic criminal law often claim that it will help "eliminate crime and corruption as a result of its deterrence and swift justice."[34] It is evident from the Qur'an and Hadith that dignity, justice, and freedom are a sacred obligation in Islam, because the Almighty God enjoins us to our Creator "not to judge among the People, and if you have to do it, do it justly" (Qur'an 5:42). Those who argue that Shariah will ensure fairness and justice base their argument on Qur'anic verses such as:

> We have already sent our messengers with clear evidences
> and sent down with them the Scripture and the balance
> that the people may maintain [their affairs] in justice . . .
> (57:25) . . . Indeed, Allah is Powerful and Exalted in Might .
> . . (58:21). Indeed, Allah commands you to render trusts to
> whom they are due and when you judge between people
> to judge with justice. Excellent is that which Allah instructs
> you. Indeed, Allah is ever Hearing and seeing. (4:58)

When criminal Shariah was codified, prominent jurists and legal scholars voiced strong support for the idea that it was the culmination of the self-determination by Muslim people in the post-colonial context. Honorable Justice Mohammed Bello, Chief Justice of Nigeria (retired), for example, stated that "Almighty Allah سبحانه و تعالى revealed in the Holy Qur'an the Law or Shariah, which he prescribed to all mankind and ordered that all shall be judged by it."[35] He further explained that "the Qur'an lays down the basic principles of Shariah, which are supplemented by the *Sunnah.*"[36] Just like Pakistan, Sudan, and Saudi Arabia, it was time for Nigeria to yield to the commandment of Almighty Allah سبحانه و تعالى and adopt Shariah.

---

34. Peters, *Crime and Punishment*, 146.
35. Bello, "Keynote Address," 7. Honorable Chief Justice Mohammed Bello, Chief Justice of Nigeria (1987–1995), is considered an erudite jurist.
36. Ibid. The Sunnah is defined by him as "a way, course, rule, mode or manner of acting or conduct of life practiced or approved by Prophet Muhammad (ﷺ), which are found in the Hadith." See also A. Khan, *Islam, Muslims, and America*, 183.

He concluded that Shariah has supremacy over all human laws in regulating conduct and action.[37]

In his paper, "Shariah: A Legal System and a Way of Life," Justice Abdulkadir Orire, Grand Khadi of Kwara State and Secretary-General of the Jama'atu Nasril Islam, opined that "nothing stands out as more symbolic of Muslim aspiration than the commitment to the re-establishment of Shariah as a code of conduct laid down by Allah سبحانه و تعالى for every Muslim to shape his or her life in accordance with its precepts. Shariah has therefore come to epitomize the goal towards whose provisions all true Muslims are restlessly trying to ensure that their lives are governed."[38]

Another proponent of the view that criminal Shariah is necessary for a moral Islamic life is Professor Muhib Opeleye, Professor of Islamic Studies and Dean of the Faculty of Arts at Lagos State University. When discussing Justice Abdallah's paper, the professor argued that "all Muslims who claim to be sincere or honest believers in God will have to accept, recognize and enforce Islamic penal code law as part and parcel of Shariah. This is because Shariah is a complete way of life and there can be no half-measure in its application otherwise one would be guilty of *kufr* (disbelief), *zulm* (wrong doing) or *fisq* (transgression) as we read in chapters 44–47 of the Holy Qur'an. Indeed the non-application of the Shariah in its totality would amount to a rejection of the faith and rebellion against the message brought by Prophet Muhammad (صلى الله عليه وسلم)."[39]

Ali A. Mazrui, a well-respected academic who has written extensively about Africa, suggests that if cultural self-determination is a factor in the implementation of Shariah law, globalization may also play a role. "The introduction of Shariah could have found a space within contending forces," Mazrui says. "What has not been discussed is whether the rise of Shariah militancy, is itself, a consequence of globalization. One of the repercussions of globalization worldwide has been to arouse cultural insecurity and

---

37. Bello, "Keynote Address," 7.
38. Orire, "Shariah," 25.
39. Abdallah, "Crime, Punishment and Evidence," 51.

uncertainty about identities. Indeed, the paradox of globalization is that it both promotes enlargement of economic scale and stimulates fragmentation of ethnic and cultural scales."[40]

One response to the fragmentation created by globalization is a desire for unity. Some argue that this desire motivated Northern Nigeria's implementation of the criminal aspect of Shariah as a way to unite against the growing power that Southern Nigeria was achieving at the federal level. Consequently, Yvonne Yazbeck Haddad suggests there is unity in diversity: Islamization and indigenization are propping up Islam as a focal point for diverse political movements and as a way of life with significant impact on the world's social fabric.[41] This line of thinking often promotes theories (known as the "clash of civilizations" and the "Islamic threat") that the Islamic religion is incompatible with many elements of modern societies and thus poses a growing threat.[42] Haddad states that Islamist activists are becoming part of mainstream society, not just its radical periphery. It is important to understand that this movement towards cultural fragmentation need not lead to greater divisions between groups, but can serve as building blocks that link our common humanity.

As a result of similar cultural misunderstandings, one of the most challenging aspects of codified Shariah law lies in its view of appropriate punishment for those convicted of crimes.[43] Many outsiders to the Islamic faith, for example, both in Nigeria and around the world, view the punishments of the codified Shariah (such as stoning to death) as ancient practices that are incompatible with modern social norms for humane

---

40.   Mazrui and Mutunga, *Debating the African Condition*, 288; see also E. McMahon and Sinclair, *Democratic Institution*, 63.

41.   Haddad et al., *Islamic Revival Since 1988*, 103. Haddad is a professor at the Prince Alwaheed Bin Talal Center for Muslim-Christian Understanding at Georgetown University, Washington, DC.

42.   The term "clash of civilizations" refers to the differences between Islamic cultures and values as well as the traditions of Western civilizations. This term will be further elaborated upon in later chapters.

43.   See also Clarke, *Fictions of Justice*, 217.

treatment.[44] A complex problem arises from these views; namely, the application of Shariah law to citizens who are not Muslim seems to many to discriminate against non-Muslims and to carry a heavy dose of unilateral religious bias. Critics believe the application of Shariah is discriminatory and argue that the Shariah penal code is evidence of a state-sponsored religion. It should be noted that the Shariah penal codes of every state that promulgated it, affirms, in no uncertain terms, that the law does not apply to non-Muslims. This concept is theoretically sound, but it has proven difficult to apply outside a society that is completely Muslim.

However, at a 2001 conference in Kaduna, Kaduna State, "Understanding *Shariah* in Nigeria," His Eminence the Sultan of Sokoto and the foremost religious leader of Muslims in Nigeria, said that the implementation of Shariah in Nigeria is not a new phenomenon. He explained that the codified Shariah is based on the Penal Code of Northern Nigeria (in place since 1959).[45] His Eminence added that "Muslims have always yearned and sought for the proper implementation of Shariah, which we regard as an integral part of our religion and our fundamental human right to freedom of worship."[46]

Distinguished and learned jurists, academicians, and religious leaders attended the seminar in Kaduna. The mostly Muslim group later issued a communiqué, expressing unanimous opinion that a misconception existed about the implementation of Shariah: its codification was a response to outside cultural pressures and Muslims' desire for autonomy. This misconception was largely a result of ignorance and misunderstanding produced by the plurality of legal systems in Nigeria. Shariah, they concluded, while an

---

44. In the case of Federation of Pakistan v. Hazoor Bakhsh, PLD 1983 FSC 255, while reviewing the constitutionality of the punishment of *rajm* (stoning to death), the Pakistani Federal Supreme Court recognized that the sentence is not provided for in the Qur'an. It is noteworthy that several instances of stoning appear in the Holy Bible, including Deut. 22:13-29, stoning for sexual misconduct; Deut. 13:6-11, stoning for stealing; and Lev. 24:10-16, stoning for blasphemy.
45. Yakubu et al., *understanding Shari'a, in Nigeria* vii.
46. Ibid.

important source of identity for Muslims is also mindful of the rights and obligations of non-Muslims.

Non-Muslim religious leaders echoed their opinion and cautioned their followers against regarding Muslims as extremists and fundamentalists. Muslim voices have also been raised in opposition to amputation and flogging of Muslims as permitted under Shariah law.[47] These acknowledgements of misrepresentations of Islam, as based on the actions of a minority of its followers, are an important step towards a more accurate and global understanding of Islam as a religion, Larbi Sadiki opined.[48]

In addition, the Council of Ulama (Muslim scholars) in Nigeria, in concurring in 2000 that the Constitution of Nigeria envisions the codification of Shariah as a right of all Nigerian Muslims, also determined that Shariah does not infringe upon the rights of others.[49] The General Secretary of the Nigerian Supreme Council for Islamic Affairs backed this belief.[50]

Some state governors have suggested that Christians in their respective states who wish to be governed by the canonical or other non-Islamic religious law should put forward a proposal for its government implementation, an idea as contrary to the doctrine of separation of state and religion as the introduction of Shariah law. The further challenge to the administration of justice under the Shariah penal codes is the fact that the Supreme Court of Nigeria has yet to decide on the issue of whether or not religious laws established by states are actually in violation of the Constitution of Nigeria, 1999, which ensures the separation of church and state.

However, these codifications of religious laws (whether Christian or Muslim) specifically state that they are not applicable to citizens who are

47.   Dr. Rowan Williams, Archbishop of Canterbury, shared this view in his "Civil and Religious Law." See also Nachmani, *Europe and Its Muslim Minorities*, 172; and *Human Right Watch Report's*, "'Political Shariah'?"
48.   Sadiki, *Search for Arab Democracy*, 121.
49.   Adegbite, "Discussion to 'Shari'a in a Multi-Religious Society,'" 155.
50.   *Nigerian Vanguard*, June 24, 2000. At the time, Sagir Mohammed, chairman of the Arewa People's Congress (APC), was the General Secretary of the Nigerian Supreme Council for Islamic Affairs.

not members of that particular faith, unless the citizen submits him or herself to the court's jurisdiction. As the Zamfara State Shariah Penal Code Law (ZSSPCL) makes clear: "every person who professes the Islamic faith and or every other person who voluntarily consents to the exercise of the jurisdiction of any of the [sic] Shariah courts established under the Shariah courts (administration of Justice and consequential changes) law, 1999, shall be liable to punishment under the Shariah penal code . . . "[51] While many differences exist, some will argue that unless one is inclined to do away with past precedent, including the pre-1999 Shariah, it may be inconceivable to maintain that Shariah criminal law (which is theoretically applicable only for Muslims) for some citizens in some states, amounts to a declaration of state religion.

Despite assurances to the contrary, whether non-Muslims in Nigeria are required to follow Shariah law is debatable. For instance, non-Muslims, especially females, who do not comply with stringent dress codes, according to some readings (or misreading) of the Shariah, are often the targets of censure by society and institutions of higher learning.[52] Also, non-Muslim merchants have suffered losses when their stock of alcohol is confiscated or destroyed by Muslims.[53] This issue of how the application of criminal

---

51.   Zamfara State Sariah Penal Code Law, 2000, No. 10,Vol. 3, Section 3.
52.   Zamfara State Hisbah Commission, Law No. 17, 2003, Section 6 (A law to provide for the establishment, composition, functions, and powers of Zamfara State Hisbah Commission); See also the Usmanu Danfodio University, Sokoto, Dress Code provision: Nudity and indecent appearance are not allowed on the university campus—violation will result to warning and rustication. Indecent dressing includes, "wearing of any dress that exposes the chest, un-buttoned or half buttoned skirts; use of tight/feature-exposing or transparent dresses, sleeveless short blouses, heavy make-ups' and excessive use of jewelry . . . " http://www.udusok.edu.ng/docx/UDUS-DRESS%20CODE.pdf.
53.   Ahmad, "Living with Conflict." The author recalls a case in which a company that distributed beer and other soft drinks had one of its trucks and its contents vandalized. Some youths, "enforcers of Shariah—*hisbah*—Shariah police," working under the contentious authority of politicians, stopped the truck as it traveled on a state highway and ordered the driver to get out. They told the driver that their state was now a Shariah state and explained why he should not drive his truck through their state. They then destroyed all of the alcoholic drinks and set the truck on fire. (Section 149 of Zamfara State Shariah Penal Code Law, 2000, No. 10, states: "Whoever drinks alcohol or any intoxicant voluntarily shall be punished with caning of eighty lashes.")

Shariah will affect non-Muslim Nigerian citizens constitutes one of the most important aspects of the debate regarding application of the Shariah law.[54] The application of the law can often be very different and even contrary to the theory behind it as a result of cultural appropriations of concepts rather than the strict interpretation of the law.

Yet, the poor and illiterate saw the codification of criminal Shariah as an equalizing agent that would bring about a more balanced society.[55] From their perspective, these new leaders of Shariah (governors, chairmen, and councilors) were finally going to stand by them.[56] Ahmad Sani, the governor of Zamfara State, capitalized on this hope when his campaign promised that the codification of Shariah would provide a new and prosperous life to the masses both in this world and hereafter. Because of the susceptibility of most of the needy and illiterate to political persuasion, Governor Sani's promises were accepted wholeheartedly and created a great excitement and expectation in the people.[57] Eight years later, when Governor Sani's term ended, opinion was divided between those who felt that the population in Zamfara (and in other states) still supported the implementation of Shariah and those who felt betrayed by the leadership.[58] Some even believed that the governor abused the people's trust to gain political power for himself, and that his administration was yet another example of the kind of corruption he had pledged to end.[59]

Dissenting Voices

Another theory traces the codification of Shariah law to a shift in Northern Nigerian sentiment after the "Northern military government leaders" cancelled the first acclaimed, internationally recognized legitimate elections in Nigeria in 1992. The alleged winner of that election, Alhaji

---

54.   Ahmad, "Living with Conflict."
55.   Kamrava, *New Voices of Islam*, 156.
56.   Chairmen are the heads of counties and councilors are local representatives.
57.   Dowden, "Africa," 445.
58.   Kirwin, "Popular Perceptions of Shari'a Law."
59.   Okike, *Practice of Sharia in Nigeria*, 29.

Moshood Abiola, was from the South (and a Muslim), and many in the North felt that the country's leaders, both military and civilian were appropriating political power for themselves and were indifferent to the South. Consequently, there surfaced among northerners a high wave of support for the South's political voice. So in 1999 when the presidential candidate Obasanjo (who was from the same southern region as Abiola) was on the ballot, most northerners voted in solidarity with Southern Nigeria for Obasanjo.[60]

However, many northerners soon realized that Obasanjo was not as supportive of the North as they thought he would be. They felt the North was losing political influence in the Nigerian Federation. As a result, the North began asserting new forms of autonomy, particularly in terms of religious and cultural self-determination—represented in this case by the codification of Shariah.[61]

Most people in Northern Nigeria expressed vigorous support for the codification of Shariah, and believed it to contain the solutions to many of the country's challenges, political and otherwise. However, another explanation for the codification of Shariah is that Shariah law is a "political bargaining chip" that the North can use to mitigate the power shift occurring in Nigeria. The influential Christian cleric Matthew Kukah, among others, has suggested that Shariah law may have been introduced to unite the North and destabilize Obasanjo's government. In the 1999 election the North "lost power" to the Christian South. However, as Obasanjo failed to fulfill some of his campaign promises to the North, Kukah argued that the Northern people realized they had no power—political, economic, or social. Moreover, Northerners realized they were educationally disadvantaged and lacking commercial viability and saw the quest for Shariah as a viable unifying force.[62] To regain some of its political power, it was suggested, the

---

60. Ado-Kurawa, *Shariah and the Press*, 88.
61. Father Matthew Kukah, personal interview with the author, Abuja, Nigeria, 2007.
62. Regarding education, one former Justice Minister from the Southwest considered the North to be "twenty years" behind the South. See Ado-Kurawa, *Shariah and the Press*, 102.

North needed to "destabilize" the new government; the codification of Shariah was a means to do that.[63]

Results from the May 1999 election, Kukah explained, reveal that Obasanjo, with no political base, had been able to win because of Northern Nigeria's support.[64] The North knew that the presidency would give Obasanjo the ability to confer many advantages to his allies, including important national and international positions, monetary assistance to individual states to address marginalization, federal presence at the state level, and recognition through appointment of senior civil service at the federal level of government. The North was particularly encouraged because the Constitution of the People's Democratic Party (of which Obasanjo was a member) set out favorable guidelines for the distribution of power, resources, wealth, and opportunities to zones, states, and localities.[65] However, this strategy seems to have backfired, as Obasanjo was perceived as failing to live up to his promises of equal access. In retaliation, it was suggested that the North decided to thwart Obasanjo's government by codifying Shariah in twelve of the nineteen Northern states in October 1999.[66]

Shariah and the Constitution

The discourse about the constitutionality of criminal Shariah centers on the 1999 codification of public law, specifically criminal law. Scholars suggest that the British colonialists prevented Shariah from influencing public and criminal law when they indirectly ruled Northern Nigeria, from 1900 to 1914 (the period before the amalgamation of Northern and Southern protectorates) through independence on October 1, 1960.[67] During Nigeria's years as a British colony, Nigerians seemed to reach a consensus

63. Kukah, *Religion, Politics and Power*; see also Ado-Kurawa, *Shariah and the Press*, 210, 324, and 60.
64. Ado-Kurawa, *Shariah and the Press*, 198 and 205.
65. Dan-Musa, *Party Politics and Personal Struggle*, 53.
66. Ado-Kurawa, *Shariah and the Press*, 360.
67. Yadudu, "Shari'a in a Multi-Religious Society," 148; see also Yadudu, "Islamic Law and Reform Discourse"; and Ojiakor and Ojih, *Nigerian Peoples and Culture*, 11.

that the application of Shariah was restricted to personal law matters such as marriage, adoption, inheritance, and bequest, but the application of Shariah to criminal law matters was not.

In contrast, many Muslims today believe the Constitution of Nigeria allows prosecution of offenses under Shariah law. For example, Governor Sani defended the legality of his declaration that Zamfara is now "the Shariah State of Zamfara," by highlighting the opening statement of the Constitution, which states that "the Nigerian Constitution is supreme and made under God."[68] He interpreted this to mean that God/Allah سبحانه و تعالى, and thus Shariah, has supremacy over the Nigerian Constitution. His interpretation may be based on Qur'an 23:88–89:

> In whose hand is the realm of all things and He protects while none can protect against Him if you should know? Rather, we have brought them the truth, and indeed they are liars . . .

We should not judge Sani's reasoning valid without first recognizing the importance of respecting the Nigerian Constitution as a reflection of the will of the people. As put by the erudite Dr. Usman Bugaje (a well respected Islamic voice in Northern Nigeria), "[as] in the Nigerian Constitution, as, in the Constitution of Western countries from whence all the [ideas are borrowed],[69] sovereignty belongs to the people. In other words it is the 'will of the people' that is supreme."[70]

Thus Section 4 of the Constitution of the Federal Republic of Nigeria, 1999, suggests that states can make laws to promote good governance. It also provides the affirmation and solemn resolve of the Nigerian people "to live in unity and harmony as one indivisible and indissoluble sovereign nation under God."[71] The central question therefore becomes: Do states of

---

68. Constitution of the Federal Republic of Nigeria, 1999, Preamble. See also Ranger, *Evangelical Christianity and Democracy*, 41; and Marshall, *Talibanization of Nigeria*, 9.
69. This author thinks that statement is verbose.
70. Bugaje, "Education, Values, Leadership."
71. Constitution of the Federal Republic of Nigeria, 1999, Preamble, No. 27, Vol. 86.

the federation, specifically the twelve Northern states in Nigeria that have adopted Shariah law since the year 1999 have the right and/or duty to promulgate the Shariah Penal Code Law? Sections 4, 5, 6, 10, 14, 15, 36, 38, 277, and 278, and the Second Schedule of the 1999 Nigerian Constitution detail the powers of the Federal Republic of Nigeria that are vested in the National Assembly for the Nigerian Federation and in the House of Assembly of individual states.[72] For example, Section 4 avails the Senate and the House of Representatives, as well as the State House of Assembly, legislative powers. The section allows the said bodies to establish laws within their domains (federal and state), to make laws for peace, order, and good governance:

> The National Assembly shall have power to make laws for the peace, order and good government of the Federation or any part thereof with respect to any matter. . . . The House of Assembly of a State shall have power to make laws for the peace, order and good government of the State or any part thereof . . . [73]

However, subsection 5 of Section 4 states that:

> If any law enacted by the House of Assembly of a State is inconsistent with any law validly made by the National Assembly [Senate and House of Representatives], the law made by the National Assembly shall prevail, and the other Law shall to the extent of the inconsistency be void.

Additionally, Section 1 subsections 1 and 3 of the Constitution underscored Section 4 when it stipules that:

> This Constitution is supreme and its provisions shall have binding force on all authorities and persons throughout

---

72. Relevant sections of the Constitution, including Sections 4, 5, 6, 10, 14, 15, 36, 38, 277, and 278 are presented in the Compendium.
73. Ibid., Section 4.

the Federal Republic of Nigeria . . . if any other law is inconsistent with the provisions of this Constitution, this Constitution shall prevail, and that other law shall to the extent of the inconsistency be void.

So therefore any law enacted by the House of Assembly of a state that is inconsistent with any law validly made by the National Assembly, shall, to the extent of the inconsistency, be void; the law made by the National Assembly shall prevail. This description of legislative powers may be examined in light of Section 10 of the Constitution, which states: "The Government of the Federation or of a State shall not adopt any religion as [a] State Religion."

According to Professor Ben Nwabueze, a constitutional lawyer and scholar, the question of whether state government can employ its power "to codify Shariah criminal law in all its plenitude and enforce it against Muslims and non-Muslim offenders," or to restrict it only to Muslims, may lay bare its character as the law, albeit in a modified form of the religion of Islam and expose it as a state sponsorship of that religion. He added, "State enforcement of Shariah in all the plentitude of its injunctions cannot in the multi-religious society of Nigeria coexist with a truly federal form of political association."[74] However, Professor Auwalu Yadudu, a legal adviser to the Nigerian government during the 1999 Constitutional conference, argues that "the demand by Nigerian Muslims in Northern Nigeria was in accordance with the provision of the Constitution."[75] Furthermore, assenting voices for the implementation of Shariah suggested that the Constitution that sets up the Shariah Court of Appeal to enforce Shariah couldn't logically make the application of Shariah a violation of the same constitution.[76]

There is affirmation that the autonomy of a constituent state in a federal system in legal and religious spheres to adopt criminal Shariah could amount

74.   Korieh, "Islam and Politics in Nigeria," 119.
75.   Ibid.
76.   Ibid.

to the adoption of Islam as a state religion, such as the case of Zamfara State. Could Zamfara State adoption of Shariah criminal law be contrary to Section 10 of the 1999 Constitution and inconsistent with Nigeria as a law-based state?[77] It was submitted that legislators administer and abide by the provisions of the 1999 Constitution and their oaths of office "to uphold and defend the said Constitution." Another assertion is that the 1999 Constitution legitimacy could be argued legally or politically—legally as an enactment of a former military government, therefore all changes made to it during the reign of the military government were "illegitimate," and that the government has no legitimate authority to enact Section 10. One of the dangers of this argument, however, is that it would nullify the 1999 Nigerian Constitution in its entirety.

Section 6 provides for the powers of the judiciary with respect to its jurisdiction to decide cases. It outlines the hierarchy of courts for the Federation of Nigeria and also allows the states to create courts to preserve justice in their jurisdiction. Likewise, Section 277 clearly defines the jurisdiction of the Shariah Court of Appeal as having appellate and supervisory jurisdiction in civil proceedings involving questions of Islamic personal law, of which the court is competent to decide. These include: questions regarding a marriage (or its dissolution) concluded in accordance with the law; questions "regarding a *wakf*, gift, will, or succession where the endower, testator, or deceased person is a Muslim";[78] questions regarding a Muslim infant or person of unsound mind; questions in which all parties to the proceedings are Muslim and have requested that the court hear the case to determine if it is in accordance with Islamic personal law, and so on.[79]

The combined effects of the Second Schedule (which provides that some sections of the Nigerian Constitution deal solely with areas of law that are reserved for the National Assembly); the provision of the Evidence Act (specifying rules of evidence), and Section 1 of the Constitution (which

---

77. Senghor and Poku, *Towards Africa's Renewal*, 328.
78. Constitution of the Federal Republic of Nigeria, 1999.
79. See also Mahmood, *Personal Law in Islamic Countries*, 14.

prevents states from enacting legislation contrary to the 1999 Nigerian Constitution) could be employed to test the constitutionality/legal grounds for criminal Shariah.[80] The Second Schedule of the 1999 Nigerian Constitution also disallows states from drafting legislation in certain areas of law. One of these areas is federal law, under which the Evidence Act was established.

According to renowned legal scholar and former Chief Justice of Nigeria, Honorable Justice Mohammed Bello, Section 4 of the 1999 Nigerian Constitution divided the legislative powers of the government between the federation and the states, specifying the exclusive legislative list on which only the National Assembly may make laws, and the concurrent list, on which both the federation and the states may make laws in the Constitution's Second Schedule. States could exclusively make laws only on matters not included in the two lists. Because Shariah falls within the residue, a state has the constitutional power to make laws relating to Shariah. The 1999 Constitution adopted all laws and courts that existed before May 29, 1999. Hence, Sections 315 and 316 of the 1999 Constitution adopted the civil aspect of Shariah and Area Courts.[81]

Justice Bello further suggested that Section 1 of the Constitution asserts its supremacy and Section 36(12) provides that a person should not be convicted for any Shariah offense unless the National Assembly or State House of Assembly enacts that offense and its punishment. Therefore, application of the criminal aspect of Shariah without codification could be unconstitutional. He observed that Shariah, as stated in the noble Qur'an, Hadith, and other sources, is not "written law" within the meaning of Section 36(12).[82] Furthermore, Section 38(1) of the constitution ensures

---

80.   The Constitution of the Federal Republic of Nigeria, 1999, Second Schedule, deals solely with areas of law that are reserved for the National Assembly. Nigerian states may not pass legislation in areas of law specifically reserved for the federal government within the Second Schedule of the Constitution of Nigeria, 1999. The Evidence Act is a federal act regarding the evidentiary procedures in Nigerian courts.

81.   Bello, "Keynote Address," 14.

82.   It has been suggested that for Muslims, Qur'an and Hadith are the universal sources of Islamic law. See Foltz, *Animals in Islamic Tradition*, 29.

for every person the right to freedom of religion, including freedom to change religion or belief, whereas under Shariah, *ridda* (apostasy) is a capital offense.[83]

The provision of *ridda*, Justice Bello opined, could be inconsistent with Section 38(1), and therefore by virtue of Section 1 could be unconstitutional. Bello suggested that the states couldn't establish Shariah law because they cannot actually regulate its evidentiary rules, as this area of law can be promulgated only by the federal legislature.[84] Because the political climate has transitioned from military to democratic rule, elected officials who govern the state are obliged to promote and protect the Constitution.[85] They cannot in the same breath make laws that are contrary to the provisions of the Second Schedule of the Nigerian Constitution. Sections of the Nigerian Constitution in relation to Shariah law will be examined in greater depth in later chapters. Worthy of note, however, is the idea eruditely stated by Abdullahi Ahmed An-Na'im that Shariah does play a fundamental role in the development of ethical norms and social values which in turn could reflect on legislation and public policy.[86]

---

83. Bello, "Keynote Address," 14; see also An-Na'im, *Islam and the Secular State*, 117.
84. Bello, "Keynote Address," 14.
85. See the Constitution of the Federal Republic of Nigeria, 1999, Seventh Schedule, which states among other things the oaths of office taken by political office holders as follows " . . . swear/affirm that I will be faithful and bear true allegiance to the Federal Republic of Nigeria; . . . I will discharge my duties to the best of my ability, faithfully and in accordance with the Constitution of the Federal Republic of Nigeria and the law . . . I will not allow my personal interest to influence my official conduct or my official decisions; that I will do to the best of my ability preserve, protect and defend the Constitution of the Federal Republic of Nigeria; . . . that in all circumstances, I will do right to all manner of people, according to law, without fear or favor, affection or ill-will; . . . and that I will devote myself to the service and well-being of the people of Nigeria."
86. An-Na'im, *Islam and the Secular State*, 1. Note also that the spirit of Shariah is one of acknowledgment, concession, and restraint. Described as bold, pragmatic, and deeply rooted in Islamic history and theology, Prof. An-Na'im is Charles Howard Candler Professor of Law at Emory University. A Muslim from northern Sudan, he promotes modernist understanding of Islam, and the cultural legitimacy and practical efficacy of international human rights standards. Particularly in relation to Islam in African societies, he is an accomplished author and directs several research projects that focus on advocacy strategies for reform through internal cultural transformation.

Summary

While considering appeals to the Shariah courts, from the Shariah trial courts, one should be mindful of the dynamics of the law, and the collateral effects these factors can have on society. It is important to understand that the codification of Shariah law intended a unified administration of the local standards, laws, and morals that would unite religion and government. Shariah does not recognize the concept of separation of religion and state as Western legal systems do. By its very nature, Shariah envisions a legal system largely controlled, ruled, and regulated by religious doctrine; thus, not only do government, law, and religion intersect, but they also merge. However, this should not be seen to trump the democratically accepted legal frameworks of countries.

Since Shariah's codification, though, the number of people who have lost their lives to violence has increased significantly. This has mainly been due to a general misunderstanding of Shariah, which has resulted in strife and violent conflict between peoples of various religions. If the cardinal principle of the rule of law is to ensure security, then the agencies of the government responsible for its enforcement, especially within the confines of the administration of the new law, must make more widespread and better efforts to maintain the peace and to guarantee the security of persons and property.

In a nation as diverse as Nigeria, it can be difficult even with the most carefully crafted and executed legislation to ensure that the law be readily understandable and enforceable through an accessible court system. The foundation of Islamic Shariah is justice, fairness, and human dignity. However, the enactment of most of the Shariah Penal Code Law was done in haste, resulting in a plethora of contextual lapses that might affect the administration of justice. When a law contains contradictions, omissions, defective wordings,[87] and so on, the power of such a law is undermined

---

87.   Peters, *Reintroduction of Islamic Criminal Law*, 18.

and the ability of a court to protect the rights of citizens could become an unattainable challenge.

Over the past years, the judicial system's efficiency has also been brought into question, owing to the fact that judges, court staffs, and lawyers have not been appropriately trained in the process of Shariah criminal issues and adjudication. For the most part, lawyers have studied common law or a combination of common and Islamic laws, and are not equipped to adjudicate Shariah criminal law, especially in cases where the death penalty could potentially result. In addition, judges and lawyers have demonstrated a tendency to be affected by the intensity of cases in which public sentiment is running high. When public emotions are allowed to color the decisions of judges and officers of the court, justice and innocent people could suffer.

Moreover, at the inception of the codification of Shariah in 1999, insufficient attention was given to other details: societal challenges, such as illiteracy in matters of religion; poverty, which had made contracting marriage a financial difficulty; the challenges posed by a new wave of attempts to imbibe "Western ways of life," especially by the youth; and issues such as equal protection under the law and unbiased application of the rule of law across varying social classes and gender. By analyzing the social, legal, and political implications of Shariah law in Northern Nigeria, we can gain a greater understanding of the social vulnerabilities that continue to foster tensions and promote an uninformed view. It feels as if there is collective failure of academics, politicians, lawyers, judges, and activists to chart a way forward that will result in less religious friction and violent conflict, and affirm Nigeria's ability to articulate a clear goal for its future. Attention to the dynamics I have described in this chapter often requires us to step outside of our role as lawyers and embrace additional roles, such as that of a psychologist, ethicist, or historian. These dynamics are an essential part of the bigger picture. Any lawyer practicing before a Shariah court could face taking into account these competing factors and learning to work with them, not against them. One must understand the dynamics of any given structure in order to succeed within it.

CHAPTER TWO

Pay Attention to Details and Look for a Creative Approach

CULTURAL NORMS EXIST THAT ARE known only in local courts and within the local society. Lawyers from outside a given jurisdiction will want to pay attention to these details, which may determine the issues before some courts more than the actual substance of the law. Beyond this, it is crucial to understand the duties and responsibilities of lawyers and of judges, before which one will be appearing. This chapter explains such duties. By applying legal theory to legal practice, lawyers are provided with a skilled understanding of the practice of law: an introduction to the sources of Shariah, its application, and the intricacies of the courtroom serve as the building blocks to this end.[88] A brief discussion about the importance of paying attention to the role of the Shariah judge within the context of the local jurisdiction is presented at the end of the chapter.

When we began arguing cases in Zamfara State in 2000, the substantive law of the Shariah penal code was in effect, but there was no codified

---

88.   Doi, *Shariah*, 21.

procedural law.[89] Subsequently, as other states adopted the Shariah penal code, courts in these states began handling Shariah cases without a procedural code as well. In the absence of a procedural code it is difficult to know how to approach and effectively argue before a court. Nearly impossible were matters such as identifying exhibits to be introduced and evidence and proof to be used; calling witnesses, expert or otherwise; and knowing what type of documentation can be established. Most importantly, because Shariah courts were newly created, having functioned as Area Courts only a few months earlier, lawyers and judges had little knowledge of how to address the Shariah penal code and its new jurisdiction for criminal cases. As a result, the effectiveness and value of the law became seriously impaired.

The case of Bariya Ibrahim Magazu is an example of how these procedural shortcomings can frustrate the defense of justice. Magazu was a physically challenged girl of about thirteen years old, who became pregnant and was sentenced to be flogged 180 times for both the pregnancy and for telling lies against the three men she alleged to have raped her.[90] As the first publicized case to come before the "new Shariah courts," widespread public support of the court's decision was not unexpected. Wishing to capitalize on his campaign promise, the new governor of Zamfara State, Ahmad Sani, was determined to make an example of Magazu. For many people her sentence underscored the moral regenerative nature of application of criminal Shariah. Unfortunately, this shifting of the scales of justice in favor of public sentiment over the rule of law leaves victims of the new system wondering why they are singled out. Having little money or means of support, many are easily cast to the sidelines. Magazu was without formal education—as were more than one hundred of the other Shariah clients in whose defense I was involved—so she was unable to read or write.

---

89. The legal team that I was part of varied from state to state, remaining cognizant of each local dynamics.

90. Depending on who and where, marriage to young girls could be frowned upon. See Bradley, *Behind the Veil of Vice*, 17; see also Pant, *It Is Continued*, 134.

The first step I took before drafting Magazu's appeal was to assemble a team comprised of local lawyers, Islamic clerics and scholars, and opinion leaders. This is an important process because each person brings a unique perspective to the trial. Our job was to look at the court records. Why was Magazu, a physically challenged, thirteen-year-old girl sentenced to be flogged 180 times for pregnancy even though she claimed she was raped? Each member of the team raised ideas and questions that helped us put together a legal appeal.

From the onset of the appeal, we became amply aware of the weight of public opinion. Although courts adjudicate at trial, the court's personnel are members of the community. Their interactions outside the courtroom may at times influence their decisions in the case. In Magazu's case it was necessary for us to state that it was not acceptable for a woman to become pregnant out of wedlock.

The key point here, which many overlook, is that taking on a Shariah defense case brings in complexities beyond the procedural issues one may face in court. If an individual lawyer or a legal team is perceived, either during or after the case, of being anti-Shariah, anti-societal values, or of seeing the case as merely a win-lose situation, rather than as an attempt to achieve justice, these perceptions may negatively affect the outcome. It is thus essential that lawyers pay attention to these details, that they observe closely, and listen to their intuition in arguing the case.

General Dynamics

Certain subtleties require a lawyer's keen power of observation and sharp intuition in order to detect details surrounding a case. Focusing one's attention on these unstated, but nevertheless critical factors can allow a lawyer to effectively determine the various details at work in a given situation. For example, observing and respecting the community's feelings, reactions, and cultural norms often impact the level of support that community will offer.

It is crucial that a lawyer's personal response to a case not veil his or her unbiased commitment to justice and the rule of law. For example, while many people might be tempted to greet an acquittal with a victory celebration, in certain cases—especially cases of *zina* (adultery/fornication)—this celebration should be avoided.[91] Such a joyous display of victory toward what amounts to a very serious breach of moral conduct within society could seriously offend the greater community. In some of these cases, victory involves crossing societal boundaries of extreme importance to the people in the community who view these values as the fabric that ties the society together and deters immorality. Whenever an acquittal is granted, we should avoid all outward expressions of any sort, although I must admit that unfortunately the media captured just such a reaction in one of our cases.[92]

It is equally important to understand that displays of unacceptable behavior or public reaction to a case could upset a victory. For example, individuals with fundamentalist views could take the law into their own hands and exact their own punishment by way of a lynch mob, resulting in the execution of the accused.[93] It is therefore important to respect the sensibilities of society and to understand that, while this responsiveness may have allowed the court to adjudicate favorably in a certain case, the community may not respond well to joyous demonstrations celebrating an acquittal for the accused. Some in the community believe that punishments like flogging or stoning an adulteress to death is the main deterrent keeping other young women from becoming pregnant out of wedlock. They fear that a bad precedent will be set if an adulterer, or one whom they perceive to be an adulterer, escapes punishment. Most members of the community will

---

91.   Doi states also that "in Islam sex is sacred and not a thing to be made cheap and lowly," that is why society should shun away from an adulteress (*Western Civilization, Islam*, 15).
92.   "Hauwa Ibrahim—2005," Sakharov network blog from Sakharov prize laureates, 2005, http://sakharovnetwork.rsfblog.org/archive/2008/12/04/hauwa-ibrahim-2005.html.
93.   For example, Asha Ibrahim Dhuhulow was executed for an alleged crime of adultery in October 2008 in Somalia. Mohamed Abukar Ibrahim was stoned to death by militants from the Hizb al-Islam group in Afgoye, a district of Somalia, in December 2009. See Mohamed, "Public anger at the recent stoning of a 13-year-old girl"; and Birt, "Let he who casts the first stone," *TimesLive*, Dec. 16, 2009. Not suggesting that the stonings were as a result of celebration.

not tolerate such a violation of their core values, especially in the presence of celebration.

When the awareness necessary for challenging situations such as this is recognized, creative approaches can be applied in a respectful manner to achieve a lasting and meaningful outcome. Having navigated through the legal and cultural labyrinths that come with taking on a Shariah defense case, our legal team found that a combination of aptitude, research, knowledge of the leading schools of thought in Shariah law, familiarity with how Shariah cases have been approached elsewhere, and attention to details within the courtroom itself all helped us argue cases successfully. As trial lawyers, we are constantly required to make immediate decisions on our feet. Often our most effective tool was following our intuition, based on important details, and our knowledge of the local environment.

When legal systems like the Shariah penal code are first codified, new ideas are often needed to help formulate their application. For example, private meetings with potentially opposing forces often diffused the opponent's adamant resistance and enabled us to achieve far more than would have been thought possible. These meetings enabled us to hold conversations with those who did not want to be publicly linked to us, including unusual allies and sometimes even direct opponents. Capitalizing on this system of details, we were able to take a more comprehensive approach to arguing our cases. When used in comparable situations, these techniques can allow a legal system such as the codified Shariah to flourish in defense of justice.

A lawyer's ability to rethink and adapt an approach to different situations is an important skill. One productive approach that has proven useful for our team is to meet with clerics before appearing in court to get their advice in a specific case as to what is in the best interest of a specific society and overall justice. Another useful approach before appearing in courts is to be educated by the *mallams* (teachers) on issues of Shariah, even where our opinions differed. These approaches help to create an impression that we are not against the opposing counsel or forcing new doctrines and trying to get the court to do our bidding, but that we are instead partners for justice—for the client and society. Creative approaches should not, however, be limited to the strategies set forth in this book. They must instead be tailored to appropriately fit a lawyer's own method and style. Lawyers must pick and choose what will provide the most success for them and their client. Creativity and innovation, especially with regards to the technicalities of the law, are essential parts of a lawyer's skill set.

Practicing and Applying the Law

Although it is important to know and respect the cultural norms of the community, attention to the law as well as to the schools of thought that might influence its interpretation is crucial. Lawyers will do well to pay systematic attention to the theoretical and methodological approaches used to explain and analyze the contents, mannerisms, and intended results of Shariah, as different approaches to the law advocate different perspectives—philosophical, political, historical, social, etc. While defending clients in Shariah courts, we are to formulate interpretations of the law that acknowledge the uniqueness of each case while still working within the Shariah penal code. For example, when arguing that there is equality before the law under criminal Shariah, we reference verses from the Qur'an and Hadith that clearly express Islamic teaching of equality and the need for our client to enjoy its benefits. By working within the system of Shariah, we also seek the court's willingness to be persuaded by the prior decisions of other courts on similar issues, both in Nigeria and in other countries with parallel Shariah laws, such as Pakistan and Sudan.

While we have handled cases on a variety of charges, the bulk of our cases are related to *zina* (adultery/fornication), which is defined, for example, in Section 124 of the Katsina Penal Code Law. "[W]hoever, being a man or woman, fully responsible, has sexual intercourse through the genitalia of a person over whom he has no sexual rights and in the circumstances in which 'no doubt exist[s]' as to the illegality of the act, is guilty of the offense of *zina*."[94] The Katsina penal code further states that the offense could be proven in seven mutually supportive ways:

---

94.   Katsina State Shariah Penal Code Law, 2001, Vol. 4, Chapters 143–180.

The conditions for proving the offences of zina (fornication or adultery) or rape in respect of a married person are as follows:

a) Islam
b) Maturity
c) Sanity
d) Valid marriage
e) Consummation of marriage
f) Four witnesses
g) Confession

If any of the above conditions has been proved by the person alleging zina or rape there is no punishment for stoning to death; the person alleging such offence shall be imprisoned for one year and shall also be liable to caning which may extend to one hundred lashes.[95]

It is important to underscore that for a conviction of *zina* to be consistent with the intent of Shariah law, all of the above may need to be considered.

Sections 130 and 131 also name the penalty to be applied should one violate this law.

Whoever by words either spoken or reproduced by mechanical means or intended to be read or by signs or by visible representations makes or publishes any false imputation of (zina) adultery or sodomy concerning a chaste person (muhsan), or contests the paternity of such person even where such person is dead, is said to commit the offence of (qadhf) false accusation of adultery or fornication . . . Whoever commit the offence of qadhf shall be punished with eighty lashes of cane, and his testimony shall not be accepted thereafter unless he repents.

---

95.   Ibid. Doi states this similar provision in his *Women in Sharīah*, 119.

In practice, our experience has been that men and women who are married, have been previously married, or have any semblance of marriage—even if they are widowed—if convicted are punished to death by stoning. In the case of a person who has never been married, however, the same statute says that the guilty party is to be flogged one hundred times and shall also be liable to imprisonment for a term of one year.[96]

Despite the detail presented in this section of the Katsina penal code, there remains much ambiguity in how due process manifests itself in cases before the trial courts. For example, who should report the case of *zina*? Should the one responsible for the act of *zina* be the one to do so, thereby gaining purification for her or him in the life to come? Can someone else report the offense? And to whom should it be reported? Can the police—whose main duties as outlined in the Nigerian Constitution are to prevent and detect crime, to apprehend offenders, and to preserve law and order—take up the responsibility of identifying infractions?[97] Did the woman accused break civil law and cause civil disorder by becoming pregnant without a "legal husband"? What is the position of the law with respect to a man who cannot naturally become pregnant but has committed *zina*? What is the role of the enforcers of Shariah (*hisbah* or *da'awah*) in these cases? Having clear and consistent answers to these questions will largely affect whether or not the accused is granted substantial due process and, ultimately, justice. To begin to sort out these ambiguities, let us turn to a review of the interpretive strands of the sources of Shariah.

The Theme of Justice Inherent in Shariah Law

The Qur'an regards justice as a supreme virtue, second only to belief in God. Justice is given the highest status in the Qur'an; the prime objective

---

96.   Section 125(a) of the said Penal Code Law states that, "whosoever commit the offense of zina shall be punished with caning of one hundred lashes if unmarried, and shall also be liable for imprisonment for a term of one year."

97.   See the Constitution of the Federal Republic of Nigeria, 1999, Sections 214–216, and the Police Act, Section 4.

of Islam is to establish justice on earth.[98] In fact, for Muslims, justice and doing good to both Muslims and non-Muslims are essential features of their religious practice.[99] Because it is understood as the means of rendering equal treatment to others within the limits of our abilities, the application of justice in Islam transcends considerations of race, religion, creed, and gender.[100] Muslims are commanded to be just to their friends and foes alike, and to be just at all levels. Scholars agree that justice is "the greatest of all the duties entrusted to the Prophets . . . and it is the strongest justification for man's stewardship of earth," since it fuels a state of equilibrium in the distribution

---

98. "Indeed, Allah orders justice . . . " (Q. 16:90) and "We have already sent our messengers with clear evidences and sent down with them the Scripture and the balance that the people may maintain [their affairs] in justice . . . " (Q. 57:25).

99. Abu-Nimer, *Nonviolence and Peace Building*, 37.

100. "And among those We created is a community which guides by truth and thereby establishes justice" (Q. 7:181); "O you who have believed, be persistently standing firm in justice, witnesses for Allah, even if it be against yourselves or parents and relatives. Whether one is rich or poor, Allah is more worthy of both. So follow not [personal] inclination, lest you not be just. And if you distort [your testimony] or refuse [to give it], then indeed Allah is ever, with what you do, Acquainted" (Q. 4:135); "[They are] avid listeners to falsehood, devourers of [what is] unlawful. So if they come to you, [O Muhammad], judge between them or turn away from them. And if you turn away from them—never will they harm you at all. And if you judge, judge between them with justice. Indeed, Allah loves those who act justly" (Q. 5:42); "O you who have believed, be persistently standing firm for Allah, witnesses in justice, and do not let the hatred of a people prevent you from being just. Be just; that is nearer to righteousness. And fear Allah; indeed, Allah is acquainted with what you do" (Q. 5:8); "And for every nation is a messenger. So when their messenger comes, it will be judged between them in justice, and they will not be wronged" (Q. 10: 47); "We have already sent Our messengers with clear evidences and sent down with them the Scripture and the balance that the people may maintain [their affairs] in justice. And We sent down iron, wherein is great military might and benefits for the people, and so that Allah may make evident those who support Him and His messengers unseen. Indeed, Allah is Powerful and Exalted in Might" (Q. 57:25); "Say, [O Muhammad], 'My Lord has ordered justice and that you maintain yourselves [in worship of Him] at every place [or time] of prostration, and invoke Him, sincere to Him in religion.' Just as He originated you, you will return [to life]" (Q. 7:29); "So to that [religion of Allah] invite, [O Muhammad], and remain on a right course as you are commanded and do not follow their inclinations but say, 'I have believed in what Allah has revealed of the Qur'an, and I have been commanded to do justice among you.' Allah is our Lord and your Lord. For us are our deeds, and for you your deeds, There is no [need for] argument between us and you. Allah will bring us together, and to Him is the [final] destination" (Q. 42:15).

of rights and duties within the human family.[101] Justice as fairness under the law is inherent in Shariah law.

Lawyers, however, are best not to confine themselves to these commentaries on justice. Those who employ with equal vigor and confidence the idea of justice that underlies the Shariah penal code will find greater avenues to success. For example, Section 65 of the Sokoto State Shariah Penal Code Law (SSSPCL), 2000, affirms that a person is criminally liable only if he or she has attained the full legal age, mental soundness, and religious capacity; or if the act or omission is done intentionally or negligently. Other similar conditions exist for conviction; such as, that the accused is intellectually competent to commit the offense and that the act was done voluntarily.[102]

The evidence for the offense of *zina*, for example, must be clear and irrefutable; the punishment requires four adult Muslim witnesses testifying that they saw and can describe the sexual act in detail (this will be dealt with in detail in chapter 6). If the accuser cannot produce satisfactory evidence, then the Qur'an indicates,

> And those who launch a charge against chaste women, and
> produce not four witnesses (to support their allegations),
> flog them with eighty stripes; and reject their testimony
> ever after: for such men are wicked transgressors;—Unless
> they repent thereafter and mend (their conduct); for Allah
> is Oft-Forgiving, Most Merciful (24:4–5).[103]

This is echoed in Sections 141 and 142 of the Sokoto State Shariah Penal Code Law, 2000:

> Whoever by words either spoken or reproduced by
> mechanical means or intended to be read or by signs or
> by visible representations makes or publishes any false

---

101. Kurzman, *Modernist Islam*, 176; see also Esposito, *Oxford History of Islam*, 98.
102. SSSPCL, Section 66.
103. See also Mansour, "Hudud Crimes," 199.

imputation of zina or sodomy concerning a chaste person (muhsan), or contests the paternity of such person even where such person is dead, is said to commit the offense qadhf (lying) . . . and shall be punished with eighty lashes of cane . . .

Where such evidence is not given within these stated parameters, it is not to be admitted. In fact, the aforementioned male witnesses are to be flogged publicly as a deterrent to others who might also be tempted to provide false testimony. Providing false testimony of fornication is itself a crime, called *qadhf.* This is a very important provision, especially to an accused person. On one hand, this certainly affirms and provides for an accused person a protection from false accusers, and on the other hand a guarantee for an individual's right to privacy and security, a provision found in both Shariah and the Nigerian Constitution.

Because the Shariah penal code is rooted in the importance of a fair trial and the goal of achieving justice, the presentation of evidence should be in accordance with, and measure up to, these standards. For instance, in the time of the prophet Muhammad (ﷺ), people could not utilize medical testing in cases of fornication. However, as technology has advanced, the presentation of an accredited paternity test in court, for example, can further the interest of justice—a major tenet, as we have seen, of both Islam and the Shariah penal code.

The demand for justice can be a powerful argument in a multitude of cases. With respect to proof of *zina*, for example, should the woman who becomes pregnant, whether by consent or through rape, report the pregnancy? In the societies where our legal team has worked this may not be so simple because sexual relationships outside of marriage are not acceptable, and the woman may be resented by admitting to fornication. The Qur'an and Hadith, however, provide some latitude, when it comes to reporting incidences of fornication, such as the one found in the Hadith of Saḥīḥ al-Bukhari. Narrated by Jabir bin Abdullahi al-Ansari, this Hadith states that "a man from the tribe of Bani Aslam came to Allah's Apostle to inform him that he had committed illegal sexual intercourse and bore four witnesses against himself . . . ."[104] Another Hadith, narrated by Abu Huraira, says, "A man came to Allah's Apostle . . . and said, 'O Allah's Apostle! I have committed illegal sexual intercourse . . . .'"[105] Yet another, narrated by Ibn 'Abbas, says, "When Ma'iz bin Malik came to the Prophet . . ."[106] In all of these episodes the guilty persons are not coerced to confess but act of their own volition.

Another important question remains. To whom should an offender report? In the above-cited cases, they reported to the prophet Muhammad (ﷺ), the Apostle of Allah سبحانه و تعالى. Who today is like unto the Apostle, a good, thoughtful statesman, truthful and trusted, to whom one could report?[107] This begs the question, and a possible suggestion by a professor at the American University in Lebanon, whom we met in 2003, that it may be impossible to have the offense of adultery/fornication in the law books. As we need a person with such qualities to sit in judgment of such an offense, and since there may be hardly such a person living, Shariah could be ridiculed to have such a provision in the law books, he added.[108] This

---

104. Abdul-Rahman, *Jurisprudence and Islamic Ruling*, 198; see also Ṣaḥīḥ al-Bukhari, vol. 8, bk. 82, no. 805, narrated by Jabir; and vol. 7, bk. 63, no. 196, narrated by Abu Huraira.
105. Rafiabadi, *Saints and Saviors*, 322; see also Ṣaḥīḥ al-Bukhari, bk. 82, no. 51, narrated by Abu Huraira, 806.
106. Unknown Author, *Hadith of Bukhari*, 541; see also Ṣaḥīḥ al-Bukhari, vol. 8, bk. 82, no. 813, narrated by Abdullah Ibn Abbas.
107. Doi, *Cardinal Principles of Islam*, 74–82.
108. See also another analogy from the Holy Bible: "But Jesus went to the Mount of Olives. At dawn he appeared again in the temple courts; where all the people gathered around him, and he sat down to teach them. The teachers of the law and the Pharisees brought in a woman caught in adultery. They made her stand before the group and said to Jesus, 'Teacher, this woman was caught in the act of adultery. In the Law Moses commanded us to stone such women. Now what do you say?' They were using this question as a trap, in order to have a basis for accusing him. But Jesus bent down and started to write on the ground with his finger. When they kept on questioning him, he straightened up and said to them, 'Let any one of you who is without sin be the first to throw a stone at her.' Again he stooped down and wrote on the ground. At this, those who heard began to go away one at a time, the older ones first, until only Jesus was left, with the woman still standing there. Jesus straightened up and asked her, 'Woman, where are they? Has no one condemned you?' 'No one, sir,' she said. 'Then neither do I condemn you,' Jesus declared. 'Go now and leave your life of sin'" (John 8:1–11).

highlights the burden Shariah places on those who must sit in judgment of others.

As listed above, one of the requirements for proof of *zina* under the Shariah penal code is the corroborating testimony of four male witnesses. Interpretation of the law further states that witnesses to *zina* must be Muslim.[109] It should be noted, however, that in the cases with which I have been involved, the standard of proof provided for under Shariah (i.e., the requirement that four adult Muslim males must have simultaneously witnessed the accused committing the act of adultery) was not met.[110]

It is necessary to underscore that, in order to convict a person of a criminal offense the evidence must be satisfactory, conclusive, clear, and convincing—according to legal standards—and must provide explicit proof that the criminal act has occurred. Any witnesses must possess a clear memory of the events surrounding the offense, they must possess good visual and auditory abilities, and they must be mature and of sound reason. In addition, witnesses must possess good character and integrity, and they must be Muslim.[111] Furthermore, the testimony of such witnesses must not be coerced.

One of the most important issues with regard to cases of fornication is confession. One of the best examples of how the prophet Muhammad (ﷺ) never rushed to judgment is in the instance of the Hadith in which Ma'iz—a companion in the Prophet's community—retracts his confession of fornication, and the Prophet admonished that he should be left free. The Hadith in which the Prophet instructed believers to "abandon doubt in favor of that which is not doubtful" and "whoever abandons his doubts purifies his faith and honor" buttressed this.[112]

---

109. Zamfara State Shariah Penal Code Law, Section 127. Note also that under the Nigeria criminal procedure code, Section 391, "in taking evidence in any criminal matter an area court (now Shariah court) may test the credibility of witness by examination." See Jones, *Criminal Procedure Code*, 243.

110. Note that under Section 518(b) of the criminal code of Southern Nigeria, adultery per se is not a crime. See Akande, *Laws and Customs*, 19.

111. Muslehuddin, *Judicial System of Islam*, 67.

112. Peters, *Crime and Punishment*, 55; see also Kamali, *Freedom of Expression*, 201.

An accused person, who, according to what the court records indicate, allegedly confessed, can withdraw his or her confession at any time before the execution of the sentence. In fact, a public or private retraction of the confession amounts to doubt (*shubha*), which should be settled in favor of the accused, and thus nullify the punishment.[113] As Shariah stipulates, confession must be made absent of external forces that can sway the accused away from his or her own will.

Aside from the right of the accused to withdraw his or her confession at any time before execution, the accused should also be encouraged not to confess. Saḥīḥ al-Bukhari and Saḥīḥ al-Muslim reported that, "a man came to the Prophet and said: 'O Messenger of Allah سبحانه و تعالى! I have mingled with a woman in the far side of al-Medina, and I fulfilled my desire short of actually having sexual intercourse with her. So, here am I, judge me according to what you decide.' Umar Ibn al-Khattab then said: 'Allah سبحانه و تعالى had kept your secret, why did not you keep your secret?' . . . He, who relieves a hardship of this Dunya (world) for a believer, Allah سبحانه و تعالى will relieve (from him) a hardship of the Day of Resurrection; he who makes easy an indebted person, Allah سبحانه و تعالى will make it easy for him in the Dunya and the Hereafter; he who covers a Muslim (meaning his mistakes and shortcomings), Allah سبحانه و تعالى will cover him in the Dunya and the Hereafter . . ."[114]

Judges must therefore be cautious when accepting confessions and give leeway for the possibility that the accused could withdraw their statement. Where there is a pregnancy, it should not be taken as conclusive proof. Where the court is disposed to facilities for a test, they may wish to seize the opportunity.

The following Hadith sheds light on some of these factors.

> One day (at the time of the Prophet) a woman left her house
> to go and pray at the Mosque. On her way she was met

---

113. Kamali, *Freedom of Expression*, 201.
114. Patel, *365*, 87.

by a man who forced her to have sexual intercourse. The woman screamed while the man raped her. After he raped her, the man ran away. A group of men (who accompanied the Prophet on his migration from Mecca to Medina) passed by the woman, and she said to them (pointing in the direction of the man running), "That man just raped me." They then ran after him and caught him and when face to face with the woman, she said, "Yes that was the person." They went to the Prophet, and the man said, "Yes Prophet, it was I who did this." The Prophet said to the woman, "Go now, God has already pardoned you." The Prophet then said to the man (while appreciating his confession), "Stone him."[115] He then changed his mind and said, "He has already learned his lesson, and if someone learns their lesson, all the people of Medina will understand."[116]

The case of Ma'iz parallels the above incident.[117] Ma'iz, who fornicated with a slave girl belonging to a clan, was told, "Go to the Apostle of Allah سبحانه و تعالى and inform him of what you have done, for he may perhaps ask Allah سبحانه و تعالى for your forgiveness." So Ma'iz went to him and said, "Apostle of Allah سبحانه و تعالى! I have committed fornication, so inflict on me the punishment ordained by Allah سبحانه و تعالى." The Prophet turned away from him, so Ma'iz came back and said, "Apostle of Allah سبحانه و تعالى! I have committed fornication, so inflict on me the punishment ordained by Allah سبحانه و تعالى." The Prophet again turned away from him, so he came back again and said, "Apostle of Allah سبحانه و تعالى! I have committed fornication, so inflict on me the punishment ordained by Allah سبحانه و تعالى." After he uttered the statement four times, the Apostle of

---

115. Ibn al-Atsir, Jami al-Ushul, IV/270, no. 1823, culled from Jahangir and Jilani, *Hudood Ordinances*, 121. See also Imams Tirmidhi and Abu Dawud through Wa'il bin Hujr (see Ibn al-Atsir, Jami al-Ushul, IV/270, no. 1823), culled from Bayrak, *Path of Muhammad*, 127.
116. Imams Tirmidhi and Abu Dawud through Wa'il bin Hujr (see Ibn al-Atsir, Jami al-Ushul, IV/270, no. 1823), culled from Bayrak, *Path of Muhammad*, 127.
117. Abdul-Rahman, *Meaning and Explanation*, 253; see also his *Tafsir Ibn Kathir Juz'*, 196.

Allah سبحانه و تعالى said, "You have said it four times. With whom did you commit it?" He replied, "With [so-and-so]." The Prophet asked, "Did you lie down with her?" Ma'iz replied, "Yes." The prophet Muhammad (صلى الله عليه وسلم) asked, "Had your skin been in contact with hers?" He replied, "Yes." The Prophet asked, "Did you have intercourse with her?" Ma'iz again said, "Yes." So the prophet Muhammad (صلى الله عليه وسلم) gave orders that he should be stoned to death.[118]

Ma'iz was then taken outside the city and, unable to bear the stoning, fled. When those who had been stoning him could not catch up with him, he encountered Abdullah Ibn Unays, who threw the bone of a camel's foreleg at Ma'iz and killed him where he stood. Ibn Unays and his companions then went to the Prophet and reported the incident. The Prophet said, "Why did you not leave him alone? Perhaps he might have repented and been forgiven by Allah سبحانه و تعالى."[119] This episode is evidence that if a punishment is based on confession alone, and the person at fault retracts the confession, it is generally acceptable and the unexecuted part of the sentence shall be stayed.[120]

In another version of the story, Ma'iz repeated his confession many times, but the Prophet turned away from him. He asked his people, "Is Ma'iz mad?"[121] This version of the story points to the prophet Muhammad's (صلى الله عليه وسلم) reluctance to punish a person who may not be of sound mind. In yet another version of the story, narrated by Abdullah Ibn Abbas, the Prophet drove Ma'iz away and later said, "You have testified of yourself four times," whereon he ordered that Ma'iz be stoned.[122] This version illustrates the preference for repeated confessions before any action is actually taken. In a fourth version of the story, the Prophet said to Ma'iz, "Perhaps you kissed

---

118. Qasmi, *International Encyclopedia of Islam*, 224.
119. Shujaat, *Social Justice in Islam*, 208; see also Doi, *Women in Shariah*, 123.
120. Jahangir and Jilani, *Hudood Ordinances*, 245; see also Rushd, *Distinguished Jurist's Primer*, 259.
121. Saḥīḥ al-Bukhari, bk. 38, no. 4407, narrated by Abdullah Ibn Abbas, culled from Younos, *Gender Equality in Islam*.
122. Ibid., no. 4412.

or squeezed or looked." Ma'iz said, "No." The Prophet then asked, "Did you have intercourse with her?"[123] Here, the Prophet clearly gives Ma'iz another chance to retract his confession and escape conviction.

While the accounts of Ma'iz vary in many ways, they can all stand out as references in cases of *zina* and similar circumstances. In all these accounts, Ma'iz confessed voluntarily, Ma'iz's state of mind was verified, the confession was given repeatedly, and the accused was given an opportunity to retract his statement. Whereas in the cases with which I was involved, the alleged adulteresses had been practically dragged out of their homes to the village leaders, and later to court, with no opportunities given to understand the circumstances of the accused or her mental or social conditions.

It is evident from the case of Ma'iz that a confession must be voluntary, unambiguous, and uttered repeatedly for it to be accepted. The prophet Muhammad (ﷺ) displayed incredible patience and understanding in response to the confession of Ma'iz. He also gave Ma'iz repeated opportunities to retract his statement and later provided an opportunity for Ma'iz to repent. This practice should be accepted and followed by judges today.

According to some Islamic courts in Pakistan—which are generally receptive to arguments based on all Islamic legal schools of thought—the only person who can report fornication is the spouse of the accused.[124] As will be discussed below, the Maliki School of law, predominant in Nigeria, is silent as to who may bring an accusation.[125] Thus, the *hisbah* or *da'awah*—the group of Muslim men, usually young, who are enlisted by the state to help enforce Shariah—are able to travel door to door and force women found to be pregnant and without a husband to come to court.

A further consideration, in ensuring that justice prevails in the application of the Shariah penal code, is required attention to the role of socioeconomic

---

123. Ibid., no. 4413.
124. Jahangir and Jilani, *Hudood Ordinances*, 87.
125. The Maliki School of law is also practiced in most parts of West Africa. See Hiskett, *Development of Islam*, 26.

factors. Scholars, and even some of our clients, have suggested that, although the law is intended for all people, it seems to be applied more to the less privileged. The less privileged are often illiterate and unaware of the content of the new Shariah and of the various other laws. In addition, they are often poor and voiceless, which hinders their defense.

As a result of this educational and informational gap, the underprivileged may not know they have broken a law until they are charged with a crime. In the rural northern villages where our team practiced, we observed that less than 30 percent of Nigerians—elites included—could speak or understand English. This means that the majority of the population has no way of reading or understanding the Shariah penal code, which is written in English. In order for the law to be effective, sound legal theory must precede legal practice; in other words, the law cannot be effective if people are unaware and unable to deduce its provisions.[126]

Sometimes, an individual's income level may affect how that individual is treated under the law. Some of the clients and their parents complained that the implementation of the Shariah penal code targets them because they are poor.[127] They say that when the children of wealthy people become pregnant, the parents fly their children out of Nigeria to have an abortion. These children then quietly come back home pretending that all is well. In contrast, the villagers and their families face the prospect of death by stoning.

---

126. Our foremost objective as we developed strategies for our various cases was not just to win the case at hand, but also to create an overall judicial environment in which justice would be assured for all men, women, and children in our society. See also Ross, *Women's Human Rights*, 500.

127. A similar view was expressed by Danny McCain in his address at the International Conference on Comparative Perspective on Shariah in Nigeria, held in Nigeria, Jan. 15–17, 2004, as reported in the *Nigerian Guardian*. In answering the question, "Why [is] Shariah implemented only on the Common Man?" he suggested that the implementation of Shariah is not evenly applied. At one point, he said, "When the Shariah courts start pushing those big people who have stolen billions of Naira and the rich men who prey upon young school girls to be their 'sugar daddies' with the same kind of penalties that cattle thieves and unwed mothers receive, only then Shariah will be viewed differently" (p. 9).

This demonstrates two standards of justice for the same crime: a favorable outcome for the wealthy and a life-altering penalty for the poor. The fact that villagers' poverty is, in many cases, a direct result of the greed and corruption of those same wealthy people further exacerbates the situation; because of this greed and corruption, many villagers find it all but impossible to escape the cycle of poverty.[128]

In many cases, our legal team has had to provide clients with transportation so that they can travel to and from court. An example of how economic inequity trumps justice is the case of Ahmadu. Sentenced to death by stoning in Niger State, Ahmadu—the breadwinner in his family—was required to be in court during the rainy season, when it was vital for him to be at his family farm. Because waiting for a court session to begin can take an entire day—and cases may even be postponed to another day for a multitude of reasons—crucial work hours can easily be desecrated. Ahmadu, on whom twelve people depended for food, decided that he could not afford to come to court because he had to be at the farm to cultivate crops for his extended family. When asked if he was afraid of going back to prison for "jumping bail"—as his absence in court could be deemed as contempt of the bail he had been granted—he said it did not matter; for however long he was not in prison, he would be on the farm, and able to feed his family.

Islamic scholars and jurists have argued that before the punishment of stoning could be rendered, there should be very strict conditions to which to adhere.[129] At a most basic level, there should be a foundational knowledge of the law and its application needs to cut across all social classes. So also, before amputation of limbs could be justly imposed, there must first be an environment without poverty where the needy can find relief through the provision of a common resource pool. There must also be a society in which all wealthy Muslims discharge the obligation of paying *zakat* (money to charity), to support the poor, to ransom slaves, and to host wayfarers.[130]

---

128. Ibid.
129. Kidder, *Jewish Nation*, 877.
130. *Zakat Handbook*, 11; see also Friedman, *Nuaayri-Alawis*, 139.

Only when the society has less want and everyone has their basic needs met
can offenses that deal with stealing be strictly imposed by the courts. Justice
can best be met in the application of Shariah law in Nigeria when the state
recognizes its responsibility to build structures that will quench the appetite
of potential offenders.

The Schools of Thought that Inform Shariah Law

The sources of Shariah are a common topic of discussion, and contention.
It was suggested that the sources could be divisible into chief and subsidiary
sources—The Qur'an and Sunnah.[131] I will limit my thoughts to the opinions
of learned scholars and jurists, including Mohammed Hassim Kamali, Majid
Khadduri, and R. K. Ramazani.[132] Shariah law draws from several sources
and is also influenced by the different schools of thought within Islamic
substantive law, or jurisprudence.[133] These are the five sources of Shariah:

1.   The Qur'an is well described by Professor Akbar Ahmed as
     sombre and meditative.[134] The Qur'an is a dialogue between

---

131. Ambali, *Practice of Muslim Family Law*, 4; see also Doi, *Cardinal Principles of Islam*, 20.
132. Kamali is a prolific writer and a professor of law at the International Islamic
University of Malaysia. He has authored several books in Islamic law and principles and his
views are wonderfully enlightening and inclusive. Khadduri (Sept. 27, 1909—Jan. 25, 2007)
was an Iraqi–born founder of the Paul H. Nitze School of Advanced International Studies,
Middle East Studies program. He was recognized as a leading authority on a wide variety
of Islamic subjects, modern history, and the politics of the Middle East. He was the author
of more than thirty-five books and hundreds of articles in English and Arabic. Ramazani
is professor emeritus of government and foreign affairs, and the author of several books,
including *The Foreign Policy of Iran, 1500–1941: A Developing Nation in World Affairs* (1966),
the first study of Iran's foreign policy in any language, and its sequel, *Iran's Foreign Policy,
1941–1975: A Study of Foreign Policy in Modernizing Nations* (1975). As such, the media
dubbed him the "dean of Iranian foreign policy studies in the United States." Ramazani
stresses the importance of historical consciousness when interpreting current events.
He also emphasizes the complex mix of factors—political, economic, cultural, religious,
historical—that combine to influence a government's actions, both domestically and
internationally.
133. See also An-Na'im, *Toward An Islamic Reformation*, 104.
134. Prof. Akbar Ahmed is the Chair of Islamic Studies, American University in
Washington, DC, Distinguished Chair of Middle East and Islamic Studies at the US Naval
Academy, Annapolis, IN, and a Nonresident Senior Fellow at the Brookings Institution,
Washington, DC.

God and humanity. As a moral earnestness, it is not an academic thesis, so it needs no structure or order; nor does it need introduction and conclusion. The Qur'an is a vibrant outpouring of divine message, of powerful reflective moods. It warns, advises, and exhorts in flashes. The language is eloquent, its imagery awesome, and its scope is mankind.[135]

2. The Sunnah is a composite of the teachings of the prophet Muhammad (ﷺ) and his works that contain commentary and episodes called Hadith.

3. Ijma is a consensus among Muslim religious scholars (*ulama*) who are consulted on many matters, both personal and political.

4. Qiyas (Analogy) whose teachings are not explicitly found in the Qur'an, Sunnah, or Ijma, consisting of new cases (or case laws) that have already been decided by a superior court judge and in which case a judge can use as legal precedent to support his rulings.

5. *Istihsan* (Preference) is to prefer something to other possibilities, such as proffering a particular judgment in Islamic law over another. Better still, to "deem proper."[136]

The major schools of legal thought within Sunni Islam are Hanafi, Shafi'i, Hanbali, and Maliki.[137] Professor Abdur Rahman Doi opined that while speaking to schools of legal thought, one needs to note that the primary sources of Shariah are two, Qur'an and Sunnah, albeit Ijma (consensus of Islamic jurists) and Qiyas (analogy) are secondary sources of Shariah.[138] Of importance, however, the final sanction for all intellectual

---

135. Ahmed, *Discovering Islam*, 30.
136. Kamali, *Shariah Law*, 19.
137. Ibid., 118. Sunni Islam is the largest branch of Islam, comprising up to 90 percent of the total Muslim population of the world. Sunni Muslims are referred to as the "people of the tradition [of Muhammad(ﷺ) and the community]."
138. Born in Ahmadabad, India, Prof. Doi was a stupendous researcher, lecturer, and administrator in Nigeria and elsewhere. An author of several Islamic books, he provided

activities in respect to the development of Shariah comes only from the Qur'an. He further suggested, "Any Hadith which is contrary to the Qur'an is considered not authentic."[139]

The Hanafi School is known for its juristic freedom and preference, recognition of an individual's ability to perceive morality, and often open-minded approach to other schools of thought.[140] It combines religious piety with a realistic understanding of the needs of a growing Muslim society. Hanafi School is characterized by its completeness, precision, and sanction of the use of science in the courtroom.[141] It bases its laws on the expediency and benefits of a system that is in accord with rational principles. It has been suggested that because the Hanafi School relies less on oral traditions as a source of legal knowledge, it conforms more closely to reason.[142] Hanafi School gives priority to the Qur'an and then Sunnah. New problems are examined and often anticipated by the use of *Qiyas*.[143]

Hanafi legal thought developed analytical interpretation of the Qur'an by the application of recognized principles governing some analogous act. It also established the principle that the universal concurrence of the community of Islam (*ummah*) on a point of law, as represented by legal and religious scholars, constitutes evidence of the will of God. The school determined that the Qur'an, the traditions of the Prophet, Ijma, and *Qiyas* were the basis of Islamic law. In addition, Hanafi School accepts local customs as a secondary source of law.[144]

Muslim students with reliable Islamic texts and syllabi. It is also suggested that the founders of the school of Figh Imam Hanafi, lived from 80–150 A. H. (After Hijirah); Imam Maliki, 93–179 A. H.; Imam Shafi'i, 150–204 A. H.; and Imam Hambali, 164–241 A. H. (Doi, *Shariah*, 86–87). Discussion is ongoing among Islamic jurists and scholars as to the closure or not of Ijtihad. Anne Sofie Roald has opined that because Ibn Hazm (d.1064) and Ibn Taimiya (d.1328) analyzed intellectual reasoning the gate may still be open (*Women In Islam*, 99).

139. Doi, *Shariah*, 64.

140. Yamani, *Feminism and Islam*, 5; see also Safi, *Tensions and Transitions*, 97; and Heper and Criss, *Historical Dictionary of Turkey*," 166.

141. Naseer and Shuraydi, *Revising Culture, Reinventing Peace*, 115.

142. Haghayeghi, *Islam and Politics in Central Asia*, 80.

143. Baamir, *Commercial and Banking Arbitration*, 16.

144. Anderson, *Islamic Law in Africa*, 317–21.

Similar to the Hanafi School, the Shafi'i School is considered an adaptable school in terms of social and personal rules. It emphasizes the consensus of the Muslim community and reasoning by analogy. Shafi'i, an Islamic scholar, was known for his remarkable abilities in the Arabic language, as a poet and philologist. His famous *Al Risalah (The Letter)* is considered the foundation of Islamic jurisprudence *(fiqh)*.[145] In his *Al Risalah*, Shafi'i set forth the classification of the Qur'an, including those general and particular dictum abrogating and abrogated conversations and the Sunnah as the authoritative source of the Shariah.[146] He brought greater clarity to what the basis for legal decisions should consist; stressing equality as an important prophetic practice recorded in the Hadith. He regarded equality before the law as more important than the composite practices of the locality in which the *ummah* live.[147]

The third school of thought is the Hanbali School, which draws from the Qur'an and the Sunnah. Imam Hanbali was said to be very inquisitive and intelligent, which lead to him becoming a great scholar of Hadith. It was suggested by Doi that he remembered almost a million Hadith, which framed his juristic mind.[148] The Hanbali School accepts as authoritative the opinion given by a companion of the Prophet, providing there is no disagreement with another companion. In the case of such difference of opinion, the opinion of the companion nearest to that of the Qur'an or the Sunnah prevails. Its founder, Hanbali, an Islamic scholar, placed a heavier emphasis on the prophetic customs than on jurisprudence. The Hanbali interpretation of Shariah suggests, for example, that judges may discount the testimony of people who are not practicing Muslims.[149] Hanbali's contribution to Islamic scholarship is a collection of fifty thousand traditions, known as *Musnadul-imam hanbali*.

---

145. Hourani, *History of the Arab Peoples*, 68; see also Sodiq, *Insider Guide to Islam*, 190–97.
146. Doi, *Shariah*, 107.
147. Moors, *Women, Property, and Islam*, 85; see also al-Qushayri, *Risalah*, 34.
148. Doi, *Shariah*, 108.
149. Deif, *Perpetual Minors*, 61; see also Lipton, *Religious Freedom*, 90.

The Maliki School differs in some ways from the three other schools of law in regards to the sources from which it derives its rulings: it employs the practice of the people of Medina as a source. Maliki, who lived his whole life in Medina, along with most of his companions, considered the practice of Medina's people a "living sunnah" because the Prophet migrated, lived, and died there.[150] Imam Maliki was born to the family of royals and scholars.[151] His grandfather was a famous scholar of Hadith. Imam Maliki learned and recited the Qur'an in accordance with the established principles of the Tajwid, under very famous scholars. Later, his reputation spread widely to different parts of the Muslim world with respect to his Hadith instructions and persuasion on various juristic and legal issues. He was a great teacher and jurist; he codified the Medinian *fiqh* (rules in relating to actions or circumstances; jurisprudence in the study of the Shariah).[152] It was suggested however, that Imam Maliki's work resulted in a more limited reliance upon Hadith than is found in the other schools. Maliki was particularly meticulous about verifying his sources when he did refer to them. His collection of Hadith, known as *Al-muwatta (The Approved)*, is highly regarded.[153] Maliki is said to have explained the title by saying he showed his book to seventy jurists of Medina and every single one of them approved it for him, so he named it *The Approved*.

The major schools of Islamic law provide universal guidelines for Muslims to follow, as well as specific guidance on issues such as the principles of administration of justice in courts. Although all of these schools of law are rooted in the same Islamic values of protection of life, morality, forgiveness, freedom, and peace, among others, it is important to note the distinctive qualities of each school. In addition, what is taught in one school may clarify an idea not fully understood by another school. All schools should be utilized, especially when it comes to finding clarity in the application

---

150. Kamali, *Shariah Law*, 73–78; see also Rauf, *What's Right with Islam*, 89.
151. S. Ali, *Scholars of Hadith*, 40.
152. Doi, *Shariah*, 100.
153. Asadullah, *Islam vs. West*, 30; see also Omran, *Family Planning*, 156.

of offenses under the Shariah penal code. Worthy of note is the fact that the four differences of opinion by leaders of the four Sunni schools of law rendered great service to the cause of Islamic jurisprudence. And, as observed in Doi, that it is about these differences the Messenger of Allah said, "my ummah (people) is blessed."[154] Through these differences, Muslims have inherited a comprehensive *corpus juris* (collections of laws) that provides guidance in every walk of life.

Nigeria generally adheres to the teachings of the Maliki School, especially within the context of the Shariah penal code. Restricting the interpretation of other schools of thought may result in locking out helpful understanding of some principles of law. For example, while the standard of proof for *zina* according to the Maliki School is considered stringent in enforcing rules, the Hanafi School evidentiary requirement of proof of illegal sexual relationship is more between sane adults. Also, the Hanafi School applies the penalty of death only when the accused is currently married to another person. Whichever interpretation is followed, the Qur'an is binding in the punishment:

> The [unmarried] woman or [unmarried] man found guilty of sexual intercourse—lash each one of them with a hundred lashes, and do not be taken by pity for them in the religion of Allah سبحانه و تعالى, if you should believe in Allah سبحانه و تعالى and the Last Day. And let a group of the believers witness their punishment . . . . (24:2)

Other Countries and Shariah Laws

It is important to pay attention to happenings in other jurisdictions, especially those countries that have an inclusive understanding of the practice and application of Shariah, where it is interpreted with human dignity and respect for the sanctity of life. This includes countries such as Morocco, Tunisia, and Turkey, among others.

---

154. Ibid., 86.

Nigeria is in a unique position to learn from other countries that have majority Muslim populations. Turkey, for example, is over 90 percent Muslim and does not currently have Shariah as its legal system.[155] Since 2001, Turkey has taken a new approach regarding family issues, as reflected by changes made to its family code.[156] Several of these changes have promoted gender equality, as the following attests: [T]he husband is no longer piled with so much responsibility for the family; spouses are partners, jointly running the matrimonial union with equal decision-making powers; spouses have rights over the family abode; spouses have rights over property acquired during marriage; and spouses have equal representative powers.[157] The family is the foundation of the Turkish society and [is] based on equality between the spouses. The state shall take the necessary measures and establish the necessary organization to ensure the peace and welfare of the family, especially where the protection of the mother and children is involved, and recognize the need for education in the practical application of family planning.[158]

Most interesting is the fact that adultery is no longer a criminal offense according to the Turkish Constitutional Court because it violates the constitutional principle of equality before the law. The Turkish Constitution, does, however, allow proof of adultery to be used as grounds for divorce.[159]

---

155. Turkish Constitution, Books LLC (Editor), Constitution of Turkey, Constitutional Court of Turkey, Turkish Constitution of 1921, Turkish Constitution of 1961, Books LLC, 2010.

156. Take note that the Turkish legal system is based on the French system of *laissez-fare* (autonomous character [i.e., the practice or doctrine of noninterference in the affairs of others]) and that it has moved toward secularism with the modernization movement of Ataturk.

157. Constitution of the Republic of Turkey, Articles 10 and 41.

158. Kardam, *Turkey's Engagement*, 66.

159. Turkish Civil Code, Articles 161, 185iii. See also Anil and Arin, *Turkish Civil and Penal Code Reforms*.

The Lawyers

While lawyers in Shariah cases are called to pay attention to the law and to the details of a case, they are also charged with remembering their oaths of allegiance to the legal profession, their commitment to justice, and their legal responsibilities. Judges in Nigeria may not necessarily have a vast knowledge of Shariah. In fact, it may be quite thin in some parts of Northern Nigeria. Accordingly, lawyers are encouraged to be very careful not to make such judges feel inadequate if the judge makes an error or omission.

As in many countries, a prospective lawyer is required to enroll and train in law school before being called to the Nigerian Bar—the accreditation after passing the bar exams—before practicing law in Nigerian courts. A lawyer may serve as an advocate or a solicitor; a prosecutor as well as a defense lawyer; private legal counsel or a state, federal, or parastatal (or similar) government counsel.[160] He or she can practice law in *any court* in Nigeria. He or she can even, as a solicitor, be solely involved in the registration of companies and deeds. The profession is guided by the Legal Practitioner's Act of 1979, which was amended in 1990.[161] It clearly delineates the responsibilities and duties of a lawyer. In the following paragraphs, I will explore this further.

A lawyer's most sacred duty is to his or her client. The interest and ultimate justice for the client is paramount and is always to be the lawyer's main focus. A lawyer has a duty to care for and protect the best interests of his or her clients and not to be negligent in this responsibility. A lawyer also has a duty to the court to present his or her case without bias.[162] Prior to appearing in court, it is imperative that he or she understand the rules and the processes of the court and prepare his or her case accordingly. In addition to the substantive law in each court, it is crucial for a lawyer to know the procedure in every court in which he or she is appearing.

---

160. An advocate is a person who pleads for or on behalf of another in a court of law. See also Ambali, *Practice of Muslim Family Law*, 103. Solicitors are lawyers who traditionally deal with any legal matters of commerce and contract, distinct from an advocate.

161. Adesiyan, *Accused Person's Rights*, 42.

162. Abdul-Raham v. COP, NWLR 87 (1971); Arzika v. The Queen, 7 WACA, 175.

A lawyer's duty includes the need to familiarize him or herself with the procedural codes for various situations. For instance, in a case involving death by stoning, it is necessary to acquaint oneself with the procedures as provided in the Shariah penal code and in the Hadith. One needs to know what documents to file, what fees and fines to pay, and how to file them. The paperwork requirements and fees/fines may differ depending on the level of court. In some states the Shariah courts have two grades of Shariah courts[163] while others have more, such as Shariah courts, Upper Shariah courts, and Higher Shariah courts.[164] It is crucial papers are served properly to the court, and that any witness who wishes to give evidence in court appears at the proper time.

Lawyers are to maintain a professional and respectful attitude toward each other, never using trickery or underhanded practices. A lawyer is required to disclose all pertinent documents and any information that needs to be legally disclosed to opposing colleagues. A lawyer will never put his or her own interests above those of the client. Nor should a lawyer take cases personally with regard to his colleagues, especially in ways that could bleed over from one case into another; clients will come and go, but the relationship with a colleague lasts forever. This cordiality includes full disclosure, especially in criminal cases, and absolute transparency with colleagues and the court. The duty of full disclosure even extends to situations in which disclosing information could result in losing the case, so that the court properly secures justice.

In Nigeria, the word *lawyer* carries no religious connotation; however, the practical reality is that religious maxims and rules exist in Shariah courts to which one must adhere. For instance, when lawyers from Southern Nigeria came to offer professional help and assistance when our team was in court and experiencing trying moments, we sometimes had to refuse their generous offers for religious reasons, such as their non-Muslim attire. Factors such as

---

163. Laws of Katsina State of Nigeria, 2002, Vol. 4, Chapters 143–180, Section 4(1).

164. Zamfara State Shariah Criminal Procedure Code Law, 2000, No. 1, Vol. 4, Section 4. Unlike Katsina State, which has three classes of Shariah criminal courts, Zamfara State has four classes, namely Shariah Court, Higher Shariah Court, Upper Shariah Court, and Shariah Court of Appeal.

a lawyer's gender or religious affiliation can often have an unintentional influence on a court case. These are challenges that together must be addressed. Wisdom is not packaged in a single color but comes in an endless variety of hues that if welcome can add depth and richness to the cases.

A lawyer has a responsibility not only to his or her client and to the court, but also to society and to justice. Lawyers are even more responsible in developing nations, where they often find themselves in the unique position of helping to frame society by drafting constitutions, penal codes, and similar legislation. This role affords lawyers great influence as they build a society's foundations. Given the amount of influence lawyers wield in such circumstances, they are commissioned with being very cautious not to draft laws that could be interpreted as inhumane, or be construed to constitute an assault on human rights, or could rob individuals of their basic human dignity.

To reiterate, a lawyer is called to always act in the best interest of his or her client. This means keeping the spotlight off of oneself and one's conduct and instead focusing it solely on the issues at hand. It is also wise to pay attention to the personalities and disposition of the judges. For example, some judges may clearly state their objections to having a female lawyer appear before them; (in circumstances such as this, female lawyers could solicit a male colleague's support and voice, or insist that the definition of a lawyer is all inclusive), other judges may show their displeasure in a different way. Remember it is not about you the lawyer, but the client(s) and that should always be the focus.

The Shariah Judge

The principles governing the appointment of Islamic judges are unique. They include governing righteously, sustaining the essence of Islamic justice. Judges are appointed when they possess an overall authority to protect individuals along with others while upholding the objective of Islamic law.[165] Islam gives importance to justice, be it political, social, or economic.

---

165. Doi, *Sharīah*, 11.

Ibn Arabi opined that divine justice expresses the essence of God; it is not intended for believers only, but for all who seek justice and each one in his own spiritual pathway.[166] This must be done at all cost so those who perform the functions of judges (khadis) must be men of deep insight, with profound knowledge of Shariah and Allah-fearing.[167] Ambali states:

> It is stipulated that for a man to be appointed a judge he should be a Muslim, free person, male, accountable for all his deeds. He should possess the capacities to hear and see. He should be literate, intelligent, conscious, scrupulous, and should be capable to make independent research and interpretation of Qur'an and the Sunnah or at least possess the capacity to interpret what an exponent of Islamic Law has interpreted on the basis of the Qur'an and Sunnah.[168]

Furthermore, a Shariah judge bears full responsibility before Allah سبحانه و تعالى for all decisions he makes in his official capacity. A judge is an Imam, the leader of the society in discharging his official functions with knowledge and piety.[169]

However, in Nigeria the Shariah judges are persons who are deemed to have obtained recognized qualifications in Islamic personal law from an institution approved by the Federal Judicial Service Commission. The 1999 Nigerian Constitution, Section 261(3), provides for such qualifications:

> A person shall not be qualified to hold office as Grand Khadi or Khadi of the Shariah Court of Appeal of the Federal Capital Territory, Abuja unless:

---

166. Ibid.
167. There are three types of judges (khadis): "One who will go to paradise and the remaining two will end up in the fire of hell. The person who will go to paradise is one who understands the truth and judges accordingly. One who judged unjustly after understanding the truth, they will go to hell. Likewise, the Khadi who judges in ignorance also will go to the hell" (Doi, Shariah, 11).
168. Ambali, *Practice of Muslim Family Law*, 85.
169. Ibid., 86.

    a. He is a legal practitioner in Nigeria and has so qualified for a period of not less than ten years and has obtained a recognized qualification in Islamic law from an institution acceptable to the national Judicial Council; or

    b. He has attended and has obtained a recognized qualification in Islamic law from an institution approved by the National Judicial Council and has held the qualification for a period of not less than twelve years; and (i) he either has considerable experience in the practice of Islamic law, or (ii) he is a distinguished scholar of Islamic law.[170]

A Shariah judge should be a free Muslim man, God-fearing, forthright, honest, and sincere.[171] He should also be a calm and composed man of integrity who is upright in his convictions and follows the path of righteousness with a dignified demeanor and sound common sense. A judge should be literate, conscientious, and capable of conducting independent research and of interpreting the Qur'an and Sunnah.[172] In fact, "it would be a travesty of justice to say that a case has been determined in accordance to the Shariah if the judge in the first instance is not qualified to judge."[173] Because judges apply a stringent rule of law, they should be of unimpeachable character and should deliver judgments promptly, without unnecessary delays or postponements.

The judge's verdicts should be fearlessly impartial, accurately reflecting what is due and right. In order to maintain the appearance of impartiality, the judge should neither accept gifts from one of the parties to the court case nor participate in private conversations with them.[174] The judge should smile rarely and speak little. The judge should neither hope for nor fear

---

170. Constitution of the Federal Republic of Nigeria, 1999, No. 27, Vol. 86. Shariah judges have hitherto been male in Northern Nigeria; however, there are female judges in some predominately Muslim countries, such as Kuwait, Palestine, and Malaysia.

171. Not in bondage or a slave.

172. Al-Ghunaimi, "Justice and Human Rights," 2.

173. Kumo, "Shari'a and the Nigerian Constitution," 169. Sulaiman Kumo is a former judge, a university don, legal luminary, and frontline politician.

174. Haleem et al., *Criminal Justice in Islam*, 153.

a particular outcome.[175] As Mohammad Talaat al-Ghunaimi, a leading modern expositor of Islam and international law, said, "A judge should avoid delivering judgment when he is hot, cold, hungry, angry, or too tired."[176] The judge is required to be intelligent, impartial, reliable, firm, and knowledgeable, and the judge must abstain from any suspicious acts.[177] He also cannot adjudicate on a matter in which he is personally involved or has any personal interest, especially cases involving his children, parents, wife(s), or people who are either qualified to inherit from him or whom he is qualified to inherit from.[178]

Caliph Ali Ibn Talib—the cousin and son-in-law of the prophet Muhammad (ﷺ) and fourth of the "rightly guided Caliphs" who succeeded the Prophet—was adopted by the prophet Muhammad (ﷺ) and educated under his care.[179] In one of Ali's earliest declarations on the importance of an independent judiciary, he envisioned a judiciary that would be "above every kind of executive pressure or influence, fear or favor, intrigue or corruption."[180] So important was this principle that some Muslim judges at that time were willing to be put to death, tortured, or dismissed rather than sacrifice the independence of their office.[181] Ali further remarked

---

175. Lampe, *Justice and Human Rights* (1997), 45; see also Hathout, *In Pursuit of Justice*. Ramadan adds that, "When a judge gives a decision, having tried his best to decide correctly and is right, there are two rewards for him; and if he gave a judgment after having tried his best (to arrive at a correct decision) but erred, there is one reward for him" (*Understanding Islamic Law*, 20).

176. Ezzati, *Concise Description of Islamic Law*, 253; see also H. A. Ibrahim, *Sayyid Abd al-Raman al-Mahdī*; and Ambali, *Practice of Muslim Family Law*, 91. See also al-Ghunaimi, *Muslim Conception of International Law*, 83, on the facts that international law was a subject of Islamic writing almost three centuries before the first codification of Western laws.

177. Cantemir, *History of the Growth and Decay*. Written originally in Latin by Demetrius Cantemir, the late prince of Moldavia 1673–1723. Translated into English from the author's own manuscript by N. Tindal, the book is adorned with the heads of Turkish emperors, engraved from copies taken from originals in the grand signor's palace by the late sultan's painter.

178. Ambali, *Practice of Family Law*; see also Rosen, *Anthropology of Justice*.

179. A Caliph is a Muslim head of state or leader of the greater Muslim community.

180. Kamrava, *Islam, Justice and Politics*, 219.

181. Ibid.

that a judge should "avoid fatigue, weariness, and annoyance at litigants.[182] Understanding the nature of the case posited before him, [the judge] must consider all people equal before [them], in his court, so that the nobility will not expect to receive partial treatment and the humble will not despair for justice. The claimant must produce proof while the court will extract an oath of truth from the defendant."[183] Caliph Umar bin al-Khattab, one of the prophet Muhammad's (ﷺ) companions and the second rightly guided Caliph, noted that "[t]he office of the Judge is a definite religious duty, and as such, is a generally followed practice."[184] Caliph Umar wrote to judges:

> Administration of Justice is an essential service and practice of the Prophet, which must be followed. So strive to understand reasons put before you and enforce the judgment on the basis of truth whenever it is clear because there is no point laboring for truth without enforcing it. Treat all manner of people who appear before you as equals showing the equality in your demeanor to the parties, the sitting arrangements and the way you dispense justice, so that the weak will not despair and be frustrated about your ability to do justice and the noble will not take you for granted. The onus of proof is on him who makes a claim and the oath is on he who denies it.[185]

In addition to the responsibilities of judges already stated, emphasis on Islamic justice is an emphasis in the process in justice delivery, in which the judges play a crucial role.[186] This process lies in the person and content of the judge; in the adjudication and application of the substantive and procedural

---

182. Khaldun, *Muqaddimah*, 173. See also Ṣaḥīḥ al-Bukhari, bk. 18, no. 4264, as reported by Abd al-Rabmin b. Abu Bakra: "Do not judge between two persons when you are angry, for I have heard Allah's Messenger (may peace be upon him) as saying: None of you should judge between two persons when he is angry."
183. Rosen, *Anthropology of Justice*, 32; see also Ambali, *Practice of Muslim Family Law*, 112.
184. Khaldun, *Muqaddimah*, 173.
185. Ambali, *Practice of Muslim Family Law*, 98.
186. Doi, *Sharīah*, 5; see also Ambali, *Practice of Muslim Family Law*, 95.

laws. It also includes the equal treatment of parties before the law and court, and the verdict where the parties will be comfortable that justice was done to them both. Heeding the concepts of Islamic justice referred to in the Qur'an should be the concern not only of judges, court staffs, lawyers, and the *ulama* (Islamic clerics), but the society as well.[187] Finally, verdicts should be delivered eloquently, in accessible language, and fairly awarding what is right and due.

Conclusion

The complexities of Shariah law can only be navigated by attention to detail. While the law profession is often revered in Nigerian society and lawyers are often referred to as honorable or learned gentlemen, this honor carries with it the equally weighty responsibility of continuing to grow in knowledge throughout one's lifetime. Legal education does not end after law school, especially in Shariah cases, where almost none of the lawyers or judges have in-depth training. (In direct conflict with constitutional provisions; extensive knowledge of Shariah is rarely found among those who frequent the courtroom, especially in the Northern region after the Shariah penal code was introduced in 1999.) The lawyer is asked to be open-minded to new information so that he or she can perform his or her duties fully, professionally, and without fail on behalf of his or her client. In the context of Shariah, active participation on the part of both the bar and nongovernmental organizations (NGOs) could help train lawyers and judges to better expedite the dissemination of information.

The more we think we know, the more we should desire to know. We must stay above the fray and anticipate the incitement of others. Doing so will allow us to formulate an appropriate response. The many nuances of language must not be lost on us.[188] Paying attention to details can help us begin to exert control over our case, and attempt to gain justice for our clients.

---

187. See also Khaldun, *Muqaddimah*, 117.
188. See Esak, *Quran, Liberation and Pluralism*, 10, because language, we now know, plays a significant role in shaping us and our consciousness.

CHAPTER THREE

Be Focused and Stay Focused

As LAWYERS WE ARE TO be focused and stay focused, even more so when the camera lights are flashing, the microphones are set up, the phone won't stop ringing, or we are traveling in the dark of night, unsure if this will be our last trip. When we are tempted to focus on ourselves by keeping and maintaining a good reputation, or when we are afraid—in those cases of life and death—we must opt for life. As lawyers we are commissioned to remain rooted in the conviction of our mission to do good and do no harm.

To remain focused is our innermost resolve. High profile media coverage is common to sensitive cases. If we are not careful, we can be drawn into the euphoria of another global picture, which can displace attention from the case and the client. It is wise to remind ourselves repeatedly that our primary responsibility as lawyers is to our client and no one else: not ourselves, an NGO, or any other agenda. Our state of mind must remain that of a minister in a temple of justice.

As lawyers our work is a constant reminder that we will sometimes be called to frequent areas outside of our usual comfort zone. In these instances, when social forces fight for our attention and veer us away from our ethic, we are to think beyond our skills and duties. Our integrity must prevail over our own personal discomforts. Our intellect generates our actions; our actions give birth to our habits; and our habits develop our character. Developing a steadfast and moral spirit will serve as our guiding light to help us walk unimpeded towards those divine sources of truth and justice. Let us not be naïve; we will certainly encounter challenges, but as lawyers, remaining faithful to our calling will lead us towards endurance, and in turn will help transform us. When faced with challenges, the question is not, "Why me?" Rather, we should have an unwavering conscience and determination to search for knowledge, while remembering that persistence develops endurance, endurance develops strength of character, and character builds our confident hope, a hope that will not lead to disappointment.[189]

Do not be overwhelmed by all there is to do; guard your motivation. Envision what you hope to achieve. To remain focused on the journey from hope to vision requires a plan. Having a strong purpose and maintaining resolution in the face of challenges is necessary if we are to stay focused. If motivation is not coupled with the capability and skills to ensure that justice, law, and its rule are administered, then our efforts and energy are not in the right place. Moreover, it is the utilization of our senses that will ensure us that we clearly perceive various situations. We are to be positive without being naïve, and know that every goal can be broken down into achievable tasks, if done consistently. So in doing, we should not lose sight of the role that social forces such as the media play in shaping society's opinions.

The Media

While we cannot control the media, we can refuse to allow the media to control us. In the capital offense cases we have tried, there was always a need to use caution and exercise measurement with regards to what we said as lawyers. We should set the agenda and speak of the law without interjecting the sentiments surrounding the case. We need not be concerned

---

189. Romans 5:3-5.

with political correctness, unless such words or actions could negatively impact our case. A news reporter may have made up his or her mind and may propose questions to which they have already presumed answers. In this instance, the reporter is merely looking for a confirming quote. In response to such media attention, it is necessary that we clearly define the law and avoid delving into facts behind the case. When we stay focused on the case, we are better equipped to not subscribe to outside influences, individual or institutional. Nor are we to tell the media what their ears are itching to hear. Our goal is simple—state the law. It is important that lawyers handling cases that have attracted local and international press clearly understand that a single action or omission can make or break the case.

The medium in which announcements and disclosures are disseminated is often one of the most important considerations in the distribution of information. Different mediums impact the flow and manifestation of information in different ways. The media, for example, often promotes awareness regarding issues of freedom and democracy that help influence public policy. At other times, as a result of its own ideological bent it can alienate groups working for social change.

In certain countries, like Nigeria, citizens face a unique situation regarding the media such as radio, television, electronic media, newspapers, and magazines that reach or influence people widely because these outlets are mostly located in the country's southern states. These media outlets seem to dominate the main form of information assimilation. As a result of a checkered past (in response to the legacy of colonial rule) defined by malfeasance and unsuccessful systems of law, the current nation of Nigeria is essentially divided into two pseudo states: Northern and Southern. Since Northern Nigeria is predominantly Muslim, the values and cultures of its people are often at odds with those of Southern Nigerians, who are commonly referred to as predominantly Christian.[190] In fact, varied forms of religious identity exist, including Protestantism, local–syncretism

---

190. Lovejoy and P. Williams, *Displacement and the Politics*, 89.

Christianity, Catholicism, African traditional religions, and other local and traditional forms of worship.

The introduction of the "new Shariah" exemplifies how these cultural contentions may take shape. The Shariah penal code brought with it religious and political publicity that was widely covered in the Western media. The case of Amina Lawal, a Northern Nigerian woman condemned to death by stoning for the crime of *zina*, was one of the most highly publicized cases of the new codified Shariah. At the time of Lawal's case, the Miss World Beauty Pageant was taking place in Nigeria, which provided an opportunity for significant media presence. The contest's preliminaries were underway at the very moment when we lost the appeal for Lawal's case before the Funtua Shariah Court in 2002. The pageant brought the international media with it too; they sometimes used an image of Amina Lawal as a way to personalize, globalize, and escalate the conflict between the Shariah law and international issues such as women's rights. Six entrants decided to boycott the contest as a statement of protest against the court's decision.[191] In such instances, it is wise to remember that our sacred duty to our client remains first and foremost. The media should not unduly affect us, nor should it interest us—unless it is in the best interest of our client.

Lawyers and the Limelight: The Legal Practitioner's Act and Global Issues

The Nigerian Bar Association's Legal Practitioner's Act (LPA) stipulates the code of conduct that a legal practitioner must follow during circumstances that attract media attention.[192] The LPA does not allow for infamous, scandalous, or otherwise unprofessional conduct.[193] It also asserts that a court could find misconduct on the part of a lawyer if he or she speaks with the press regarding a case that is pending before the court. The

---

191. "Unwed Mother's Plight in Nigeria Sparks Global Outcry," *Des Moines Register* (Iowa), Sept. 24, 2002.
192. Laws of the Federation of Nigeria, 2004, Vol. 8, Chapter 118.
193. Ibid., Section 11.

rules further state that lawyers in Nigeria can only argue the case exclusively before a court of law, not in the public sphere. The professional ethics are spelled out clearly and Nigerian lawyers, regardless of the jurisdiction under which they may practice law in Nigeria, must adhere to them to avoid disciplinary action. A breach of these rules could seriously compromise a client's case.[194]

When contacted by the media, it is important to be cautious with our words and not comment on any extraneous issues such as the "clash of civilizations" debate or "the West v. Islam" discussion in Nigeria. Within these two specific issues, it has been suggested that the current trend of globalization has encouraged a melting pot of sorts in countries around the world.[195] Within this melting pot, various cultures begin to mesh where possible, and clash where they may be in conflict. This may have begun to happen around the world, especially between Islamic culture and Western values. As participants in Amina Lawal's case, we found it necessary to make it clear that as lawyers we were merely trying to use the Shariah law and court process to obtain justice for our client. By shying away from questions such as: "Don't you think this case is a . . . clash of civilizations?" or "Is this case an example of West v. Islam?" we were able to maintain a level of professionalism. When responding, we emphasized that we knew one thing and one thing alone—our client was sentenced to death by stoning and it was our duty to utilize Shariah law to ensure her deserved justice and freedom.

Expression and the Power of Language

While Southern Nigeria may have opposed the new Shariah of the North, if the media had shown more prudence in their use of insensitive language and demonstrated an overall responsible, comprehensive, and

---

194. Worthy of note is that ethics is one of the cornerstones of Sufism (esoteric dimension of Islam). See Douglas, *Mystical Teachings of al-Shadhili*, 8.
195. Kumaravadivelu, *Cultural Globalization*, 74.

respectful analysis of the volatile issues surrounding the new law when reporting about the pageant, it is possible that the media's agenda would have been better served. During this time, however, the publicity garnered from the boycotting of the pageant and the appellate decision in Lawal's case contributed to the unfortunate hardship inflicted on the psyche of Nigerian society. Unthinking and insensitive reporting such as the use of descriptive characterizations about the Holy Prophet (ﷺ) inflicted deep wounds of mistrust upon Northern Nigeria, and at times made it challenging to engage in peaceful and diplomatic discussions, and even resulted in regrettable and unnecessary deaths.[196]

Though first reported by local correspondents of the international media, Lawal's case was afforded little coverage by the local media in Northern Nigeria. While a few local media houses in Northern Nigeria covered the case, their attention abated as the issues became more intense and somewhat embarrassing to the elites in the North; finally only a few media outlets picked up the story. In contrast, the national (Southern) media covered the case from its inception. Unfortunately, the voice of the national media mainly stems from the South, where the new Shariah does not exist. As a result, the national media's publications (over 60 percent of the national print and electronic media are in Lagos and in the South) are not necessarily reflective of what Shariah practice entails. Not surprisingly, a mutual distrust and suspicion exists between North and South; it has been alleged that most things written by the media in reference to the implementation of the Shariah Law, then, in the Northern states, may not be accurate.

The challenges presented by a common misperception and general lack of understanding between the North and the South is numerous and extends far beyond issues of media coverage. Many Northerners suggest that the South does not fully understand what is happening in the North, least of all concerning Shariah, and should not be meddling in their affairs. Unfortunately, there have been instances where certain reports were not

---

196. Ado-Kurawa, *Shariah and the Press.*

properly investigated or just poorly reported. When journalists portray court proceedings inaccurately, lawyers, clients, and society are all endangered. For instance, *The Guardian's* headline story, "Hauwa's Anti-Shariah Advocacy," is an example of sensationalism that may have put the author in danger by completely mischaracterizing her goal of working within the new Shariah to achieve justice.[197]

Working Within Shariah Law to Achieve Justice

The approach of following due process and working within Shariah law and Shariah courts to acquit those who have been sentenced to penalties under the same system of laws has proven to be very effective. Shariah law is very rich and contains all possible advocacy strategies and defense provisions to enable a lawyer to argue on behalf of his or her client. The number of accepted exegetical interpretations of the religious texts by the courts can provide lawyers with tools to convincingly mount a legal argument. However, this approach requires a vast amount of research. In essence, working from within Shariah law entails having the courage to think beyond what is simply stated in legal books. For example, as taught by Maliki School, if a person is found guilty of stealing and, as Qur'an 5:38 commands, sentenced to amputation, the sentence carries no legal weight if the person at fault did so because poverty fueled the act.[198] According to the Zamfara State Penal Code Law, the crime of theft should not be prosecuted " . . . Where the offence was committed under circumstances of necessity and the offender did not take more than he ordinarily requires to satisfy his need or the need of his dependents . . . "[199] This exception

---

197. "Hauwa's Anti-Shariah Advocacy," *Guardian* (Lagos, Nigeria), Aug. 31, 2002.
198. Maliki Manual, Al'Risala 37:27, p. 7520. Qur'an 5:38 provides for the punishment of amputation for stealing. Note, however, some of the conditions necessary. The alleged theft must be a Muslim, sane, adult, had not been compelled to steal, and was not hungry while committing the theft. Other conditions with respect to the property include, that the stolen property must reach *nisab* (it must have value), it must be in a custody, and must be owned by someone. See Doi, *Shariah*, 257.
199. Zamfara State Shariah Penal Code Law, 2000, No. 1, Vol. 3, Section 147(c).

stresses Qur'anic teaching that punishments should not be given lightly and without careful thought for actions not reflective of a person's character or condition. For example, in the famous case of Caliph Umar, "he cancelled the *hadd* punishment for theft due to famine and the resulting hunger."[200] Of importance is going above and beyond normal resources and using all possible solutions, which may require the use of multiple scholarly opinions and schools of thought.[201] By attacking an issue from all angles and considering many schools of thought, a lawyer can take the chaos and uncertainty of a new legal system and transform it into one that promotes greater calm, clarity, and confidence.

When working within the framework of Shariah law, there is a need to demonstrate an understanding of the legislation relevant to each case and to identify the specific legal obligations of key concepts within the proper legal context. These concepts also require acknowledgment by courts of their fundamental responsibility to ensure citizens' basic human rights. As upheld by the Nigerian Constitution and widely accepted by many Muslim countries, citizens have the right to dignity, honor, freedom of thought, belief, and speech; freedom of religion, freedom of conscience, freedom of worship, and freedom of association and protection from abuse of power, physical and mental torture; and undue interference in one's personal life.[202] Lawyers can use the above-enumerated rights, either as legally binding rules or as the commonly accepted Islamic perspective on human rights, to sway the courts toward a comprehensive view of the case and of Shariah law.

---

200. Abiad, *Shariah, Muslim States*, 22.
201. To ensure integrity, avoid the "begging bowl" syndrome, especially from donor organizations. The begging bowl is employed when funds are solicited from the international community and not properly utilized. The begging bowl and broken promise syndrome, though a sort of international phenomena, is creeping into developing societies in different phases, at times compromising lawyers' integrity. See Prof. Ibrahim Gambari, United Nations Under-Secretary and Special Adviser on Africa, "Africa and the United Nations," 9.
202. Universal Islamic Declaration of Human Rights, Articles 12 and 13; see also Constitution of the Federal Republic of Nigeria, 1999, Chapter 4.

Many local communities follow our most difficult cases with intense interest. The key here is to ensure that we are also winning the case *out of court*: in the hearts and minds of the local people and in society in general. Our greatest desire is to make certain that our clients are able to return to live in their societies. Achieving this is the biggest victory.

It is necessary for a lawyer to research and review relevant legislation and rulings that express social policy and allow for protection and a duty of care in a prudent and responsible manner. We are called to demonstrate the willingness and the ability to push ourselves beyond the envelope.

As a defense team, it is very important for us to identify key members in our client's local communities and assure them that they are an integral part of the process. This will help the community's psyche when the accused re-enters society, as community members will have been involved in the case, and will share the client's sense of justice. When done successfully, the client can live without fear of retribution; society will protect him or her. For this purpose, it is vital to get input on how to best conduct the cases socially. We have also used our allies in local communities to learn how to speak the language of that community and conduct the social aspect of our case. By communicating our motives transparently, we avoid the otherwise frequent misunderstanding between the community and us that is often conveyed by the media.

Within this framework of working in the community many questions arise: How can cases heed the law, its rule, and its processes? What is the rule of law? Or is it rule by the law? Whose law? What law? What process is due to whom and in what context? These questions raise the concept of the rule of law as an empty vessel, the content of which is dependent upon local legal culture and historical contexts that affect the application of laws in practice. In all these incessant challenges, it is important to remember that the rule of law is about unrestricted justice; bearing in mind that legal culture and historical context can differ greatly between communities that could at times lead to confrontations. The establishment and maintenance of the rule of law in this atmosphere can often be a slippery slope. Simply put, rule of law should be consistent with liberty and justice.[203]

While it is historically true that "foreign" legal principles, rules, and institutions have been voluntarily and involuntarily adopted by societies, there still may be inevitable clashes with existing local laws, culture, customary practices, and behavioral patterns. For example, Islam and Christianity share a common historical origin, through ancient Semitic traditions; both Muslims and Christians believe that there is only one God and that one's faith must be integrated into all aspects of life.[204] Yet, today as a result of Western secularization in the public sphere, their belief systems seem to be mutually exclusive. While Christianity and many other religions may distinguish between the State and Religion, Muslims do not distinguish between the civil and religious spheres.[205] For Muslims, Islamic law is an integral part of their faith. In this context, the rule of law means extending the Shariah; in Islam, religion and law are "indivisible." From the orthodox point of view, Islam is timeless. As a faith based on complete submission to the will of Allah سبحانه و تعالى, Islam has neither beginning nor end. Islam seems to have a stronger sense of the indivisible nature of law and religion.[206]

Rule of Law and its Role in Shariah Law

The rule of law, precious words of power, is what protects us all from tyranny and injustice. Depending on the speaker, the call for the rule of law may be narrow or broad. This relates not only to its content, but also to the rule of law's very existence.

---

203. Casper, "Rule of Law? Whose Law?"
204. The articles of Islamic faith as enumerated by Doi include, belief in Allah سبحانه و تعالى, His Angels, His Books, His Messengers, in the Last Day, pre-measurement of good and evil, and life after death (*Cardinal Principles of Islam*, 20).
205. Hood et al., *Psychology of Religious Fundamentalism*, 172.
206. See Outhwaite, *Blackwell Dictionary of Modern Social Thought*, 309; see also Karibi-Whyte, *History and Sources*, 76.

Some suggest that the rule of law is no more than legal certainty, independent judiciary, or a concept incorporating several principles that govern the intricate workings of a legal order, that it envisions equality before the law and effectiveness of its own principles.[207] Others assert that the rule of law must meet certain substantive requirements in addition to legal certainty. These requirements range from the recognition of private property rights and the freedom to contract, to the call for sophisticated securities laws, transitional transparency, and good corporate governance. In addition, the rule of law stands for the protection of a wide range of rights identified as fundamental human rights. These include freedom of speech; freedom of association; freedom of religion; the right not to be discriminated against based on sex, race, nationality, and ethnicity; and the right to due process.

Gerhard Casper and others have suggested from these two views that there is a *Rule of Law* and *rule of the law*.[208] As a general concept, *Rule of Law* allows checks and balances to further order and good governance within society.[209] *Rule of the law*, on the contrary, could establish a harmful hierarchy where the law and those who create it reign supreme and unchecked by the government.[210]

Casper further argues that law is universal in nature and has three major strands: divine law, natural law, and public law. All three are universal and continue to have followers all over the world.

In opposition to the universal views of law, however, the modern world has been focused on particularistic law, where there is a specific emphasis determined by a region's specific legal code. Sovereign nations constitute largely autonomous legal systems. The autonomous system of different countries may at the same time reflect historic legal traditions such as

---

207. Finckenauer, *Russian Youth*, 14.
208. Casper, "Rule of Law? Whose Law?"
209. Maravall and Przeworski, *Democracy and the Rule of Law*, 172.
210. Casper, "Rule of Law? Whose Law?"

Roman law in civil law countries, the French Code of civil law, the German civil code, or the Swiss civil code.[211]

In the 1990s, Desmond Tutu, Nobel Peace Prize laureate, opined that the rule of law is defined as respecting the law and its rules, including court judgments. Where the rule of law is not upheld, there will be danger and the law will subvert itself; people will approach a slippery slope, leading to perdition.[212] In other words, where rule of law does not exist and is not practiced, peoples' daily lives, as well as the broader society, are adversely affected. In the past and in some societies today, laws in individual villages were first based on customs, administered and interpreted by the village head/chief in a manner that was sometimes arbitrary and rigid.

Then came the king's law, which altered the existing village-by-village system; subsequently, the new king's law became rigid and infallible.[213] For centuries it was recognized that the king's law or any other human authority could only declare the existing law, or modify abuses that had crept into the law. These powers could not create law.[214] It is only proper that the law, rather than any one citizen, should govern;[215] the persons holding supreme power should be appointed only guardians and servants of the law; and that he who would have supreme power in mind would place it in God and the laws.[216]

The rule of law can also be defined as the need to simply follow the law as set down by constituted authorities. This interpretation, however, raises a few questions: What law should apply? Has that law been validly written? Is the law internally consistent and equally applicable to all? Where the answers to the above questions are consistent with the basic provisions of the rule of law, then the law should be neutral and apply equally to all in its substantive content. The application of the law should be fair, transparent,

---

211. Steers and Nardon, *Managing in the Global Economy*, 72.
212. Gish, *Desmond Tutu*, 164.
213. Goebel, "King's Law and Local Custom," 416–48.
214. Ibid.
215. Aristotle, *Politics*, 77.
216. Hayek, *Constitution of Liberty*, 165.

accountable, consistent, predictable, and binding. Adjudicatory mechanisms, such as the judiciary should be independent and equipped with necessary structures while assuring equality of access and treatment to all.

The seventeenth-century political philosopher Thomas Hobbes, for example, believed that in a well-ordered commonwealth, the law, rather than man, should govern. Hobbes's contemporary, James Harrington, also proposed that "the art whereby a civil society is instituted and preserved upon the foundations of common rights and interest . . . [is], to follow Aristotle and Livy, 'the empire of laws not of men.'"[217] During the classical period of Roman law it was fully understood that no conflict exists between law and freedom. Freedom is dependent upon certain attributes of the law:[218] its generality, its certainty, and the restrictions it places on the discretion of right delegated, given, or authorized authority. This classical period was also a time of complete economic freedom, to which Rome largely owed its prosperity and power.[219]

The first maxim of a free state, other early jurists have written, is that the laws be made by one set of men, and administered by another. In other words, that the legislative, executive, and judiciary be kept separate.[220] When these offices are unified in the same person or assembly, a government by them is similar to slavery. Montesquieu puts it succinctly,

> When the legislative and executive powers are vested in
> the same person or in the same body . . . there can be
> no liberty because apprehension may arise, lest the same
> monarch or senates should enact tyrannical laws to execute
> them in a tyrannical manner. . . . Again, there is no liberty
> if the power of judging is not separated from the legislative
> and executive. If it were joined, with the legislative, the life

---

217. Coker, "James Harrington 1611–1677," 357; see also Frost and Sikkenga, *History of American Political Thought*, 114; and Wren, *Inventing Leadership*, 71.
218. Mudambi et al., *Economic Welfare*, 268.
219. Hayek, *Constitution of Liberty*, 162–75.
220. Hammond et al., *American Political and Constitutional Thought*, 491.

and liberty of the subject would be exposed to arbitrary
control; for the judge would then be the legislator. If it
were joined to the executive power the judge might behave
with violence and oppression. There would be an end to
everything if the same man or the same body, whether of
nobles or of people were to excise those three powers that
of enacting laws, that of executing public affairs and that of
trying crimes of individual cases.[221]

In a similar context of separation of powers, Indonesia, which enjoys the
largest population of Muslims in the world, has fashioned its constitution to
make Islam its source for the formation of values, norms, and behaviors of
its people. However, the country has established the separation of state and
religion based on the *Pancasila* (philosophical foundation of the Indonesian
state).[222] The basis of the Indonesian state includes five principles: belief in
God, belief in a just and civilized humanity, belief in the unity of Indonesia,
belief in democracy guided by inner wisdom, and belief in social justice.[223]

The citizens of Indonesia have the rights inherent in a democratic
system; however, there are additional terms and authorities, as well as various
concepts of rights, within Muslim countries. Like Indonesia, most Muslim
countries stipulate the separation or distribution of powers. Turkey, for
example, prides itself as the most democratic country in the known Muslim
World, and provides for effective electoral control of government and free
elections, as well as the protection of democratic culture and the will of the
people. Both Indonesia and Turkey celebrate themselves in the rule of law
where separation of power reigns.

Incontestably, the rule of law is a concept incorporating several principles
that govern the intricate working of a legal order. These principles include
supremacy of law; separation of powers; protection of life, liberty, safety, and
property of persons; legal certainty and equality before the law. The rule of

---

221. Masterman, *Separation of Powers*, 13.
222. Riddell and Street, *Islam*; see also Darmaputera, *Pancasila and the Search for Identity*.
223. Darmaputera, *Pancasila and the Search for Identity*, 253.

law also envisages stability, maintenance of law, public order, and security. The alternative is instability at best and anarchy at worst. Until another comes about, this is the general perception of the rule of law.

It has also been suggested that the rule of law is merely a legal order that follows certain principles for the exercise of state power.[224] Essentially, a regime of the rule of law envisions the existence of state power and individual transactions as regulated by law. The rule of law could be stated as the law of rules, or commitment to the enforcement of laws that already exist.

Whether it is the rule of law or law of rules or yet another idiom, organizations and institutions are introducing several rules of law projects and concepts. Programs such as the American Bar Association Rule of Law project, the United Nations Rule of Law enterprise, and Transitional Justice projects are all excellent initiatives meant to promote legal systems that conform to principles of separation of powers, independence of the judiciary, human rights, the suppression of corruption, and the commitment to good governance.[225] Societies and countries should, however, be measured in adopting rule of law programs into their systems *in toto*. What needs to be done by these wonderful organizations that are kind to assist, and the societies that will benefit, include encouragement of a workable system of laws that are adaptable and strengthen the existing laws; while making clear the broader system of the "rule of law project." Sometimes the rule of law projects may not account for cultural nuances that exist within societies seeking to incorporate rule of law into their legal framework. Adopting the "rule of law project" should ultimately assist societies in ensuring justice, freedom, and peace. Nevertheless, the many positive developments of the

---

224. Sevastik, *Legal Assistance*; see also Hayek, *Road to Serfdom*, 117; and Bingham, *Rule of Law*.

225. American Bar Association is the largest voluntary professional association in the world with about 400,000 members. Serving equally its members, the profession, and the public by defending liberty and delivering justice as the national representative of the legal profession (http://www.americanbar.org/utility/about_the_aba.html).

rule of law within national borders across regions should be utilized within and calibrated to better serve local jurisdictions.

While there is compatibility between democracy and good governance in the pursuit of systemic reforms in many countries, the rule of law should also be explicitly considered and incorporated as a primary concern by the local community as well as all other interested parties involved be they regional, national, or international. This form of intentionality around this fundamental value strengthens local authorities in their reform efforts toward human and economic development. The past, present, and anticipated future leads these societies to understand that traditional culture has a role in promoting rule of law as a key feature of conflict resolution. Indubitably, the rule of law should apply equally to everyone, and citizens should be allowed to participate equally in the process of its adoption and development. This will help to ensure personal freedom as well as the maintenance of the interests of the state as superior to the interests of individual groups. Integration of the value of rule of law with traditional judicial institutions will not only promote lawfulness and local justice systems, but also broaden and ensure individual freedom. Additionally, it should encourage the development of cooperative responsibility and promote legal order and security in peoples' lives.

To achieve this order and security, the rule of law, when exercised in local cultural settings, should not promote torture, repression, detention, kidnapping, nor should it detain an individual in solitary confinement under any pretext. If the rule of law allowed such abhorrent actions, it could undermine its basic tenets of human rights principles. The World Justice Project has recently emphasized the substantial role of the rule of law in material and multidisciplinary matters as well as local and global collaboration efforts.[226] The rule of law can help encourage developing societies to foster mutual relationships between nations across the world.

---

226. The World Justice Project is a leader in a global effort to strengthen the rule of law for the development of communities, opportunity, and equity. One of its purposes is the advancement of the effectiveness of the rule of law.

The World Justice Project also suggests that when addressing the rule of law in different societies stability, economic development, good governance, and freedom of civil societies should be emphasized.

This emphasis will help to enhance the idea of law and justice while improving progress. Furthermore, access to justice needs to be provided by a sufficient number of competent, independent, and ethical law enforcers, as well as lawyers, representatives, and judges, all of who have access to adequate resources within the communities they serve. Theoretically, this fundamental principle appears very plausible. However, upon examination within the context of the Shariah, specifically in regards to the Shariah Penal Code Law of Northern Nigeria, one must ask if the government and its officials and agents can be held accountable. The ability of a people to hold their government accountable is largely rooted in the principle of separation of powers.

In some developing societies that lack a clear separation of powers, the rule of law does readily apply. In some of these cases, the executive branch wields its power, as it controls the instrument of coercion and the resources of the state. In other circumstances, government officials often use a lack of security as an excuse to violently suppress any opposition or alternative voice. In such cases, a national goal of unity is perverted into a trend of government-backed suppression, and the rule of law becomes a function of rule by law. When government becomes more interested in ruling by law, rather than achieving any semblance of the rule of law, the path often leads away from unity, peace, and progress.

When it is apparent that the executive branch of government seeks to ignore principles of the rule of law and interferes with functions and/or processes of the judiciary, bar associations need to insist on the independence of the judicial branch. This can be accomplished in a variety of ways, and especially through the encouragement of a credible bar association. While this author has advocated the adaptation of the rule of law to work within many different systems, certain cultural values remain inconsistent with human rights and the rule of law. In the case of the *Attorney General of the Republic of Botswana v. Unity*, one of the cultural practices at issue was the provision that stated that a child born to a Botswanan man was automatically a citizen of Botswana; whereas a child born from a marriage between a Botswanan woman and a foreign man could not attain Botswanan citizenship.[227] In a progressive judgment for the rule of law, the High Court held that, " . . . custom as far as possible [must] be read so as to conform to the Constitution. But where this is impossible, it is the custom and not the Constitution, which must go."[228] This ruling affirmed the Botswanan Constitutional principle of equality of its peoples.

One of the greatest challenges encountered by the Nigerian judicial system has been establishing a rule of law that incorporates local customary laws and practices while modifying some of the new Shariah laws to promote rule of law principles. Indeed, societies across the world have enjoyed the fusion of customary law in the adjudication of dispute for centuries. When this can be incorporated within Nigeria its ripple effect will be felt across Africa. Nigeria wields tremendous influence throughout the continent, especially along the western coast. The examples set in Northern Nigeria in the interpretation and application of the law will influence other Muslim societies in the region and elsewhere in the Muslim world.

The provision against discrimination in the Nigerian Constitution guarantees that citizens of Nigeria from any state cannot be discriminated against on any basis whatsoever. It seems, however, that a Muslim who resides within a state that does not practice the new Shariah will be treated differently from a non-Muslim who resides in a state that practices the new Shariah. Thus, discrimination may arise and defeat the provision of Sections 15(2); 17(3)(a)(e); 19(c); and 42 of the Nigerian Constitution; whereas, citizens of Nigeria of any community, ethnic group, place of

---

227. United Nations General Assembly, A/HRC/WG.6/3/BWA/1, Sept. 5, 2008, Human Rights Council. Working Group on the Universal Periodic Review, Third Session, Geneva, Dec. 1–15, 2008. See also Heyns, *Human Rights Law in Africa*, 31.
228. Beyani, "Toward a More Effective," 295.

origin, sex, religion, or political opinion shall be accorded equal privileges and advantages accorded to any other citizen of Nigeria.

Staying Focused While Taking Advantage of a Globalized World

In today's globalized world, it may behoove us to look beyond our various local jurisdictions to the international community. While remaining focused on a particular case, one may encounter useful thoughts and decisions from the international community that could be persuasive in national courts. With respect to Shariah cases, a lawyer's comprehensive skill set may be more adequately used to pinpoint jurisdictions that have similar progressive views to the jurisdiction in which their case is being tried. For example, the development of the Northern Nigerian penal codes in the late 1950s, which extends to the Shariah penal codes as currently applied in Northern Nigeria, was traced back to sources from India, Pakistan, and Sudan. The use of some of the progressive courts' current decisions in these countries will be pragmatic for persuasion.

Additionally, the use of decisions by international human rights bodies can broaden a lawyer's perspective and add value to arguments in local courts. Human rights commissions, committees, and treaty bodies' decisions, such as the United Nations Human Rights Committee (UNHRC) have been upheld in national courts. It follows that national courts could utilize the reasoning and findings of treaty bodies while highlighting the range of issues that come before local courts.[229] This is reasoning that will work within local and grassroots settings that allow the lawyer to identify his or her most effective methods. Indeed, the principles outlined in many human rights treaties and declarations are synonymous to those that have been forwarded for centuries by Islam and Shariah law; justice, fairness, and human dignity breathes life into the spirit that illuminates human rights law and Shariah law.

---

229. Louw, "Domestic Effect."

Cases from countries such as Pakistan, Indonesia, Malaysia, Turkey, and Africa that practice Shariah, as well as cases from international bodies, such as the Human Rights Committee (HRC) of the United Nations could prove beneficial. For instance, when considering the HRC's adjudication on individual cases that had an impact on domestic jurisprudence, some of the case arguments were adopted by national courts in regards to issues such as torture and the Convention on the Elimination of all Forms of Discrimination Against Women (CEDAW).[230] Use of these materials also increases their accessibility and dissemination while simultaneously promoting knowledge of their existence. Furthermore, where the findings of these bodies have been applied, it was mostly used as an interpretative guide to clarify and validate the application of constitutionally guaranteed rights in domestic law. While this reasoning may not be adopted in its entirety within a local jurisdiction, the analogy or factual reasoning of a case can often be creatively used.

For example, in a ruling on the constitutionality of the crime of sodomy in the Zimbabwean case of *S v. Banana*, the court ruled, "the social norms and values of Zimbabwe did not push the Court to decriminalize consensual sodomy."[231] Similarly, in the case of *National Coalition for Gay and Lesbian Equality v. Minister of Justice*, the Constitutional Court of Zimbabwe held that the common law offense of sodomy and accompanying legislation was unconstitutional.[232] Citing yet another example, in the South African case of *S v. Makwanyane*, the Constitutional Court abolished the death penalty; ruling that the death penalty is not a competent sentence for murder by contending that it was in conflict with the provisions of Sections 9 and

---

230. Convention on the Elimination of Discrimination Against Women, "Convention on the Elimination of all forms of Discrimination Against Women."
231. Amar and Tushnet, *Global Perspectives on Constitutional Law*, 58; see also Bernstein and Schaffner, *Regulating Sex*.
232. National Coalition for Gay and Lesbian Equality and Another v. Minister of Justice and Others, ZACC 15 (1998), 114. See also Van der Merwe and du Plessis, *Introduction to the Law*; and Gutto, *Equality and Non-Discrimination in South Africa*.

11(2) of the Constitution in that it prohibits "cruel, inhuman or degrading treatment or punishment."[233]

In its decision, the South African court referenced two decisions of the HRC: *Chitat Ng v. Canada* and *Kindler v. Canada*.[234] However, the court clearly stated that "we can derive assistance from public international law and foreign case law, but we are in no way bound to follow it."[235] The court concluded its discussion of the committee's findings by stating,

> Despite these differences of opinion, what is clear from the decisions of the Human Rights Committee of the United Nations is that the death penalty is regarded by it as cruel and inhuman punishment within the ordinary meaning of those words, and that it was because of the specific provisions of the International Covenant authorising the imposition of capital punishment by member states in certain circumstances, that the words had to be given a narrow meaning.[236]

Alternatively, the Supreme Court of Nigeria held in *Onuoha Kalu v. The State*, that the death penalty is not unconstitutional in Nigeria.[237] The court came to this conclusion despite the advocate for the appellant's submissions that referred the court to the decisions of *Chitat Ng v. Canada* and *Cox v. Canada*.[238] In another South African case, *Bon Vista Mansions v. Southern Metropolitan Council*,[239] the court stated that "general comments

---

233. Lauterpacht and Greenwood, *Interntational Law Reports*, 103; see also Van der Walt, *Law and Sacrifice*, 507; and Franck et al., *Barbaric Punishment*, 75.

234. Schabas, *Death Penalty as Cruel Treatment* (Chitat Ng v. Canada, Communication No. 469/1991, [1994]), 260 and (Kindler v. Canada [Minister of Justice], 2 S.C.R. 779 [1991]), 236.

235. Ibid., 236.

236. Schabas, *International Sourcebook on Capital Punishment*, 143.

237. Onuoha Kalu v. The State, 13 NWLR 531 (1990).

238. Pollis and Schwab, *Human Rights*, 206.

239. Bon Vista Mansions v. Southern Metropolitan Council 2002 (6) BCLR 625. See Donders and Volodin, *Human Rights in Education*, 110; see also Brand, *Socio-Economic Rights in South Africa*.

have authoritative status under international law" and quoted General Comment 12 of the Committee on Economic, Social and Cultural Rights in explaining the duty to respect "rights of access."[240] A. J. Bundler, the South African Judge, further made it clear that he relied upon international law to interpret the Bill of Rights "where the Constitution uses language similar to that which has been used in international instruments."[241]

The Globalization of Human Rights Within the Rule of Law

While the above cases indicate how international norms and thinking could affect state court decisions, it is important to mention that there is an integrated and, sometimes, national rule of law engraved in most legal systems. Sometimes customary law reflects fundamental human rights; not so much with regard to language, but assuredly in respect to the sanctity of life. Human rights language is generally expressed more comprehensively in international human rights law than in customary law. However, provisions similar to those found in international human rights instruments exist in local jurisdictions, though they may not necessarily be framed in the same sophisticated manner.

Most communities, and indeed international laws, hold that the right to life is sacred and invaluable; so, too is the right to freedom of equality. Before the law, all people are equal and entitled to equal protection. No individual should be discriminated against or exposed to greater risk based on their religious beliefs, race, language, circumstances of birth, or other similar incidences. In addition to other human rights instruments, protocols, and treaties, the Universal Islamic Declaration of Human Rights (UIDHR) proclaims the right of justice for every person. Each individual is entitled to be treated in accordance with the law and has both rights and obligations. In fact, in this author's opinion, the UIDHR is more comprehensive than the United Nations Universal Declaration of Human Rights (UDHR) because it includes an individual's obligation to others.

---

240. Donders and Volodin, *Human Rights in Education*, 117.
241. Kravchenko and Bonine, *Human Rights and the Environment*, 135.

The domain of human rights and constitutionalism within the rule of law is not a recent Western conceptualization; nor is it new to Islam. According to Noah Feldman, a constitutional theory developed by scholars implied that a Caliph had paramount responsibility to fulfill the divine injunction to "demand the just and prohibit the awry," which in turn required him to delegate responsibility to befitting judges who would apply God's law as they construe it.[242] The Caliphs had a plethora of power and could issue commanding guidance as beseeched.[243] Shariah law favors the just rights of its *ummah* (followers), and was seen by the spiritual leaders of Islam as doing so.[244] However, many of the legal matters fell outside the specific rules given by Shariah. Shariah functioned as a constitution that safeguarded against injustice and the trespass of power; though the Constitution was not enforceable because neither scholars nor subjects could compel their ruler to observe the law in the exercise of government.[245]

According to historical accounts, the Ottoman Empire, at the height of its power (1299 to 1923), controlled much of Southeastern Europe, Western Asia, and North Africa, with authority over distant overseas lands. The Empire responded to military setbacks with an internal reform movement. The most important reform was the codification of its civil laws. While this process was extraneous to the Islamic approved tradition, it metamorphoses the Islamic law from a body of beliefs and regulations to be enunciated through the undertaking of the scholars, to rules that could be found in a book. Meanwhile, the Ottoman leaders constituted a council comprised of dual legislatures, one elected by the people and one designated by the sovereign ruler.[246] Promulgated in 1876, the Mecelle Code had been suggested to be the first attempt to codify part of Shariah law.[247] The Ottoman lawmakers

---

242. Feldman, *Fall and Rise*, 28.
243. Bennison, *Great Caliphs*.
244. Harnischfeger, *Democratization and Islamic Law*, 88; see also Otto, *Sharia Incorporated*, 455.
245. S. V. R. Nasr, *Mawdudi and the Making*, 4.
246. Faroqhi, *Ottoman Empire*; see also Sufian and LeVine, *Reapproaching Borders*.
247. Esposito, *Oxford Dictionary of Islam*, 199.

encouraged a consciousness that the populace embodies the decisive source of legal connoisseur. Here the law became a tool of the ruler, not an authority to be used indiscriminately by the ruler. This could prevent absolute rule and other forms of executive command and control that may soar as a result of a nonfunctional rule of law. Caution must therefore be exercised so that the rule of law safeguards justice and restores confidence among Muslims who wish to see the implementation of Shariah law.[248]

Divinity of Shariah

The national or state assemblies are best suited to address the colloquy of Shariah as the source of law in Nigeria. Their power, generally, allows them to make laws for peace, order the good governance for a federation or state; for example, Section 4 of the Nigerian Constitution, 1999 (or similar provision of governance) in accordance with the provisions of a national constitution or other binding legal documents. Muslims will be glad to have judicial review of legislative actions; it is a sure way to guarantee that they do adhere to the human dignity provisions of the Qur'an and Hadith as well as Islamic values. Such a review is incorporated into constitutions that seek to harmonize Islam and democracy.[249] For example, in the Afghan Constitution of 2004[250] and the Iraqi Constitution of 2005,[251] both the legislative assembly and/or a single court may not deliver the rule of law alone.

In spite of this separation of powers, the issue still remains that basic human rights must stem from the rule of law. Human rights must be understood within local traditions and cultures, without disregard to other forms of religious faith and worship. Shariah upholds law that applies equally to every Muslim believer; such as provided for by the Qur'an in several verses, especially 33:35:

---

248. Mani, *Beyond Retribution*, 76.
249. Feldman, *Fall and Rise of the Islamic State*.
250. Constitution of Afghanistan, 2004, Chapter 7, Article 121.
251. Etzioni, *Security First*, 21. Article 14 of Iraq's Constitution states that "Iraqis are equal before the law without discrimination . . ."

Indeed, the Muslim men and Muslim women, the believing men and believing women, the obedient men and obedient women, the truthful men and truthful women, the patient men and patient women, the humble men and humble women, the charitable men and charitable women, the fasting men and fasting women, the men who guard their private parts and the women who do so, and the men who remember Allah often and the women who do so—for them Allah has prepared forgiveness and a great reward.

Furthermore, as American President Abraham Lincoln succinctly put it, "My friends," he thundered, "let me make one thing clear . . . No one is above the law, no one is below the law. And we're going to enforce the law."[252] Nor should anyone be discriminated by it, and everyone at all times is bound by the rule of law.[253] A state needs competent institutions that recognize that it benefits most by continuing to acknowledge citizens the enabling freedoms to practice their faith with fairness, justice, tolerance, and equity.

Of interest is the discussion surrounding divinity and spirituality.[254] Can Shariah be a universal religion applying a legal system whose sources are divine and whose rules are thought to be eternal? The rule of law ideally allows at least the possibility of evaluating the adequacy of legal orders and establishing whether legal orders comply with certain requirements. As aforementioned, the rule of law requires that the legal rules be open, clear, and adaptable; and that legal institutions be effective. This approach examines the difficulties for legal orders in which Shariah maintains an important place. While Shariah is often cited as divine law, it should strive in its application to comply with the criteria of the rule of law ideal that is conceived in this manner.

---

252. White, *Making of the President*, 361.
253. Neal, *Rule of Law*, 67.
254. Khaldun, *Muqaddimah*.

With respect to constitutionality and codification of the Shariah, progress has been immense. At least in Nigeria, the 1999 Constitution included provisions that upheld basic fundamental human rights. The Shariah Penal Code Law (SPCL), adopted by the twelve states in Northern Nigeria (though all different), are mostly codified; creating a tangible and specific example to refer to by insisting that the provisions of the SPCL be interpreted by an independent body and applied impartially. Furthermore, a unification of the codes by legislation and conformity of provisions to Section 1 of the 1999 Constitution of Nigeria will certainly bring justice closer to citizens and noncitizens alike.

Each of the Shariah cases should be analyzed in light of the Qur'an, Hadith, court practices, and issues surrounding sex, gender, and equality, to name a few, as well as theory of proof of the hudud offenses and/or punishment.[255] For instance, if we examine the case of *zina*, must we first inquire as to the stipulation required by the Qur'an and the method of proving the offense? Or will the Hadith be the basis of our defense in court? The Shariah penal code of the states proffer that the proof of *zina* must include all of the following: a confession, sanity, valid marriage, maturity, and the confirmation of four male witnesses who must be Muslim.[256] By concentrating on the code of each state regarding matters such as the proof of *zina*, strategies can be developed to ensure that all necessary legal authorities are relevant. Authorities such as the Qur'an, the Hadith, prior cases, the Constitution, and relevant statutes can be cited to illustrate each issue. For example, confession: How was the confession made and by whom? Was it a repeated confession? Was the accused coerced or was the confession voluntarily given? Did the accused possess the proper mind (mental faculty) at the time of confession? Questions such as these acknowledge that the accused can withdraw the confession at any time prior to execution of the sentence.

---

255. Sidahmad, *Hudud*, 173.
256. Katsina State Shariah Penal Code Law, 2001, Vol. 4, Chapters 143–180, Section 127. See also Ashrof, *Islam and Gender Justice.*

The ability to stay focused in the midst of controversy is a skill that I was constantly learning throughout the cases with which I was involved.[257] Professional and personal challenges are part of the work, but to be focused and stay focused requires a certain mindset: it's not about me, it's about standing and doing what is professionally and personally right. In conclusion, reverence for the rule of law and protection of basic human rights should be the guiding principles. As ministers in the temple of justice, we must remain focused and learn from every opportunity presented.

---

257. This author has been involved in 157 Shariah cases at the time of this writing (2012).

CHAPTER FOUR

Be Firm and Flexible

BE FIRM YET FLEXIBLE. CONSIDER each case on its merits and do not take for granted the power of one. Acknowledge an even greater strength in the vigor of a team. Even though we might not always sway things our way, firmness and flexibility remain our greatest virtues. We are to be firm in the fidelity to our ideals and principles while remaining flexible in recognizing our professional imperfections and personal ambitions. We should embody the patience of the bamboo tree that spends the first year of its life growing very little in stature yet spreads a wide root network so as to eventually become tall and flourishing. Similarly, we allow for spending the necessary time to learn the diverse contemporary nuances and distinctiveness of the "new Shariah" law, becoming thoroughly conversant in its intricacies so as to be able to assist future clients in obtaining justice.

Our professional life and clients are constantly changing, presenting us with new roles, goals, and relationships; thus, ever new opportunities to improve ourselves. As time passes, we find ourselves making better choices by learning from our mistakes and building upon our past successes. In the midst of these seemingly tumultuous challenges, it will serve us well to remain mindful of the principles we learned in law school, our professional ethics (as alluded to earlier), and our firm belief in justice and human rights, which we must hold dear. We are charged to stand unfailing in the values that create the individuals we are. As the Greek biographer Laërtius Diogenes put it succinctly:

> We have two ears and one tongue so that we would listen more and talk less. We have been given two ears, one on each side of our head so that we can hear things from two different perspectives. We have been given two eyes on either side of our face to see things from two different views. We have two hands to feel things from both sides. Two feet to help us gain steady footing; and even right and left hemispheres of our brain that perform different but equal tasks, all to give us every physical opportunity possible to find balance. If we can only gain control of our mouths, we might just find it.[258]

Thus, we have two ears and one tongue so that we will listen more and talk less.[259] As we redefine and think comprehensively through each case using all available tools and, where necessary, applying *legal game theory* (forming a unified set of strategic solutions), we help redefine the rest of society. It is crucial that we allow ourselves to be influenced by our legal practice, our clients, the law and its rules, its processes and procedures, the evidence, and witnesses, as they all stimulate new and different ways of thinking and acting. Ultimately, these influences lead us to become "agents of positive change." It is an opportunity and a privilege to be part of such a role in the development of our societies and its systems. We are consciously creating new realities and opening new horizons; we are creating the

---

258. Laërtius, *Lives, Teachings, and Sayings*, 37. Diogenes Laërtius was a third-century biographer of the Greek philosophers. His *Lives and Opinions of Eminent Philosophers* is one of the principal surviving sources for the history of Greek philosophy.
259. Sherburn, *Caring for the Caregiver*, 37.

reality in which we will pave a path for generations yet unborn. As Thomas Edison admonished, in a life filled with so many possibilities, there are no mundane moments, for each moment is the performance of a lifetime. It beholds on us to continue to find our greatest pleasure (more so, when it is attuned with God's justice) in our work and not necessarily in the reward or successes.[260]

Being a good advocate involves approaching cases in both a firm and flexible manner. These two tactics may seem to be mutually exclusive, but they can actually be mutually beneficial when applied correctly. Being firm when it comes to the core principles of law—particularly the principles mentioned earlier—adds value. Evidently, equality before the law and the knowledge that laws are made for man and by man—to reflect dreams and aspirations, hopes, fears, and insecurity—help to secure justice. According to these primary principles, man made all laws and man was not made for the law. Therefore law should not only be attributed to divinity and royalty alone, but rather the law should synthesize the divine and human in a respectful and inclusive manner to better appreciate its possibilities.

By allowing for flexibility and adopting local understanding of social values, one affords oneself the opportunity to better navigate the terrain and offer valuable assistance. Learning to be flexible within local cultural norms is a continual process of investigation, analysis, interpretation, and trial. At times, even of adaptation. Each situation or question is an opportunity. People are entwined with their histories, of *what it used to be*, with their ancestors and its specific nuances and traditions. The people we work with at the grassroots have an in-depth intuition, with creative problem-solving skills. They continuously interpret interactions, words, and body language within social and political contexts to process and see *if it fits*. Attempting to recognize societies' heterogeneity, traditions, and multiple objectives is one way to be flexible. When local communities are interested, there is great

---

260. See also Burlingame, *Engines of Democracy.*

value in approaching them to negotiate, to conduct fact-finding, or to offer legal assistance in a way that respects their sensibilities and values.

Take for instance in the cases of *zina* (adultery/fornication), which is considered by local societies to be a shameful and degrading act. Yahaya Yunusa Bambale (an erudite academician in Northern Nigeria), quoting from the Qur'an has this to say about *zina*, "And do not approach unlawful sexual intercourse. Indeed, it is ever an immorality and is evil as a way" (17:32). And, "They who guard their private parts; Except from their wives or those their right hands possess, for indeed, they will not be blamed—But whoever seeks beyond that, then those are the transgressor—" (23:5–7). He further said it is "religiously sinful, morally wicked, socially evil, shameful and objectionable. It is a social crime against the institution of the family and an offense against public morality."[261] Local traditional societies believe that *zina* is disgraceful and brings dishonor to the family and communities. Any attempt to minimize this stigma to such clients will not be acceptable to the communities and will not be helpful for the legal assistance a lawyer may wish to render. The lawyer may have to consciously acknowledge this dynamic where necessary. The Holy Qur'an is emphatic about the act of *zina*:" . . . Nor come near to adultery: for it is a shameful (deed) and an evil, opening the road (to other evils)" (17:32). Because the Qur'an is foundational for creating and sustaining individual and collective identity, the need to be aware of like sensibilities and to seek to work within the system cannot be over emphasized.

By allowing for flexibility in the area of social values, we are able to keep our focus while remaining calm and rational. In our experiences, this flexibility makes it possible for us to attempt to open channels of communication with potential adversaries in the hope of finding common ground, and hopefully allies. Trusted relationships with allies can help to mitigate hostile feelings post-trial while also quelling some of the intense feelings that often surround issues such as *zina* in the Shariah courts.

---

261. Bambale, *Crime and Punishment*, 65.

Creating allies is ultimately what makes it possible for clients to reenter their communities and find acceptance.

Simultaneous to building relationships within the community, we work diligently to become fully grounded in the facts of the case. This permits us to be far less susceptible to frustration and emotion and allows us to focus clearly on each case. We are then able to earn the trust, confidence, and respect of the courts and our clients. Being firmly grounded in principles, however, does not preclude lawyers from allowing themselves to be flexible. Being a good lawyer involves approaching cases in both a tenacious and adaptable manner. If the occasion arises where a lawyer is in harm's way as a result of his or her professional service, the lawyer will do well to put two of his or her greatest virtues in action: firmness and flexibility.

Being Firm Regarding the Principles of Law

Western and non-Western societies alike commonly uphold that some principles, such as *equal treatment under the law* cannot be negotiated. In order for progress to be made, certain legal doctrines should be upheld and defended. Among these are supremacy of the law, separation of religion and state, separation of powers, equality of the law, independence of the judiciary, respect for fundamental human rights, and certainty of law, all of which ensures that within the law, punishments are not inhumane, degrading, nor contrary to the principles of equity, fairness, and good conscience.

Equality before the law in Islam is beyond the argument, beyond winning a case. As Yusuf al-Qaradawi observed, it stems from the honor Islam bestows on every human being regardless of race or creed.[262] The only yardstick here is that "the most honored of you in the sight of God is (he/she) who is, the most righteous" (Qur'an 43:13). Islam aspires to unite humanity in a single family that is based on the equality of its members and on oneness and a common origin of people. Qur'anic verses provide for human equality and negate all inequalities based on race, color, nationality,

---

262. Al-Qaradawi, *Islam*, 187.

tribe, etc., because all humans spring from a single source.[263] As the Qur'an states " . . . O mankind! We created you from a single soul . . . male and female. . . . Verily the most honored in the sight of Allah is he who is the most righteous . . . " (49:13). In Islam there is no privilege granted based on race, ethnicity, color of skin, or any other identities. The most important criteria of judging a human being is his or her faith and good deeds; most importantly, his or her devotion to Allah سبحانه و تعالى . . . only Gods-fearing people merit God's preference.[264]

Take for instance the major Islamic schools of thought, like the establishment of proof of the crime of *zina* to be based on the Qur'an and Hadith. Prosecution must be by eyewitness testimony; neither confession nor circumstantial evidence alone is permitted without the application of the strict proof requirements. Thus, unmarried pregnancy, being neither eyewitness testimony nor confession, simply may not be admissible as proof in a *zina* case. The Hanafi, Shafi'i, and Hanbali schools of law seem to take this position.[265]   Others should take this view into consideration when passing judgment for the well being of society and the defense of justice.

Pregnancy is not generally accepted as conclusive proof of *zina* because of its circumstantial nature and its element of doubt. As Tirmidhi Hadith observed: "idra'u al-hududa bi'shubhat [Raise the defense against *hudud* in all cases of doubt]."[266] Classical muslim scholars have also suggested that pregnancy could occur through other means—for example, unawareness of sexual relationship while in a state of sleep, a mistaken belief of one's marital status, or use of force or intimidation to obtain compliance; to have intercourse against one's will.[267] With modern medical advances, this cautionary approach to some provisions of Shariah penal codes is commendable. We now understand that one can become pregnant through

---

263. El-Nimr, "Women in Islam," 91.
264. Abu-Nimer, *Nonviolence and Peace Building.*
265. Quraishi, "Her Honor," 115.
266. See also Anderson, *Islamic Law in Africa.*
267. See al-Mughni al-Maqdisi, vol. 8; see also Abdallah, "Crime, Punishment and Evidence," 44.

artificial insemination where there is no sexual coupling. Unmarried women, partnered or single, in increasing numbers are becoming pregnant through artificial insemination. Even as far back as 1970 there were hundreds of thousands of such cases.[268]

The principles as encapsulated in Shariah issues with respect to *zina* that remain unresolved—result in doubt (*shubha*), and cause confusion between truth and falsehood, and where neither is proof, the Hadith of the Prophet said,

> That which is lawful is plain and that which is unlawful is plain and between the two of them are doubtful matters about which not many people know. Thus he who avoids doubtful matters clears himself in regard to his religion and his honor, but he who falls into doubtful matters falls into that which is unlawful, like the shepherd who pastures around a sanctuary, all but grazing therein. Truly every king has a sanctuary, and truly Allah's sanctuary is His prohibitions. Truly in the body there is a morsel of flesh which, if it were whole, all the body is whole and which, if it were diseased, all of it is diseased. Truly it is in the heart (Hadith: Bukhari and Muslim).[269]

The point is that doubt vitiates the case of *zina* and the court should settle it in favor of the accused/defendant; it makes for common sense, to be apt in using this provision as most of the facts and procedural process at trial raises multiple issues of doubt. It is indeed better for a guilty person to be set free than an innocent person to be convicted of a crime.

In addition, the Qur'anic verse referred to above protects women against charges of *zina* that offer as evidence anything short of four eyewitnesses. Therefore it becomes necessary that lawyers and the court understand the general principles of Islamic law mentioned earlier, but it

---

268. Maier, *Human Sexuality in Perspective*, 228.
269. At-Tahan, *Perfect Muslim Character*, 9.

remains important that they also stay firm within the general procedural principles of proving *zina* as laid out.[270] To be clear, pregnancy simpliciter is not sufficient evidence for a woman to be convicted of *zina*.

Principles of law to which lawyers are to stand firm require that proving the guilt of the accused lies on the accuser, especially in cases carrying capital punishment. This was the position in the case of *Ms. Rani v. The State*.[271] Proof of adultery ought to be based upon an incidental and intentional act, as well as upon the lawful presence of the witnesses at the location and time of the act; having taken place within a reasonable period of time following the act of the alleged *zina*. Cases involving the slightest doubt should be settled in favor of the accused.[272] Instances regarding the proof of *zina* will be expounded upon in subsequent chapters, but it is important to note that lawyers practicing in Shariah courts in Nigeria will benefit from exposure to all available opinions on this topic.[273] The point to be made is that when it comes to principles of law, the standard of proof should not be negotiated.

There exists a significant amount of literature written on issues of legal philosophy and interpretation about these principles of law. However, I will briefly mention two relevant issues—*Equality before the law* and *Separation of powers*—as they illustrate "gray" areas we encountered at the beginning of our defense of "Shariah cases." I hope that in the future, lawyers will navigate them even more creatively.

---

270. Imber and Calder, *Islamic Jurisprudence,* 26; and Engineer, *Rights of Women in Islam,* 79.
271. Ms. Rani v. The State, PLD Karachi (1996). The court held *inter-alia* that, "The prosecution would have to discharge the heavy onus of proof by bringing forth positive and independent evidence that the woman actually and in fact had committed zina with her own free will and consent with another man to whom she was not lawfully married to. In this regard, it may also be stated that the mere proof of pregnancy or some form of medical testimony/report on its own could be of no consequence as the latter would at best only be corroborative in nature" (p. 316).
272. Doi, *Sharīah,* 224.
273. Anderson, *Islamic Law in Africa.*

Equality Before the Law

Equality is sometimes described as a "Western concept," a culture whose legal thinking originates from a vision of equality as a revolution "celebrating equal rights and equality before the law of all men and women."[274] However, the notion of equality has been practiced by many societies in many different forms. While the "new Shariah" in Nigeria may logically and rightfully be referred to as "developing gradually," it still must confront the issues of equality before the law. Given that almost all our clients demonstrated hardship and helplessness, this issue is especially relevant when considering whether all people receive equal treatment, regardless of their social class. We asked ourselves: Is this equality available to all? Or could it be said that, for many, justice consists of "treating equals equally and unequals unequally?"[275] Because almost all of our clients are illiterate and impoverished, are unaware of why they are in court at the time of their arraignment before the Shariah courts, and are unable to secure legal counsel, their sentence and conviction renders the concept of equality under the law fluid and capricious. When describing equality, the Honorable Justice Aguda, an eminent Nigerian jurist and author, had this to say:

> To the best of my acquaintance with facts, cognitions and perception, there is nothing like equality before the law, at least not the way the law is administered today [in Nigeria]. It is nothing but an allegory created by our political rulers and the lawyers to give cold consolation to the "common man," so that they, "*political majesties*" and the lawyers, can have peace of mind.[276]

Realizing that the concept of equality before the law can be perceived as novel or rare, thereby contributing to its failure in some societies, the

---

274. Siddiqui, "Concept of Justice," 29; see also Orens, *Muslim World*; and Mathur and Mettal, *Spectrum of Nehru's Thought*.
275. Bowie and Simon, *Individual and the Political Order*, 72; see also Cohen, *Justice*, 17.
276. Aguda, "Common Man and the Common Law," 25.

renowned Nigerian intellectual Claude Ake characterized equality as the "inheritance elite" that internalizes and fulfills many European ideals.[277] Notwithstanding, equality before the law is, in reality, an aspect of formal justice; that is to say, a presumption of equality of status.[278]

One issue that arose at the inception of our defense of "Shariah cases" was that our clients convicted for the offense of *zina* were mainly women. About two dozen cases with which I was involved where stoning was a possibility, only two involved the conviction of men. One wonders what happened in the trial courts to the men in the cases of *zina*? Especially in societies where a woman cannot become pregnant *suo motu* (on her own motion), in societies where techniques such as artificial insemination or other technologies to help treat fertility are not available, who impregnated her?

Granted, we are defending our clients and that should be our main focus. But, the fact that the trial records of the courts repeatedly indicated that the men were allowed to swear an oath and subsequently discharged and acquitted, while the women were not allowed the opportunity to swear to a similar oath—an inconsistency that belittles the equality provision—cannot be ignored. There also seems to be procedural challenges when prosecuting a man for the crime of *zina*. In some cases, the men are not included as part of the court record, while sometimes the men's statements are recounted orally. When the men are mentioned, court records often indicate a trial with both an accused and a co-accused at the commencement of the trial. However, at the end of the trial the accused (the woman) was often convicted while the co-accused (the man) was either allowed to take an oath, be discharged, or omitted completely from the court records. This happened in the cases of Ahmadu Ibrahim and Fatima Usman.[279] Both were

---

277. Sindjoun, *Coming African Hour*, 364; see also Kohnert, "New Nationalism."
278. Doi, *Women in Shariah*, 134.
279. Ahmadu Ibrahim and Fatima Usman v. The State. The case was tried in Upper Area Court, Gawu, Babangida in Gurara local government of Niger State in 2002, but is not recorded in the official law report, to the best of the author's knowledge. See also Weimann, *Islamic Criminal Law*, 41.

earlier sentenced to stoning and later imprisoned in Suleja, Niger State, the court record was mutilated at some point, and part of Ibrahim's statements disappeared. It also happened in the case of Amina Lawal, where the court records indicated that the prosecuting police officer, Corporal Idris Adamu, had on the First Information Report (FIR), dated January 15, 2002, an accused, Amina Lawal, and a co-accused, Yahaya Mohammed. Upon the co-accused's denial of the alleged offense of *zina*, the court administered him an oath, and thereafter satisfied, accepted his oath and discharged him.[280]

The Qur'an makes it clear, in numerous places, that men and women are equal before their creator. It states *inter alia* (among other things) that, "I never fail to reward any worker among you for any work you do, be you male or female—you are equal to one another" (3:195). Also, "As for those who lead a righteous life, male or female, while believing, they enter Paradise without the slightest injustice" (4:124). Indeed, "Anyone who works righteousness, male or female, while believing, we will surely grant them a happy life in this world, and we will surely pay them their full recompense (on the Day of Judgment) for their righteous works" (16:97). Furthermore, the Qur'an states: "O people, we created you from the same soul, male and female, and rendered you distinct peoples and tribes, that you may recognize one another. The best among you in the sight of GOD is the most righteous. GOD is omniscient, cognizant" (49:13). Although Shariah receives its legitimacy from various sources, the bedrock of Islam remains the Qur'an and lawyers in Shariah courts should not shy away from using it to forward justice and fairness, which, after all, are pervasive themes in Islam.

The Qur'an further demonstrates women's equality to men before their maker when it affirms that Adam and Eve are equally guilty for listening to Satan—the fall of mankind from the Garden of Eden is not blamed on Eve. This is shown more than once in the Qur'an:

---

280. See the certified true copy of the proceeding of the Shariah Court of Appeal of Katsina State Holden at Funtua, (Jan. 15, 2002). Certified court proceeding dated Sept. 10, 2002.

And [mention] when We said to the angels, "Prostrate before Adam"; so they prostrated, except for Iblees. He refused and was arrogant and became of the disbelievers. And We said, "O Adam, dwell, you and your wife, in Paradise and eat there in [ease and] abundance from wherever you will. But do not approach this tree, lest you be among the wrongdoers." But Satan caused *them* to slip out of it and removed *them* from that [condition] in which *they* had been. And we said, "Go down, [all of you], as enemies to one another and you will have upon the earth a place of settlement and provision for a time" (2:34–36). "O Adam, dwell, you and your wife, in Paradise and eat from wherever you will but do not approach this tree, lest you be among the wrongdoers."—But Satan whispered to *them* to make apparent to *them* that which was concealed from *them* of their private parts. He said, "Your Lord did not forbid you this tree except that you become angels or become of the immortal."—And he swore [by Allah] to them, "Indeed, I am to you from among the sincere advisors."—So he made *them* fall, through deception. And when *they* tasted of the tree, their private parts became apparent to them, and they began to fasten together over themselves from the leaves of Paradise. And their Lord called to them, "Did I not forbid you from the tree and tell you that Satan is to you a clear enemy?" (7:19–22). O children of Adam, let not Satan tempt you as he removed your parents from Paradise, stripping them of their clothing to show them their private parts. Indeed, he sees you, he and his tribe, from where you do not see them. Indeed, We have made the devils allies to those who do not believe (7:27).[281]

---

281. Italics mine.

This repeated affirmation of equality in both the Qur'an and Sunnah maintains over and over again that Allah سبحانه و تعالى only favors one person over another based on that person's awareness, consciousness, fear, love, and hope of Allah سبحانه و تعالى. All other criteria are excluded, including gender, ethnicity, class, and so on.

While defending clients, we, as lawyers, sought to answer the question: Do these clients have the right to be treated equally before the Shariah law, in the Shariah court, and by the Shariah judges? The answer was affirmative. In our research, we ventured into an interesting verse in the Holy Qur'an that says:

> O you who have believed! The law of equality is prescribed to you in . . . the free for the free, the slave for the slave, and the female for the female. But whoever overlooks from his brother anything, and then there should be a suitable follow-up and payment to him with good conduct. This is alleviation from your Lord and a mercy. But whoever transgresses after that will have a painful punishment. (2:178)

Both Muslim men and women seem to be given the opportunity, according to this verse, to be treated equally before the law. It is worth positing the meaning this has in Islam as well as the contribution it can make in Shariah courts.

Within the social structure and teachings of Islamic Shariah in Northern Nigeria, the role of the family as the central unit of society is emphasized. In the Islamic faith, the Muslim family is a microcosm of the entire Muslim community (*ummah*) and is its firm foundation. In it, the man, or father, functions as the *Imam*, or leader, in accordance with the "patriarchal nature of the religion." The religious responsibility of the family rests upon his shoulders. In the family, the father upholds the tenets of the faith and his authority is final. He is respected in the family precisely because of the "sacerdotal function" that he fulfills. Qur'an 4:34 is rooted in this opinion:

Men are in charge of women by [right of] what Allah has given one over the other and what they spend [for maintenance] from their wealth. So righteous women are devoutly obedient, guarding in [the husband's] absence what Allah would have them guard. But those [wives] from whom you fear arrogance—[first] advise them; [then if they persist], forsake them in bed; and [finally], strike them. But if they obey you [once more], seek no means against them. Indeed, Allah is ever exalted and Grand.

Although this verse has been interpreted and reinterpreted—sometimes for the right reasons and sometimes not—it is beyond the scope of this book to discuss its detail. Suffice to say however, that women are not the same as or like men, neither are women inferior to men; as the Qur'an proclaims: "We have created you out of the same substance."[282] Islam envisions the roles of men and women in society not as competing, but as complementary. Each has certain duties and functions in accordance with his or her nature to further the cohesion of the family and thereby the society.

Some who have questioned the assumption of equality before the law have gone so far as to suggest that "the lady of justice should, perhaps, from time to time, peep through her blind-fold in order to acknowledge the inequality of litigants and tilt the scales of justice a little bit in order to compensate for the material inequality of the under-privileged."[283]

---

282. Qur'an 22:5: "O People, if you should be in doubt about the Resurrection, then [consider that] indeed, We created you from dust, then from a sperm-drop, then from a clinging clot, and then from a lump of flesh, formed and unformed—that We may show you. And We settle in the wombs whom We will for a specified term, then We bring you out as a child, and then [We develop you] that you may reach your [time of] maturity. And among you is he who is taken in [early] death, and among you is he who is returned to the most decrepit [old] age so that he knows, after [once having] knowledge, nothing. And you see the earth barren, but when We send down upon it rain, it quivers and swells and grows [something] of every beautiful kind."

283. Akin Oyebode, personal email communication with the author, April 21, 2011. In Nigeria, Oyebode was the dean of law at Ondo State University and later the vice chancellor of Ado-Ekiti University.

While equality between man and woman and husband and wife remain questionable in practice, economic inequality is clearly evident in the public square and is a chief deterrent to social justice. The truth is that the burden of poverty constitutes a tremendous disadvantage whenever members of the subordinate class have to confront the legal system. It might as well be said that in Nigeria, "equality before the law operates with a discount."[284]

The fruits of equality under the law cannot be achieved where the people are impecunious, illiterate, powerless, and voiceless. Dame Barbara Ward cautioned that if the rich refuse to listen to the cries of the poor, then the cries of the poor would deprive them of their sleep at night.[285] There is no legal, constitutional, or ethical justification for discrimination. All litigants should face the law on equal terms irrespective of gender, race, class, or any other characteristic. When the term "gender" is used only to refer to women, it is germane to note that it might provoke male resistance or backlash as it obstructs male participation. Gender should remain all-inclusive.

The 1999 Nigerian Constitution provides for the equal treatment of all Nigerians, regardless of their ethnic origin. Section 42 goes on to state:

> A citizen of Nigeria of a particular community, ethnic group, place of origin, sex, religion or political opinion shall not, by reason only that he is such a person, be subjected either expressly by, or in the practical application of, any law in force in Nigeria or any executive or administrative action of the government, to disabilities or restrictions, to which citizens of Nigeria of other communities, ethnic groups, places of origin, sex, religions or political opinions are not made subject.

---

284. Ibid.
285. Lean, *Tribute to Barbara Ward*, 62. Ward was a British journalist, economist, conservationist, and later, an advocate for developing countries.

Furthermore, Section 42 states that, "No citizen of Nigeria shall be subjected to any disability or deprivation merely by reason of the circumstances of his birth." Nigeria is signatory to several international human rights treaties that make it incumbent upon Nigeria to treat each of its citizens equally.[286] One such treaty is the International Covenant on Civil and Political Rights (ICCPR). Article 26 of the ICCPR states that "all persons are equal before the law and are entitled, without any discrimination, to equal protection of the law," and further stipulates that "the law shall prohibit discrimination and guarantee equal and effective protection against discrimination on any ground such as national or social origin." These rights and freedoms are also guaranteed to citizens without distinction.[287]

The right to freedom from discrimination is also recognized in the African Charter on Human and Peoples' Rights (Ratification and Enforcement) Act (ACPRA), which has become part of Nigeria's national laws.[288] Article 2 of the African Charter states: "Every individual shall be entitled to the enjoyment of the rights and freedoms recognized and guaranteed in the present charter without distinction of any kind such as race, ethnic group, color, sex, language, religion, political or any other opinion, national and social origin, fortune, birth or other status." Article 3 further promises individual equality before the law and Article 26 proscribes "every individual shall have the duty to respect and consider his fellow beings without discrimination, and to maintain relations aimed at promoting, safeguarding and reinforcing mutual respect and tolerance." Likewise, as the

---

286. Nelson, *Nigeria*.

287. In addition, Islam offers views on basic freedom. Abdul Hamid Siddiqui claims that Man's physical being is hemmed in by time and space, but not his ego . . . He is made the trustee of free personality for which he has been charged with moral responsibilities in regards to all his thoughts and deeds. Morality, essential in Islam, presupposes freedom, ability to choose, select, accept, or repudiate. And where there is no freedom, there can be no morality, for moral conduct applies just to action in respect to which man enjoys the freedom of choice (Siddiqui, "Concept of Justice," 31).

288. African Charter on Human and Peoples' Rights, (Ratification and Enforcement) Act, Chapter A9, (Chapter 10 LFN 1990), (No. 2 of 1983) in Laws of the Federation of Nigeria, 1990.

African Commission on Human and Peoples' Rights said in its twenty-first activities report:

> Together with equality before the law and equal protection under the law, the principle of non-discrimination provided under Article 2 of the Charter provides the foundation for the enjoyment of all human rights. . . . The aim of this principle is to ensure equality of treatment for individuals irrespective of nationality, sex, racial or ethnic origin, political opinion, religion or belief, disability, age or sexual orientation.[289]

These laws, rights, and principles are especially relevant in Northern Nigeria, which has long been an area where treating women differently on the basis of gender and beliefs is a challenge.

Discrimination against women is defined in Article 1 of the United Nations Convention on the Elimination of all forms of Discrimination Against Women (CEDAW) as follows:

> Any distinction, exclusion or restriction made on the basis of sex which has the effect or purpose of impairing or nullifying the recognition, enjoyment or exercise by women, irrespective of their marital status, on a basis of equality of men and women, of human rights and fundamental freedoms in the political, economic, social, cultural, civil or any other field.

Unequal treatment, especially against women, differs in form depending on the societal and historical epoch, thus requiring it to be addressed through different strategies in each unique place and time. The content of domestic, regional, and international legislation concerning equality should guarantee,

---

289. African Charter on Human and People's Rights, Article 2. See also *Evans and Murray, African Charter on Human and Peoples' Rights.*

de jure, protection reflecting women's *de facto* condition in society. Though there are regional, cultural-religious, traditional, and ethnic variations in the pattern of discrimination against women, deliberate efforts need to be made to reshape customary practices, thinking, language, ethics, and morals. Legal and substantive efforts to enhance both status and situation of women must be coordinated at the grassroots of regional, state, national, and international levels. The promotion, protection, and defense of these rights will remain only in theory if conscious actions are not put in place to actualize them, one of which could be advocacy in court rooms.

Concerning the Separation of Powers *(Trias Politica)*

Separation of powers has been described as a "model for the governance of democratic states."[290] The ancient Greeks first developed this model and the Roman Empire later adopted it as part of an un-codified constitution.[291] This classical model provided the paradigm for the division of government into three branches that were to be separate and independent, yet equal. The term *trias politica,* or "separation of powers," is said to have been coined by Charles-Louis de Secondat, baron de La Brède et de Montesquieu, the eighteenth-century French socialist and political philosopher.[292] Under Montesquieu's model, the political authority of the state was to be divided into three powers: the legislative, the executive, and the judicial. He asserted that in order to most effectively promote liberty, these three powers would have to be separate and act independently.

Similarly, Thomas Jefferson stated that checks and balances are our only security for the progress of mind, as well as the security of body; assurances that people are the ultimate rulers, so that those who make the law should not also judge or punish violation of it. It is incumbent to ensure the independence of each institution in performing its function.[293] These

---

290. Pound, *Separation of Powers*, 323.
291. Hutchison, *Foundations of the Constitution.*
292. Labuschagne and Sonnenschmidt, *Religion, Politics and Law*, 92; see also Montesquieu, *Spirit of Laws*; and Northrup and Turney, *Encyclopedia of Tariffs and Trade*, 263.
293. Witte, *God's Joust, God's Justice*, 178.

are guiding principles that to this day have informed democratic societies. While other models for the separation of powers and governance are indeed recognized, governments internationally widely accept this model. A contemporary of Jefferson, Thomas Paine, further opined that, "For as in absolute governments the King is law, so in free countries the law ought to be King; and there ought to be no other."[294]

Essentially, the separation of powers is the idea that a government functions best when its powers are not concentrated in a single authority, but are instead divided among different branches.[295] In the aforementioned model, the three branches of government each exercise unique powers: the legislative branch has the power to make the law, the executive branch wields the power to enforce the law, and the judicial branch holds the power to interpret the law. When the system works, the branches are separate but unified in working for the common good, with each branch serving as a check and balance on the powers of the others.

The judiciary is free from political interference on the part of the legislature and the executive branch likewise has specific powers protected in a constitution. The executive and legislative branches each have powers that check and balance the judiciary. For example, the courts must rely upon the executive branch for the enforcement of their decisions. Checks and balances on specific powers include, for example, the Supreme Court's ability to review the constitutionality of a law if it is challenged in a case brought before it, the judiciary's power to declare executive actions unconstitutional if they are challenged in court, or the President's ability to veto proposed legislation. Separation of powers is a hallmark of most democratic governments, but the balance of powers among branches can differ widely depending on the political system.[296]

---

294. Carper et al., *Understanding the Law*, 52.
295. Flynn, *Separation of Power*, 78; see also Judge Carolyn B. McHugh, "Separation of Powers," 1.
296. Montesquieu, *Personal and the Political*.

In some African societies, this concept of separation of powers is referred to as "three cooking-pot supporting stones" that make every meal possible. Once they are well organized to function in the interest of the people as a whole, the common good of the nation is served and the country can be nourished to develop in stability and joy.[297]

In some instances, however, the independence of these three powers from each other may be blurred by the attempt to promote the same democratic ideals they seek to promote and protect. In the Shariah court cases with which I was involved, at times our team encountered challenges in which one branch was unjustifiably attempting to extend its reach into the rightful domain of another branch. For example, in the case of Bariya Ibrahim Magazu, the appeal filing by counsels was truncated by the administrative structure, under the guise that the court needed to verify information from higher authorities.[298] Such attempts accomplish very little in terms of achieving the ultimate goal—to bring about justice that is readily identifiable and satisfying for all.

The suggestion that power should not reside in one person is not new or exclusive to the West, as is generally assumed; it has long been established in non-Western societies, even at the grassroots level; so also in Muslim societies. Islam encompasses every facet of a Muslim's life, and because Islam has a number of tenets that seem in line with the general principles of democracy, many conclude that Islam is compatible with democracy.[299] "Islam contemplates an embodiment of nations and tribes as a facet of a Muslim's life; therefore, one may conclude that Islam requires Muslims to organize their nations and tribes by Islamic principles."[300] Conversely, it would be considered incongruous for Muslims to set aside their religious principles when carrying out the conduct of the state as neither the prophet

---

297. Waliggo, *Struggle for Equality*; see also Werner, *Natives of British Central Africa*, 101.
298. The State v. Bariya Ibrahim Magazu, unreported, 2000. The case was tried in 2001 in Tsafe, a small village in Zamfara State, but is not recorded in the official law report, to the best of the author's knowledge.
299. Hudson and Azra, *Islam Beyond Conflict*, 2.
300. Asad, *Islam and Politics*, 38.

Muhammad (ﷺ) nor any of his companions did so when entrusted with government positions.

The concept of political power in Islam suggests that appointments to positions of responsibility should not be given to those who aspire to them, much less to those who openly hanker after them. Shehu Uthman Dan Fodio who was an Islamic reformer, teacher, writer, and the most influential Islamic scholar in the history of Islam in West Africa, as well as the founder of the Sokoto Caliphate of Nigeria in 1809, had this to say, "first that the emirate (head of governance) be not given to one who aspires to it, because the Hadith of Saḥīḥ al-Bukhari said, 'We do not give charge of this affair of ours to one who seeks after it.' The reason is perhaps very obvious; people who aspire to posts either fail to appreciate the weight of responsibility it entails or have some sinister motives other than discharging the obligations of the trust."[301]

Sultan Muhammad Bello (the second Sultan of the Sokoto Caliphate who, as is custom, took over the throne after his father, Shehu Uthman Dan Fodio) further made it clear that political leaders should do well to:

> Know also that most of the evil that befalls the state comes from the appointment of officers who are anxious to have the appointment because none would be keen on such but a thief in the garb of a hermit and a fox in the guise of a pious worshipper, someone who is keen in the collection of money, sacrificing for such his religion and integrity; all his endeavors are for the fruits of this world, not portraying zeal and honesty, and that is the very sign of treachery. Such a person would enslave the slaves of Allah سبحانه و تعالى and use their wealth for his own ends; once the rights of the Muslims are usurped and their wealth unjustly taken, their souls are corrupted, their obedience diminishes, and the

---

301. Bugaje, "Islamic Political System," 3. For more information on Dan Fodio, see H. A. Ibrahim, *Sayyid Abd al-Raman al-Mahdī*.

affair of the state become shaky and corruption pervades the state.[302]

Dr. Bugaje, an eminent Islamic scholar and writer on the political power struggles in Nigeria, has suggested that it is difficult, if not contradictory, to advise someone who claims to have a monopoly on wisdom while holding political power. Even more difficult is advising a man who takes his instructions directly from God while in a democratic setting where power rests with ordinary mortals. This is an assault on the intelligence and integrity of the people on behalf of whom power is held in trust. The peoples' confidence and trust is destroyed, undermining the freedom of expression, of association, of choice, and the freedom to pursue legitimate economic activities. Dr. Bugaje writes that these freedoms are what guarantee justice and equity. Justice and equity, in turn, bring about stability and progress of human society.[303]

The issue of separation of powers becomes the point of understanding or departure in some Muslim countries where rulers are, sort of, divinely appointed. They represent a break in the democratic process because they are commanded religiously, a position which is not necessarily open to full democratic governance. Events in North Africa and the Middle East since December 2010 are bringing about revolutionary fervor that has spread across countries from Tunisia to Egypt to Libya. Meanwhile, according to Jim Finnegan, "the average time in power for leaders in the 33 countries in this region of the world is nearly 19 years, the leader's average age is nearly 67, and the gap between their age and the median age of their countrymen is slightly over 42 years, or nearly two generations."[304] This certainly becomes a dilemma when making demarcations and assertions in the realm of Islam and/or holding an office in a political capacity, and the extent to which it becomes democratic or autocratic, better still, divine. In any event, checks

---

302. Bugaje, "Islamic Political System," 7; see also A. Ali, *Islamic Perspectives on Management*, 137.
303. Bugaje, "Islamic Political System."
304. Finnegan, "Turmoil in the Middle East."

and balances should be valued principles in societies that aspire toward the core values of humanity, freedom, and justice.

The judge, having been given independence with the judiciaries, can, however, have his decision and interpretation reviewed and/or evaluated on appeal; in essence, it is legitimate to determine if they conform to the principles of Islam.[305] This review is analogous to the powers a Supreme Court holds to review the constitutionality of laws promulgated by a sovereign or parliament. Second, the judge or person in a related position is enjoined to seek opinions or *shura* (consultative decision making) as suggested by Qur'an 3:159:

> So by mercy from Allah, [O Muhammad (ﷺ)], you were lenient with them. And if you had been rude [in speech] and harsh in heart, they would have disbanded from about you. So pardon them and ask forgiveness for them and consult them in the matter. And when you have decided, then rely upon Allah سبحانه و تعالى. Indeed, Allah loves those who rely [upon Him].

This verse is a highly regarded principle in Islam. Contrary to the organization of most democracies, a Muslim state may not need to make a distinction between the religious and secular components of life. In its proper context, "Islam shows a religious law which is more voluntary than enforced, more passive than aggressive and more considerate of social and financial conditions than applying broad, general, and inflexible rules across different classes of people."[306]

---

305. Sulami, *West and Islam*, 141.
306. Farooqi, "Islamic State in the 21 Century"; see also Esposito and Voll, *Islam and Democracy*, 270.

Flexibility When Trying Cases

The idea of flexibility within contextual parameters leads to the question: In a constitutional democracy that has a separation of powers and a supremacy clause, how can one be flexible with regard to various cultural and/or traditional dynamics when a society derives a person's worth from contemporary values about excellence, and still communicates traditional ways of life from generation to generation? Sometimes cultures create changes. Culture can encourage creative thinking and challenge the way we've always done things to generate innovative ideas and solutions to problems. At other times, culture can deal constructively with failure and mistakes by creating tools and techniques with potential for social change. From this creativity emerge practices that can take society to the next level.

In the evolving practice of Shariah courts, much of what we do takes place outside the courtroom and within the culture and traditions of society. We try to create awareness and enhance communication strategies in each local entity, starting with engaging the religious clerics and heads, *Sarki* or villages (chiefs). When these authority figures understand our mission and provide leadership, everyone benefits. Furthermore, religious and village leaders are not the only ones who should be conferred with and their wisdom utilized.

As lawyers, it is imperative that we strive to work—when not in conflict with our professional etiquettes—with nonlocal organizational stakeholders such as community-based organizations (CBOs), nongovernmental organizations (NGOs), civil society, and other partners that may be powerful catalysts for boosting flexibility. When we endeavor to use technology in new ways to facilitate communication and to develop our legal practice in areas such as sharing useful resources, interaction, and research, we will be served well. We will also find it very useful to explore new opportunities and move toward accomplishing goals while developing new approaches based on core values, culture, and traditions. Be bold and confident, but do so respectfully. Establish networks and collaborate with various legal organizations such as Lawyers Without Borders (LWB) and international bar associations across the region and in Islamic-related jurisdictions. The journey may be complex and challenging, given the variation in codes and cultures, but it will be more successful if you maintain your firmness while being flexible.

In an effort to serve your client well, it is best to be flexible with how you obtain information. Much can be accomplished by creating an environment where you begin to understand the culture and, sometimes, become a part of it. When you are in villages gathering information to prepare a case for court, the villagers feel good and are developing a sense of trust when they follow custom by offering you water to drink and food to eat, and you accept it. Our experience has indicated that one of the biggest barriers to implementing flexibility successfully is the failure to maintain a connection to the culture. For instance, it is customary to remove footwear before entering the home of a Muslim, so as not to track in dirt or possibly soil the sacred space where they pray. If it will not be harmful for you to observe some basic societal norms such as this, then do it.

Furthermore, interaction within societies indicates social differences; the hierarchical ranking among peoples is clearly displayed. In some cultures in Northern Nigeria, a young person will not stand in the presence of an elder; he or she should not look the elder in the eye and will not speak to an elder in the first person. A young person needs to bow or prostrate before an elder. While this may be a stretch for a lawyer, I would be remiss not to note, consequently, that flexibility may require an acclimation of attitude about traditional ways of thinking, and true flexibility requires this shift in disposition. Be aware that the locals are able to read facial expressions well. Always present a "good face" and be polite when venturing to accommodate local courts.

Where a seemingly logical point of argument is met with opposition, posit understanding for what is relevant to your case. Refrain from over-analyzing the situation. Some people are truly simple and what they say is what they mean. Place emphasis on the specific descriptions of incidents and statements of facts, found not through words but through experience. Be flexible; don't wait to start the journey, but take it now!

Flexibility entails tolerance of others' ways of life and perspectives. It further entails being humble, acknowledging that we know only as much as we know, and recognizing the beauty of our humanity in the differences of various people. We need to show kindness while cultivating compassion and knowledge of a new environment and its people. One can build trustworthiness by using an adaptable sense of personal steadiness, sincerity, perseverance, and patience. One can also cultivate the trust of local communities by showing interest, respecting their traditions, observing their rites and social rituals—and trying not to be dismissive. This can be as simple as performing traditional greetings, removing one's shoes before entering a place of worship, announcing one's presence before entering a private home, reciprocating greetings offered to you, showing solidarity with others, and practicing moderation without the sense of cultural superiority.

True to its teachings, Islamic law is an advocate of a just, equitable judicial process.[307] It is a concept that is rooted in the Qur'an itself; the ultimate source of guidance for Muslims. The Qur'an places tremendous emphasis upon judging between people in a just and equitable manner. For instance:

> O ye who believe! Stand out firmly for justice, as witnesses to God, even as against yourselves, or your parents, or your kin, and whether it is [against] rich or poor: for God can best protect both. Follow not the lusts [of your hearts], lest ye swerve, and if ye distort [justice] or decline to do justice, verily God is well acquainted with all that ye do. (4:135)[308]

---

307. Muzaffar, *Human Rights*, 38.
308. See also Ambali, *Practice of Family Law*, 107.

In Islamic jurisprudence, "political power must be exercised within the framework of the Shariah."[309] This could mean being able to submit control and power to laws and the principles of the law, such as the principles of equal treatment under the law and respect to human dignity. Understanding that the criteria for evaluating equality of human beings either as equality of sexes or equality of status is beyond the scope of this book.

While the "new Shariah" system of law attempts to control the vices of society through the application of severe and difficult punishments, it has not been found, most times, to be effective in fighting crime. The transparency and simplicity that Shariah law offers could enable a quick trial and swift justice as opposed to a long legal process that could last many years. However, one must be cautious regarding the approach taken when combining the Shariah legal system with other legal systems (such as the common law), as the two must maintain a delicate balance in order to be effective. Aside from legal concerns, it is worth noting that within societies where the roles of Imams and judges have long been distinct, some Imams might feel their honored positions threatened in the event they may be forced to share them with judges.[310] A lawyer will do well to always be aware of the dynamics of any situation so that he or she can effectively work within them to achieve the maximum effect.

In appreciating the essence of new law and its contents, we need to understand that some words in the Shariah Penal Code Law are not terms that are used in everyday vocabulary. Both judges and lawyers will at times debate their meaning in Hausa, translating it into other local languages and at times into Arabic. This amount of uncertainty can, in the worst scenarios, result in a miscarriage of justice. In some states, such as, Katsina, Niger, and Bauchi, there are still vacuums of procedural law that can result in frustration

---

309. Hallaq, *Introduction to Islamic Law*, 26.
310. Imam (Liman) in the context of Northern Nigeria are Muslim spiritual leaders, heads of mosques.

when attempting to discover which procedural law to adopt.[311] Be ready to be adaptable and flexible to succeed in the Shariah courts.

Flexibility allows lawyers to adapt to a variety of situations and to maintain a balance between differing viewpoints in order to achieve the highest probability of success. While balancing various interests can be challenging at points, it is a crucial element of success. Law is based on competing interests; this is why cases are brought to court. The lawyers who can recognize these competing interests and balance them throughout his or her argument, exercising flexibility where possible and firmness when necessary, will be closer in his or her pursuit of achieving justice for clients.

---

311. In the case of Audu Magaji v. COP, (2007) NNLR, 336, where the Court of Appeal held *inter alia*, that "There was no law of criminal or civil procedure promulgated for the Shariah courts of Katsina State."

CHAPTER FIVE

Play to Your Strength—The Law

THE STRENGTH OF A LAWYER'S ARGUMENTS in Shariah courts should come from multiple legal sources. These include Shariah laws, such as the Qur'an, Hadith, and additional sources of Islamic law; the Nigerian Constitution and other national laws; and relevant international human rights instruments, such as the Universal Islamic Declaration of Human Rights (UIDHR). When a lawyer is able to master and apply many laws, echoes of success will spread from individual clients to the larger society. The lawyer who is willing to confront new challenges and demands as they arise, while being diligent and faithful to the law and the legal profession, will help deliver a valuable edge. Although mastery of the many laws in their entirety is virtually impossible, knowledge of the principles of law will provide a firm and likewise abiding foundation for securing justice.

Legal principles are commonly defined as, "regulations established in a community by authority and applicable to its people, whether in the form of legislation or of custom and policies recognized as a consequence of being enforced by judicial decision."[312] Although at times it is claimed that

---

312. Wallace and Roberson, *Principles of Criminal Law*, 75; see also Soukhanov, *Webster's II*

these systems or rules are divinely appointed or are codes based on morality, conscience, and/or nature, these various legal systems—each one intricate and unique—have all been recorded by man.

The essence of Islam and of Islamic law is respect for the dignity of humanity and the need for compassionate justice. Punishment is not the objective of the criminal law, nor is it the spirit of Islamic practice.[313] Indeed, Islam is primarily concerned with keeping Allah's trust, as expressed in its five pillars: testifying that there is no God except Allah سبحانه و تعالى and that Muhammad (صلى الله عليه وسلم) is His Messenger, keeping up the prayers, giving the zakat, fasting during the month of Ramadan, and making the pilgrimage to Mecca. Many Hadith teach us not to be judgmental, and call for punishments only when absolutely necessary. For example, "Drive off the ordained sentences [Hudud] from a Muslim as far as you can. If there is any place of refuge for him, let him have his way, because the leader's mistake in pardon is better than his mistake in punishment."[314] And, "None of you believes until he loves for his brother what he loves for himself."[315] Furthermore, according to a tradition reported by A'isha,[316] the Messenger of Allah سبحانه و تعالى said:

> Whosoever removes an affliction from a believer, Allah سبحانه و تعالى will remove from him one of the afflictions of the Day of Resurrection; whosoever brings ease to a person under hardship, Allah سبحانه و تعالى will bring ease to him in this world and Hereafter. Whosoever shields a Muslim, Allah سبحانه و تعالى will shield him in this world and

---

New Riverside University Dictionary, 680.

313. Justice A. Ali Hyder of the Pakistani Court, quoting Maulana Maudoodi, said, "the spirit of Islam is toward understanding human nature" (Jahangir and Jilani, Hudood Ordinances, 27).

314. Chaudhry, Human Rights in Islam, 32.

315. Ibid., 34.

316. A'isha, the wife of the prophet Muhammad, was described by one of her pupils, 'Urwa ibn al-Zubair, as a great school in learning of the Qur'an, obligatory duties, lawful and unlawful matters, poetry, literature, Arab history, and genealogy. See Yamani, Feminism and Islam.

the Hereafter. Allah سبحانه و تعالى will help a bondman [of
his] so long as the bondman helps his brother. Whosoever
follows a road to seek knowledge therein, Allah سبحانه و تعالى
will make easy for him a road to the garden. No people
gather in one of the houses of Allah سبحانه و تعالى, reciting
the Book of Allah سبحانه و تعالى and studying it among
themselves, without tranquility descending upon them,
mercy enveloping them, the Angels surrounding them
and Allah سبحانه و تعالى making mention of them among
those who are with Him. Whosoever is slowed down by
his deeds, will not be hastened by his lineage.[317]

Lawyers will find it helpful to keep this in the forefront of their minds.
Recognizing that justice is the essence of Islamic law will help to structure
and sustain legal arguments, while navigating through the complexities of
the system.

Islamic Law

Islamic law is very broad and encompassing. In some circumstances,
it may lead to conflict between social, moral, and political understandings.
Interpretation, translation, and passion have resulted at times in a dogmatic
appropriation of the language and intent of the Shariah law, bringing about
uncertainties and complications. Within the Muslim community as well
as between Muslims and non-Muslims, an ocean of voices argues about
what constitutes legitimacy and order in a just society. Shariah law and its
jurisprudence are not always clearly understood by societies that wish to
apply the law. At times, this causes disputes and the misappropriation of
justice.

Because Islam is "submission or surrender to Allah's will," hence it
concedes no separation of religion from other institutions such as legislative,
executive, and judicial. Additionally, Shariah is suppose to be applied to all

---

317. Ghali, *Selection of Hadiths*, 44.

Muslims; herein, questions abound as to the partiality before the law in a society that is not 100 percent Muslim. Can one religion have a set of rules that govern it within a larger society with multiple beliefs? And can one belief be favored above another, especially when dealing with crime? Debates are ongoing between scholars and intellectuals. Attempts are also being made to answer the questions. It would seem prudent that the Supreme Court may at some point proffer some direction toward answering these questions arising from what seem to be conflicting legislations, between the states and federal laws.[318]

Although we should nurture with our actions the unseen reality of our divine humanity, we can do better by working to strengthen the ties that connect us as human beings. Where religious legal systems exist with written laws and punishments, lawyers in a pluralistic society need to work diligently to find their own niche within the particular legal system in order to ensure that justice is achieved for all. Appreciating that, unlike laws that are developed to meet changing needs of society, Shariah law, for instance, is suggested also to be, "Allah's law, present outside space and time."[319] Therefore, the offenses and proof thereof require strict evidence to establish the certainty of guilt. Its guiding principles as expressed in the Shariah, include protection against attacks, insults, humiliation, making unwarranted accusations, and the protections of rights to privacy.

There are several Hadith that describe the commitment to and unwavering trust in justice and its administration by the prophet Muhammad (ﷺ). Abu Sayeed reported that the Messenger of Allah سبحانه و تعالى said:

> Verily the dearest of men near Allah سبحانه و تعالى on the resurrection day and the nearest of them before Him for company will be a just ruler, and verily the most disagreeable of the people near Allah سبحانه و تعالى on the resurrection

---

318. In Nigeria the Supreme Court interprets the Constitution.
319. Lippman et al., *Islamic Criminal Law and Procedure*, 2.

day and the most distant of them in company of Him will
be a tyrannical ruler. (Tirmizi)[320]

A'isha also reported from the Messenger of Allah سبحانه و تعالی who
said:

> Do you know who will be the foremost unto the shade
> of the Almighty and glorious Allah سبحانه و تعالی on the
> resurrection day? They replied: Allah سبحانه و تعالی and His
> Apostle knows best. He said. . . . Who dispense justice for
> the people like they are doing justice to themselves.[321]

And Abdullah bin Amr and Abu Hurairah reported that the Messenger
of Allah سبحانه و تعالی said:

> When a judge wishes to pass a decree, and then strives
> hard and decides justly, there are two rewards for him; but
> when he wishes to pass a decree, and then strives hard but
> commits a mistake, there is but one reward for him.[322]

Appropriately, the concept of justice in Islam is more comprehensive, vital,
and sacred—more than in any other system of life.[323] Justice is a trust, a sacred
responsibility that is to be performed in conformity with the provisions of
the Qur'an and the Sunnah.[324] And the administration of Islamic justice
constitutes one of the most important acts of devotion.[325]

---

320. Unknown Author, *Hadith of Bukhari*, 662.
321. Chaudhry, *Human Rights in Islam*, 43.
322. This Hadith conveys the importance of clarity of decision and lack of haste when a
judge is making a ruling. When a judge spends adequate time on his decision and decides
justly, his reward will be greater.
323. Singh, *Social Justice and Human Rights*, 138.
324. Ashrof, *Islam and Gender Justice*, 292.
325. Shah-Kazemi, *Justice and Remembrance*, 49.

Nigerian Legal System

The heterogeneity of cultures can be seen as much in their legal systems as in their populations. This diversity can easily be traced to the composition of a country's ethnic groups, tribes, cultures, religious sects, languages, dialects, and history. In addition to the provision of beautiful panoply, all these variations exacerbate the issue of the application of multiple legal systems and the quest for harmonization in adopting law. Nowhere is this more self-evident than in Nigeria.[326]

The Nigerian legal system is fairly complex, and has several sub systems. "At the Federal level, the legal system is applicable throughout the country. At the lower levels, each state (including Abuja) has its own legal system. At the local level, both Shariah and customary laws are applicable in some states."[327] The system is based on the English common law tradition, a byproduct of colonization. The recognition and adoption of English law was achieved by transferring British laws to its colonies' systems of laws, sometimes for the better, sometimes not.

Nigerian author and former judge Akintunde Olusegun Obilade notes that "English law has had a tremendous influence on the Nigerian legal system and forms a substantial part of Nigerian law"[328] At present, Nigerian law consists of many sources: the Constitution, legislation, English law, Islamic (Shariah) laws, customary law, and judicial precedents.[329] The 1999 Nigerian Constitution, which has been revised several times, regulates the legislative arm of government, the National Assembly. The assembly has been vested with the power to make laws for the peace, order, and good governance of the federation.

---

326. This may not be new in Nigerian society, as suggested by Aharon Layish, but in Libya the intensive interaction and mutual fertilization of systems culminated into integration of Islamic and customary laws. However, in its practical application, customary laws in tribal areas enjoy autonomy. See Layish, *Shariah and Customs*, 2.

327. Elias, *Nigerian Legal System*, 19.

328. Obilade, *Nigerian Legal System*, 54.

329. Tobi, *Sources of Nigerian Law*, 66.

The Nigerian system of law has adopted a considerable number of laws from diverse external sources. It requires that all criminal laws must be written.[330] For example, Northern Nigeria incorporated a great deal of Islamic law (civil provisions) into its codes in the aftermath of the nineteen-century Fulani Jihad.[331] Today, Shariah laws have, to a large degree, supplanted the indigenous customary and traditional laws in many communities, following their acceptance of Islam. Nevertheless, Shariah law in some communities still reflects much of the indigenous African character, as evidenced by the strong role the rules of customary law still play in society. While the Nigerian laws today are mostly codified, there are (also) unwritten laws that emanate from custom that still hold great sway.

Laws promulgated during the occupation of a country may come to be regarded as established legislation. However, failure to review such laws to determine if they are in conformity with societal norms, especially in the field of criminal law, can occasion the existence of what may be described as impracticable laws or legal provisions that are disregarded more often than they are observed. Even apart from the influence of foreign laws, countries' legal systems are generally very complex due to legal pluralism.[332]

Prior to Dan Fodio's Jihad and British rule, the part of Nigeria now known as the Northern region was organized around kingdoms based in large walled cities, mostly pagan and animist, and engaging in the worship of ancestral spirits and Bori cults.[333] Accompanying the Jihad of Dan Fodio, which took place at the turn of the nineteenth century, an Islamic system of justice was put in place, administering both the civil and criminal aspects of Islamic law.[334] It was applied mainly to Muslims, and to all aspects of their lives. Nonetheless, Shariah laws have a distinct status, a separate foundation of sovereignty and their own attributes in terms of origin, nature, and scope

---

330. Constitution of the Federal Republic of Nigeria, 1999, Section 36(12).
331. Wallace, *Africa Today*; see also M. Smith, *Government in Zazzau*, 84.
332. Legal pluralism is the existence of more than one legal system within a society.
333. Yadudu, "Islamic Law and Reform Discourse," 17.
334. Ibid., 32.

of application.[335] During Dan Fodio's rule, the Islamic system of law usually worked with thoroughness and precision, especially in those areas where preexisting systems of customary law were in place. In some areas, it even became incorporated with customary law and the two systems fused and were jointly administered in Shariah courts.[336]

Shariah Penal Codes

The Shariah Penal Code Law (SPCL), introduced in twelve of the thirty-six states of Northern Nigeria between 2000 and 2003, along with subsequent amendments, varies in scope and operation according to the state. The SPCL is to some extent the extension of the pre-1999 Penal Code Law of Northern Nigeria, with the addition of religious-based criminal offenses.

The details of the legal provisions in the SPCL are extensive and cannot be covered in depth here. Nevertheless, a quick survey of some of the more common provisions that one may encounter in the various states' codifications of the SPCL could prove helpful to lawyers as they seek to navigate these issues more creatively. These areas of law include, but are not limited to, offenses, punishments, constitutionality, jurisdiction, and legislative powers.

Offenses and Punishments

Islamic law divides criminal acts into *hudud* (crimes against God as provided for in the Qur'an and Sunnah), *qiyas* or *qiyas*-related crime (including but not limited to assault and murder), and *Ta'azir* (discretionary punishments not fixed in the Qur'an). This classification is basically organized according to the punishment delivered for the offense. Offenses in Islamic law include murder, assault, theft, highway robbery, embezzlement, rebellion,

---

335. The concept of sovereignty is sometimes confused. Muslim intellectuals and religious leaders interpret state power as comparable to divine authority and others reject Muslim kings as the true representatives of God. See M. A. Khan, *Human Rights*.
336. Vikør, *Between God and the Sultan*, 247; see also Bonner, *Jihad in Islamic History*.

perjury, adultery, fornication, sodomy, apostasy, public drunkenness, drug offenses, and defamation.

For example, according to the SPCL, cases concerning manslaughter and bodily injury can be privately prosecuted (i.e., the accused can be sentenced and punished if the victim or victim's relatives demand the punishment [*qiyas*]).[337] Likewise, other crimes are punishable at the discretion of the judge (*Ta'azir, siyâsa*).[338] Even where the SPCL has not clearly defined certain offenses, judges may, at their discretion, punish individuals whom they deem guilty of a sinful or undesirable act. Section 92 of the Zamfara State Shariah Penal Code Law (ZSSPCL) provides *inter alia*,

> Any act or omission which is not specifically mentioned in this Sharia penal code but is otherwise declared to be an offence under the Qur'an, Sunnah and Ijtihad of the Maliki School of Islamic thought, shall be an offence under this code and such act or omission shall be punishable . . . [339]

Although this is permitted under the SPCL, the provision may not be desirable as it could allow passions to cloud judges' judgment. It is important to note that in certain Shariah courts, a trial is to be presided over by one judge and two other members; not by a judge alone. There is a strong moral tradition to this requirement. As the Holy Prophet said in a conversation with the fourth Caliph Ali:

> I said to the Prophet of Allah سبحانه و تعالى, peace be upon him, if a situation arises after you, about whom there is no specific guidance in the Qur'an or in your own tradition, what should we do in such a situation? He said "gather

---

337. Kano State Shariah Penal Code Law, Section 143(c) and Zamfara Shariah Penal Code Law, Section 200(c). See also Peters, *Reintroduction of Islamic Criminal Law*, 60; also cited at Harvard Law Library as NIGE, 980, PET48, 2001.
338. Zamfara State Shariah Penal Code Law, 2000, Section 92.
339. Ibid.

the righteous learned persons in my Ummah, consult them and do not decide the matter on the opinion of one person."[340]

Also of concern are the discrepancies in punishment for similar offenses under the states' penal codes. In the twelve Northern Nigeria states that have codified Shariah, different definitions and punishments can be found for a single offense, such as theft, under the varied Shariah penal codes.[341] Theft by Muslims can result in a sentence requiring amputation of the right hand at the wrist.[342] For more serious cases of theft (or *hirabah*/robbery), where bodily harm is inflicted and property seized, the sentence is severe, ranging from life imprisonment, to amputation, death, or crucifixion.[343] For example, Sections 153(d); 156(d); and 155(d) of the Zamfara, Bauchi, and Sokoto Shariah penal code, respectively, provide the punishment of crucifixion, where robbery results in death and seizure of property. But Kaduna State, Section 148(d) spells out that whoever commits *hirabah* shall be punished. . . . "With *salb*, where murder was committed and property seized."[344] The word *salb* is not defined in Schedule A, chapter 1, which defines terms and words in the law, while Section 140 (punishment for *hirabah*) omitted the subsection on crucifixion. The Niger State Shariah Penal Code Law on the other hand just adopted the penal code law.[345] The penal code has no provision for robbery, but the punishment for theft under

---

340. See Hefner and Horvatich, *Islam in an Era*, 59; also Qur'an 42:38 on consultation.
341. The Kano and Zamfara penal codes define theft as covertly, dishonestly and without consent—taking any lawful and movable property belonging to another, out of its place of custody (*hire*) and valued not less than the minimum stipulated value (*nisab*) without any justification. The Niger State penal code, Section 68(s)(2)(a) does not adopt the Shariah definition, but refers to the sections on theft of the 1960 penal code (Sections 287–290) and stipulates that the stolen goods must have a minimum value of 20,000 Naira (about $150 US) and must have been stolen from proper custody.
342. The Kano (Section 134) and Zamfara (Section 145) penal codes stipulate that in the event of subsequent recidivism the left foot, the left hand, and the right foot will be amputated.
343. Zamfara State Shariah Penal Code Law, 2000, Section 153.
344. Kaduna State Shariah Penal Code Law, 2000.
345. Northern Nigeria Penal Code Law, 1960, Cap 96.

Sections 287 to 290, ranges from fine to flogging to imprisonment. Also, in both Kano and Zamfara, the penalties vary from single amputation of the wrist to cross amputation and flogging. The punishments for these offenses also differ from those listed under the leading Maliki School of law,[346] which, for example, precludes the application of the penalty of amputation of Muslims.[347]

The Constitution and Jurisdiction

The working relationship between the Shariah and the Nigerian Constitution is important to understand for the proper administration of justice. Section 4 of the 1999 Constitution articulates the respective legislative powers of the federation and the states. The Exclusive Legislative List (incorporated in the Constitution in the Second Schedule) delineates those matters upon which the federal legislature alone, to the exclusion of state legislatures, retains the power to legislate. Alternatively, matters mentioned in the Concurrent Legislative List can come under both the legislative power of the federation and the legislative power of the states.

---

346. Kano State Shariah Penal Code Law, Section 143(c) and Zamfara State Shariah Penal Code Law, Section 200(c). See also Peters, *Reintroduction of Islamic Criminal Law*, 18; cited at Harvard Law Library as NIGE, 980, PET48, 2001.

347. "The penalty of hadd for theft shall be remitted in any of the following cases: (a) Where the offense was committed by ascendant against descendant; (b) Where the offense was committed between spouses within their matrimonial home; provided the stolen property was not under the victim's lock and key; (c) Where the offense was committed under circumstances of necessity and the offender did not take more than he ordinarily requires to satisfy his need or the need of his dependents; (d) Where the offender believes in good faith that he has a share (or a right or interest) in the said stolen property and the said stolen property does not exceed the share (or the right or interest) to the equivalent of the minimum value of the property (nisâb); (e) Where the offender retracts his confession before execution of the penalty in cases where proof of guilt was based only on the confession of the offender; (f) Where the offender returns or restitutes the stolen property to the victim of the offense and repents before he was brought to trial, he being a first time offender; (g) Where the offender was permitted access to the place of custody (hirz) of the stolen property; (h) Where the victim of the offense is indebted to the offender and is unwilling to pay, and the debt was due to be discharged prior to the offense, and the value of the property stolen is equal to, or does not exceed the debt due to the offender to the extent of the nisâb" (Zamfara penal code, Section 147).

Any remaining matters not mentioned in the Exclusive Legislative List
or in the Concurrent Legislative List are reserved for the states alone to
legislate upon. Since penal code law is not mentioned in either list, it can be
concluded that it properly belongs to the domain of state legislatures.[348]

However, the Exclusive Legislative List does contain certain domains
related to penal code law that are regarded as federal, such as evidence,
the police, and prisons.[349] State legislatures may not address these topics.
In light of these specific restrictions, the issue is not whether states may
introduce their own penal laws, but whether or not they may introduce a
religiously inspired law that could infringe upon the federal constitution.[350]
There is no dispute about the rightful exercise of the Shariah in some fields,
such as personal law. In fact, this is provided for in the Constitution, which
authorizes the states, if they deem it necessary, to establish Shariah Courts of
Appeal which are to have jurisdiction in matters of Islamic personal law.[351]
Nevertheless, there remain questions about the application of criminal
aspects of the codified Shariah in societies with multiple legal systems and
religions.

Jurisdiction is the right, power, and authority vested in the courts
to administer justice by hearing and determining issues before them.[352]
While this is often a simple matter, it can occasionally become quite
complex. As a general rule, Shariah courts in the current dispensation have
jurisdiction over all civil and criminal matters, but exceptions do exist, such
as if the parties are non-Muslim and have not agreed to the jurisdiction of
the Shariah court. Before filing a case, a lawyer must first determine whether
or not the court in which the case is to be filed will have jurisdiction over
the parties and the subject matter.

---

348. Constitution of the Federal Republic of Nigeria, 1999.
349. Constitution of the Federal Republic of Nigeria, 1999, Second Schedule, Item 23,
Legislative Powers, Part I, Exclusive Legislative List. (Item 23 governs evidence.) See also
Item 45, Police and Other Government Security Services Established by Law, and Item 48,
Prisons.
350. Hayek, *Road to Serfdom*.
351. Sections 275–277.
352. American Law Reports, 654.

The Shariah Court of Appeal for each state has jurisdiction to hear all appeals from Lower Shariah courts in their states. Since the introduction of the new Shariah Penal Code Laws in 2000, the purview of these courts of appeal has raised some constitutional questions. According to Section 277 of the 1999 Nigerian Constitution (printed in its entirety in the Compendium), their jurisdiction seems to be limited to matters of civil law.[353] However, this section (as well as Section 244 of the 1999 Constitution) is not clear upon which court is the final arbitrator in these matters. For instance, the question could be posed: Can a judgment on a criminal matter from a state Shariah Court of Appeal be appealed to the Federal Court of Appeal when the Federal Court of Appeal seems to be limited in its jurisdiction to civil law matters, with respect to cases coming from state Shariah courts?[354]

The Constitution stipulates that the Federal Court of Appeal is the appellate court for state Shariah Courts of Appeal.[355] However, such appeal is restricted to matters of Islamic personal law. Because the application of Section 244(1) has a restrictive application clause,[356] it may only be applied if it is neither in conflict with written laws nor with the mandates of natural justice, equity, and good conscience. It is important to note, however, that some have argued that the repugnancy clause may not apply, as the enacted

---

353. Any question of Islamic personal law regarding a marriage—family relationship or the guardianship of an infant; any question of Islamic personal law regarding a *wakf*, gift, will or succession; any question regarding an infant, prodigal, or person of unsound mind—maintenance or the guardianship of a Muslim who is physically or mentally infirm; or where all the parties to the proceedings, being Muslims, have requested the court that hears the case in the first instance to determine that case in accordance with Islamic personal law.
354. Constitution of Nigeria, 1999, Section 244(1): "An appeal shall lie from decisions of a Shariah Court of Appeal to the Court of Appeal as of right in any civil proceedings before the Shariah Court of Appeal with respect to any question of Islamic personal law which the Shariah Court of Appeal is competent to decide."
355. Section 244(1).
356. "An appeal shall lie from decisions of a Shariah Court of Appeal to the Court of Appeal as of right in any civil proceedings before the Shariah Court of Appeal with respect to any question of Islamic personal law which the Shariah Court of Appeal is competent to decide."

laws to introduce a criminal aspect of Shariah law were in accordance with
Section 275(1) of the Constitution.[357]

Less contested is that Shariah penal codes may be in conflict with
the Constitution of the Federal Republic of Nigeria, 1999, with regards
to evidentiary rules. The Exclusive Legislative List includes evidence as
one of the domains in which only the federal legislature may enact laws.
Nevertheless, some Shariah penal codes do contain evidentiary provisions.
For example, the Kano penal code, Kebbi penal code, and Niger penal
code all stipulate that four male witnesses are required to prove unlawful
sexual intercourse.[358] This falls short of the provisions of the Evidence Act
that apply to all judicial proceedings in or before any court established
in the Federal Republic of Nigeria (including Shariah courts adjudicating
criminal matters).[359] It also falls short of the provisions that apply to *hadd*
(offenses with capital punishment), and the offense of confession in *zina*
(adultery) cases. An accused could confess to the offense, but is allowed
to withdraw the confession at any time before execution, which does not
ensue with the provisions of the Evidence Act, especially, Sections 27–32.
Since the *hadd* offenses in particular are subject to strict rules of proof, the
constitutional position regarding evidence represents a potential obstacle to
the strict application of these rules. The evidentiary provisions outlined in
many Shariah penal codes differ from the provisions of the Evidence Act.

Complexities nonetheless exist in understanding the application of the
Shariah Penal Code Law within evidential rules. The Nigerian Evidence
Act is applicable to judicial proceedings in any criminal cause or matter in
or before an Area (Shariah) Court.[360] Section 1(3) of the Evidence Act says,

---

357. Yadudu, "Islamic Law and Reform Discourse."
358. Kano State Shariah Penal Code Law, Section 127; Kebbi State Shariah Penal Code
Law, Section 127; and Niger State Shariah Penal Code Law, Section 68(a)(3)(b).
359. Nigerian Evidence Act, specifically, Section 163, regarding competency in
proceedings relating to adultery, other relevant sections on examination of witnesses and
more.
360. Laws of the Federation of Nigeria, 1990, Evidence Act, Chapter 112. Area Courts
became Shariah courts after the introduction of Shariah penal code in states that are
applying the Shariah penal law.

"The court shall be guided by the provisions of the Act." This is so especially in areas where "If the commission of a crime by a party to any proceeding is directly in issue . . . it must be proved beyond reasonable doubt."[361] Also, "The burden of proving that any person has been guilty of a crime or wrongful act is, subject to the provision of Section 141 of the Act, on the person who asserts it . . . "[362] However, where the prosecutions prove the commission of a crime beyond reasonable doubt, the burden of proving reasonable doubt is shifted to the accused.[363]

Indeed, the "burden of proof as to any particular fact lies on that person who wishes the court to believe in its existence . . . "[364] For example, in at least one of the Shariah cases where a trial court's conviction was stoning, the prosecuting police officer, in trying to prove his case, presented to court a child of the accused, allegedly born out of wedlock, as evidence, exhibit, and witness (the child was less than three weeks old). The trial court record of this case demonstrates the inability of the prosecutor to take advantage of the provision of the Evidence Act to prove the case against the accused. Prosecutors and defense counsels in Shariah courts should be desirous of ensuring justice under law. In this regard, conscious attempts should be made to comply with the provisions of the Evidence Act.

Several questions arise, for example: Who should be the witness(es)? How can their testimony be presented and admitted? Essentially, what evidential proof rule is to be adopted? Did the Evidence Act provide for relevancy of facts and how that process can be established? If yes, which relevant fact? Could the fact(s) be admissible? When should oral evidence be admitted? In terms of confession, how is it made or obtained? Is such confession relevant in proving the offense? These are questions that will

---

361. EA, Section 138.
362. "A person accused of any offense whose burden of proving the existence of circumstances bringing the case within any exception or exemption from, or qualification to, the operation of the law creating the offense with which he is charged is upon such person . . . "
363. EA, Section 138(3).
364. Ibid., Section 139.

be relevant to facts in issue in trying to establish a case, especially cases that carry the capital punishment of death. It is pertinent to note though, that the Evidence Act does provides for the relevancy of the evidence of character of an accused person, as well as facts that need to be proven and those that do not need proof.[365] Additionally, the Nigerian Evidence Act provides for relevance principles before admission of facts or facts in issue.

Proof of confession is even more arduous. For example, the Evidence Act provides *inter alia*: "A confession is an admission made at any time by a person charged with a crime. . . . confessions, if voluntary, are deemed to be relevant facts as against the persons who make them only . . . A confession made by an accused person is irrelevant in a criminal proceeding, if the making of the confession appears to the court to have been caused by any inducement, threat or promise having reference to the charge against the accused person . . . "[366] Meanwhile, from the record of the trial Shariah courts, if the alleged confession of the woman convicted for adultery seems to have been induced or obtained by threat, in this respect, where a court so declared, such confession cannot stand the weight of Sections 27–37 of the Evidence Act.

Consequently, will the Evidence Act be relevant and applicable to witnesses under the Shariah penal law? Will the evidence of these witnesses be admissible? Will the Evidence Act be used in cases of adultery? And to what extent? The Evidence Act procedure seems to be restrictive; for example, are only relevant parties competent to be witnesses before a court for the Act to apply? If competent, will the testimony be admissible? In relation to the proceedings for adultery, the Evidence Act provides *inter alia:* "The parties to any proceeding instituted in consequence of adultery and the husbands and wives of the parties shall be competent to give evidence in the proceedings, but no witness in any such proceedings whether a party thereto or not, shall be liable to be asked or bound to answer any question tending to show that he or she has been guilty of adultery, unless he or she

---

365. Ibid., Section 69, Part III.
366. Ibid.

has already given evidence in the same proceeding in disproof of the alleged adultery . . . "[367] Will such a proceeding be accepted in an adultery trial conducted before Shariah courts? If not, then what proceeding of evidential proof procedure is to be adopted in Shariah courts? These I believe are issues that need to be settled when it comes to the application of evidence and due process. For the most part, lawyers stand at the center of these two legal forces, and must learn to navigate the terrain and how to best move toward a legal defense that would prove successful for the client.[368]

Furthermore, the Constitution declares that all criminal offenses should be codified.[369] The SPCL of most states contains a provision suggesting that offenses codified in the Shariah Penal Code Laws shall be applied in the state.[370] It falls on the state legislators, in states where the codes are not enacted in a codified form to so do, if they so desire, to have its provisions adjudicated upon by an independent judiciary.[371] Almost all the states that have introduced the criminal aspects of Shariah law have codification with jurisdictional modification over civil litigation where the two opponents are Muslim. Of special interest are cases involving criminal matters. If the accused is non-Muslim, the court will not have jurisdiction over him or her unless the accused voluntarily accepts such jurisdiction.[372] However, there are exceptions that must be accounted for. For example, it is the position of some state Shariah penal codes that if an individual has been accused of *juju* (witchcraft), the courts will have jurisdiction even over non-Muslims.[373]

---

367. Ibid., Section 163.
368. For more on the examination of witnesses, see Richardson and T. Williams, *Criminal Procedure Code*, 399.
369. Constitution of Nigeria, 1999, Section 36(12): "Subject as otherwise provided by this Constitution, a person shall not be convicted of a criminal offense unless that offense is defined and the penalty therefore is prescribed in a written law and in this subsection, a written law refers to an Act of the National Assembly or a Law of a State, any subsidiary legislation or instrument under the provisions of a law."
370. Bauchi State Shariah Penal Code Law, 2001, No. 16.
371. Niger and Gombe States do not have codified Shariah penal codes or procedural codes.
372. Zamfara State Shariah Penal Code Law, Section 3.
373. Bauchi State Shariah Penal Code Law, 2000, Sections 404 and 405.

Diversity in Shariah Penal Codes

It is likewise important for lawyers to understand the diversity in the structure and the language within the Shariah penal codes of the different states. For example, while Section 93 of the Zamfara Shariah penal code provides for punishments and compensation, the Sokoto penal code provides for the same provision under Section 95. The punishment of *hadd* (flogging), for example, provided for in subsection (r) of the Sokoto code is not present in the Zamfara code. The same provision is also missing in the Katsina penal code, and in its place, Section 92(1)(r) provides for stoning instead of flogging, while Section 96 of the Bauchi Shariah penal code is silent on both flogging and stoning.

Similarly, Section 92 of the Zamfara code—general offenses, and punishments—went further to state an omnibus statement, suggesting uncertainty of law and legal process.[374] It states among other things that "any act or omission not specifically mentioned in the Shariah penal code of Zamfara State, but is declared an offence in the Quran, Sunnah and Ijtihad of Maliki School of Islamic thought, shall be an offence under the code ... " These certainly open up lots more windows of uncertainty, both in text and in its application, that lawyers may need to weigh. Meanwhile, the Katsina and Sokoto codes do not have such a section. More so, Sections 153(d), 155(d), and 156(d) of the Zamfara, Sokoto, and Bauchi Shariah penal codes, respectively, provide crucifixion as punishment for cases of *hirabah* (robbery) where death was caused and property seized. This provision is missing from the Katsina penal code.

---

374. "Any act or omission which is not specifically mentioned in this Shariah Penal Code, but is otherwise declared to be an offense under the Qur'an, Sunnah and Ijtihad of the Maliki School of Islamic thought shall be an offense under this code and such act or omission shall be punishable (a) with imprisonment for a term which may extend to 5 years, or (b) with caning which may extend to 50 lashes, or (c) with fine which may extend to N5,000.00 ($33) or with two of the above punishments." Uncertainty of the law may increase failure to settle litigation, which in turn affects persons who may be shy to resort to judiciary to seek for the enforcement of their fundamental human rights.

Also, although there is no offense for female homosexuality under the Katsina penal code, a punishment of flogging and/or imprisonment is listed in Sections 134 and 135 of the Zamfara penal code and in Sections 137 and 138 of the Bauchi penal code. There is no such offense or punishment listed for male homosexuality in the Shariah penal codes.

Human Rights and the Law

Another major concern regarding the constitutionality of Shariah law arises in regards to basic human rights guaranteed under chapter 4 of the 1999 Nigerian Constitution.[375] The possibility that harsh sentences could be carried out may potentially violate these human rights provisions. It could represent a further constitutional issue that Shariah law must face, especially issues of inhumane and degrading treatment under Section 34(1) of the 1999 Nigerian Constitution.[376]

As previously noted, one of the most fundamental principles in human rights discourse maintains that all persons are equal before the law and entitled to the same legal protection. Although this principle is embodied in Section 42 of the Constitution, it can easily become eroded in actual practice. For example, in detailing the requisites for proving the offense of *zina,* the Niger penal code asserts that the evidence of men is of greater value than that of women .[377] As of yet, no case has gone forward to serve as a litmus test on this issue.[378] Clearly, punishment is not being meted out equally in these cases, particularly in cases of *zina*, where the author participated in defense of clients. Women are mostly convicted and the men go free. Attention should be paid though not to create an environment where rapists could find safe haven.

---

375. Within this book, this current section on "Human Rights and the Law" will be building on the study conducted by Rudolph Peters in 2001 on the reintroduction of Islamic criminal law in Northern Nigeria.
376. Constitution of the Federal Republic of Nigeria, 1999.
377. Section 68(a)(3)(b).
378. This work was completed in 2011, at which time this author was not aware of any case regarding the weight accorded to evidence when given by men versus women.

This unequal treatment before the law is also in evidence with regard to a person's religious affiliation. For example, and as discussed earlier, whereas the punishment for certain forms of theft is amputation for Muslims, it is only imprisonment for non-Muslims. This is in direct conflict with Section 42 of the Nigerian Constitution in as much as it distinguishes between two individuals who have committed identical crimes. Such discrepancies in the treatment of Muslims versus non-Muslims can be found with regard to a number of offenses (e.g., drinking alcohol, clothing of dress, and mode of transportation).

Section 38 of the Constitution guarantees freedom of religion for all. However, there is a need to evaluate whether Shariah puts this principle in jeopardy through the provision of Apostasy (*ridda*), even though none of the Shariah penal code seems to have expressly included it as an offense.[379] This does not mean that Apostasy cannot be punished under the laws in the states; take for instance, Section 92 of Zamfara penal code, which provides for an omnibus language, thereby allowing a charge for Apostasy to be fit in *mutatis mutandis* (matters that are generally the same). Yet if Section 1 of the Nigerian Constitution, affirming its supremacy is to be applied, the codification of Apostasy as a crime would violate Section 38 of the Constitution by punishing a person for exercising the right to freedom of religion.

Conflict may also arise under the new SPCL. Some punishments espoused under the criminal aspect of Shariah law are thought to run afoul of the principle of *nulla poena sine ledge* (no penalty without a law), as mentioned under the Zamfara provision. For instance, Section 93(2) of the Zamfara penal code[380] promotes the principle that all persons are equal before the law and speaks against restrictions on the freedom of religion and

---

379. The discussion about Apostasy had Muslim scholars, academics, clerics, and intellectuals opining on the distinction between Apostasies simply or Apostasy with treason. While the latter falls within the ambit of freedom of religion, the former is treated with severe punishment.

380. " . . . Nothing in this section shall prevent a court dealing with an offender in accordance with the Probation of Offender Law. . . . "

inadvertently harming the basic rights of children.[381] So also Section 94 of the Sokoto State penal code, which provides "any act or omission which is not specifically mentioned in this Shariah penal code but is otherwise declared to be an offense under the Qur'an, Sunnah and Ijtihad of the Maliki School of thought shall be an offense under this code as such act or omission is punishable . . ."

The Sokoto, Zamfara, and Bauchi penal codes are silent on, among other things, the need for four eyewitnesses to prove the offense of *zina*. This silence can prove threatening for women as it can allow a faulty charge of *zina* to proceed. In unclear circumstances, rape can wrongly be associated with *zina,* which places women at a further disadvantage. If a woman reports to the police that she was raped, her report can easily be misconstrued as a confession to unlawful intercourse, thus exposing her to the possibility of *hadd* punishment for *zina*, unless she can prove that intercourse took place without her consent, which may be tantamount to proving a camel can pass through the eye of a needle.

By trying to report the crime of rape, women can inadvertently shift the burden of proof against *zina* onto themselves, thus putting themselves at even greater risk. Likewise, if her attacker does not confess, her accusations against him can amount to defamation *(qadhf)*, for which she can receive an additional eighty lashes as punishment.[382] This was the case with Bariya Ibrahim Magazu, our first client under the "new Shariah." Bariya was found guilty of *zina* and sentenced to 180 lashes: one hundred lashes for *zina*, since she was unmarried, and eighty for defamation. She was later given one hundred lashes; the governor was said to have forgiven her the eighty lashes as an extension of his prerogative of mercy.

In practical terms, women's subordinate status has roots in religion, culture, traditions, and secular services. Dominance and sometimes control over women by patriarchal, tribal, and monarchial structures is believed appropriate and necessary for the protection and security of the women.

---

381. "Convention on the Rights of Children," Articles 1, 37, and 40.
382. *Qadhf* translates as unfounded allegation of unlawful sexual intercourse.

These claims are based on the idea that women are the symbol of honor and chastity, the custodians of culture, tradition, and values, and because of that, they need protection. However well intended, in certain societies such claims can bring untold hardship to women and make them susceptible to being wounded or hurt.

Human Rights and Islam

Recognizing that the concepts of equality and social belief vary between jurisdictions, and being aware of the impact that the current application of Shariah law has on Muslims, especially women, is germane. The question of gender relations is a particularly important one. In Islamic belief, women are not equal to men; but neither are men equal to women.[383] Islam envisages their roles in society not as competing but as complementary. Each has certain duties and functions in accordance with his or her nature and constitution.[384] These functions are further defined in Qur'anic verses and Hadith that expound upon the position or role of women in Islam. Included in the Compendium is a collection of Qur'anic verses and Hadith that may be useful for practitioners in defending women in cases involving marriage, divorce, inheritance, maintenance, right to give evidence, rights in Pudah, rights in a polygamous relationship, and property rights.

Generally, women's role is more clearly defined as mothers, as stated in Qur'an 31:14 and 46:15; their status as wife, Qur'an 16:72; and their position as daughters.[385] Another Hadith reported by A'isha on the position of woman as a daughter is reported thus,

> A woman came to me, while there were two of her
> daughters with her. She was begging of me, but found

---

383. Bayes and Tohidi, *Globalization, Gender, and Religion*, 20.
384. Osman, *Malaysian World-View*, 31.
385. Chaudhry, *Human Rights in Islam*, 139. The Hadith of Saḥīḥ al-Muslim states that Anas reported that the Messenger of Allah سبحانه و تعالى said, "Whoever maintain two girls till they attained maturity, he and I, will come on the Resurrection Day, like this; and he joined his fingers."

nothing from me except one date, which I gave her. She divided it between her two daughters and she herself did take nothing out of it. Then she got up and went away. The Holy Prophet (ﷺ) came and I informed him (of it). He said: "Whoever suffers for any thing on account of these daughters and (still) treats them with kindness, they will be a shield for him from hell."[386]

A woman's position can also be that of a sister, Qur'an 4:176. The Qur'an is explicit about a woman's right on issues of marriage and divorce, 2:232; 4:4; 4:35; 2:228–229, and 2:241. Right of maintenance is provided for in 4:34; 2:233; 65:7; rights of inheritance in 4:7; 4:176; 4:11–12; right to give evidence, 2:282; 24:6–9; her rights in a polygamous relationship, 4:3; 4:129; her rights in Pudah, 24:30–31; 33:59; and her rights to property in 4:7, 11–12, 32, 176. Women have in the past taken leadership roles and their role is now increasing in public and socio-political life. Qur'an 9:71 states that as Muslims, both men and women need to take responsibilities to ensure that the Muslim *ummah* uphold what is right and rebuke what is wrong in the society; we all are stakeholders. So also, women can form or be in a political party and participate in governance; it is by so doing that women can advance Islamic values, give counsel (Q. 42:38) and govern on a societal level. Women leaders certainly could be powerful tools in advocating for equality before the law; and justly so, both because the Qur'an provides for women to take a responsible role in their society and this is because both men and women would likely benefit from such active participation.

Islam's position on discrimination has been clearly laid out and absolutely does not embrace discrimination based on race, gender, or circumstance of birth. Practitioners in Shariah courts can thus continue in this realm by ensuring that women's issues are respected when it comes to the following: inclusion of women in the labor market; sex discrimination and protections;

---

386. In the Hadith of Saḥīḥ al-Muslim as reported by A'isha. See Chaudhry, *Human Rights in Islam*, 139.

ensuring justice and fairness in the administration of sex discrimination; allowing for stringent burden of proof in challenging cases; and seeking new initiatives across the board for the implementation of the principles of equal opportunities by giving women access to the media, information, and communication technologies. They will provide an inclusive society where everyone is treated with respect and where there is opportunity for all, to play his or her full part in social and economic life. The need to tackle barriers to universal participation and to change the culture so that equal opportunities and equal treatment become a priority for all cannot be understated.

When our legal team started to appear in court, gender consideration made it difficult for me as a woman to argue before some Shariah courts. Initially, this forced me to play a "minor" role in the proceedings. Depending upon the jurisdiction, even possession of specific and important knowledge may not be sufficient to afford a woman the same status as a male in attempting to further the adjudication of justice. As women's rights advocate, I disagreed with this general dismissal of my worth; however, it was important to remind myself that my standing before the court was not the issue at hand. Rather, this case was about something far more important than me, the fact that a woman had been sentenced to death by stoning. The true challenge here was to attempt to work within the framework of the SPCL to try to win her freedom. All the same, the court could learn from the example of other Muslim countries regarding the value that women can add to a legal system.[387] Especially in family cases and cases of alleged adultery, women can bring a very important perspective to the surrounding issues, which could prove critical in ensuring that justice is served for all.

The Qur'an provides: "O mankind, fear your Lord, who created you from one soul and created from it its mate and dispersed from both of them

---

387. On Feb. 25, 2008, Egypt appointed its first female marriage registrar as reported by Farah El Alfy, "Focus on Muslim Women," *Al Jazeera*, Cairo, Egypt, Nov. 19, 2008. Also in November 2008 the United Arab Emirate appointed Fatima Saeed Obeid Al Awani as a marriage registrar in Abu Dhabi.

many men and women. And fear Allah, through whom you ask one another, and the wombs. Indeed Allah is ever, over you, an Observer" (4:1). There is equality of all mankind in an Islam that believes men and women were created from one soul.

As the book of Kitab-ul-Haj states: "No Arab has any superiority over a non-Arab, neither any superiority over an Arab; nor does a white man over a black man; you are all children of Adam and Adam was created from clay."[388] This wisdom is an example for all states implementing the Shariah penal code, to emulate.

Farid Esack, in explaining how Muslims ought to see the Holy Qur'an in what he calls "our realities," has said, "If we are true to the Qur'an, we have to discern that message in terms of our own experience [today]—we have to see how God speaks to us today—through that same Koran—in terms of our new realities and our deeper understanding of what it means to be human in the 21st century."[389] Dr. Esack further opined that, "Islam stands for the absolute sacredness of God, not the sacredness of religion or of Shariah." He believes that "Muslims should make a distinction between the objectives of Islamic law and the letter of the law." And he says, "It is the objectives of the law—its underlying principles—which must be met."[390]

Society will benefit when the Shariah legal system raises the level of propriety in the justice system by becoming inclusive of other jurisdictional understandings of Islamic text and open to other schools of thought in interpreting an issue of law, fact, and/or procedure.[391] The Shariah justice system will become more humane if judges exercise restraint by imposing

388. Maudoodi, *Human Rights in Islam*, 20. Also, the Book of Pilgrimage to Mecca is a basic guide on how to perform Umrah and Hajj.
389. D. Smith and Burr, *Understanding World Religions*, 369. Dr. Esack is a South African Muslim scholar, writer, and political activist.
390. Eagle, "Sharia/Comparison."
391. Doi, *Sharīah*, 85; see also El Fadl, *Speaking in God's Name*. El Fadl argued that Imam Malik says, "no one jurist or juristic tradition may have an exclusive claim over the divine truth, so therefore, one school of thought should not be legitimately supported to the exclusion of another" (p. 10). Not being inclusive could amount to being ignorant and uninformed. The words Maliki and Malik are used inter changeably when referring to Imam Maliki. See Sheikh and Al-Khajnadee, *Should a Muslim?* 12.

less severe punishments. Efforts by Shariah or Muslim countries, such as the Cairo Declaration of 1981, which promote human rights values, should be echoed in other Islamic societies, especially ours.[392]

Argue Your Strengths

As mentioned earlier, the rule of law can be the lawyer's strength in navigating the relationship between Shariah law and its application. Rule of law is a constitutional doctrine that emphasizes the supremacy of the law as administered by courts of law. Literally, the rule of law means the governance of law. That is to say, "The entire society including democratic institutions, organs of government and the civil society must be subject to legal rules."[393] As Nobel Prize-winning economist F. A. Hayek observed, when vested with absolute power, man has a tendency to "subordinate, manipulate and oppress his fellow man. The old adage stands, that power corrupts, and absolute power corrupts absolutely. Thus, the only apparatus available to check and restrict the excesses of man within the ambit of the law and to preserve social harmony is the rule of law."[394]

Asserting the supremacy of the law affirms the fundamental and lawful right of every citizen to appeal his or her case to the highest court of the land. Under the Nigerian Constitution, this right should not be denied to individuals, even within Shariah states. When convicted of an offense, everyone should have the opportunity to appeal the sentence and its judgment without hindrance. Such areas where Shariah practices come into direct conflict with the nondiscrimination clauses in the Nigerian Constitution will need to be addressed in due course, especially in those cases where a weightier punishment is meted out to a Muslim than a non-Muslim for the same crime.

---

392. Universal Islamic Declaration of Human Rights, 1981. See also Hussain, *Human Rights in Islam*, 108.
393. Cheema, *Building Democratic Institutions*, 169.
394. Hayek, *Road to Serfdom*, 18.

Summary

Shariah court judges have demonstrated bravery in their rulings and judgments and displayed a virtuous independence from outside influence. At its outset, the new Shariah also gave clients faith in the process and structure of justice, which in turn gave our team the courage to go further. During these cases, media attention played a huge role in the promotion of justice by keeping all parties honest and on target. It was never about us; nor should it ever be. Justice is what we promised to uphold and bear as a trademark, and so it should remain. Through the practice of intense strategies and pragmatic thinking, the treatment of human rights and rule of law becomes an object of devotion rather than a computation.

In conclusion, know your strength and play to it. A lawyer's strength is the law; its rules, processes, and procedures. It is important for counsel representing an individual accused under Shariah to grasp the dynamics of the Shariah legal system itself, which include the court procedures, the judges' understanding and perceptions of the issues, and the attitudes and understanding held by the people toward their culture, traditions, and values.

CHAPTER SIX

Plan a Defense

HAVING MANY DIFFERENT PLANS WHILE preparing a defense may seem obvious; it is, however, a necessity, given the climate of the Northern Nigerian Shariah courts, and will serve one with propriety, justice, and reason in other courts as well. I had the privilege of serving as a prosecutor prior to my involvement in the defense of Shariah cases, which helped me to realize that a lawyer can tear down various boundaries, especially working at the grassroots level within the society. No individual can claim these achievements as his or hers alone; it is "we" doing it together. Achieving justice and freedom together, and having clients return safely to their societies is what we collectively strive to accomplish. Winning the case in the minds and hearts of the villagers is at times more important than winning the case in court. Most of the cases I was involved with, especially cases in the first few years following the introduction of the new Shariah penal code, involved a large collaborative effort of preparation, planning, and strategizing with senior colleagues, Muslim clerics, scholars of Islamic law, and many members of the Muslim society. The process of collaboration enriches a lawyer's skill set and paves the way to justice.

What It Was

Tradition plays an influential role when understanding issues of crime and punishment in rural societies. Some societies are guided by a collective sense of responsibility, which dictates that they first attempt negotiation, conciliation, mediation, and other alternative forms of conflict resolution before they turn to adjudication. This collective approach to dealing with crime is illustrated in the Native American tale "When Two Twists Led the Cheyenne against the Crows." In the story,

> A man named Red Robes had two sons who died in battle protecting their community. Red Robes' grief for his only sons led him to abandon his entire herd, and thereby all his wealth, not keeping a single animal for himself. Recognizing his pain, the community gathered his herd and watched over it for him, trying several times to convince him to take back his herd, but he refused. In their support of Red Robes, the community joined together *en masse* to avenge the death of his two sons. Two Twists, a member of the community unrelated to Red Robes, fearlessly led the assault against the enemies, not knowing whether he would live or die. During the assault, the women of the community sang a beautiful song: "*Only the rocks lie here and never move—human beings vapor away*." The community won the battle and thereafter Red Robes took back his herd. In the spirit of solidarity and gratitude, he later gave away most of the herd to his fellow citizens.[395]

Happy ever after, the community bonds remained strong. The story of Red Robes exemplifies the power of collective responsibility for justice. A society that solves challenges together becomes a community bound by the glue of camaraderie.

---

395. Llewellyn and Hoebel, *Cheyenne Way*, 3.

The reaction of local communities to cases filed in courts follows a similar path. The initial response to almost all of the *zina* cases handled by this author was to get the local head of the community or village (*Sarki;* sometimes *Mai Gari*) involved, as the first point of call. In fact, the chiefs resolve and adjudicate dispute.[396] The natural place to call on a chief is his *zaure* (parlor). When the unusual happens—an unmarried woman shows signs of pregnancy and is in her father's or male relation's home (a female is not allowed to live by herself), the father or male relation will call a family meeting to discuss the challenges that have befallen the family—a woman becoming pregnant without a husband is considered a shame and embarrassment. This meeting then moves from the family to the *Sarki*. A traditional council is convened and the issues are discussed, along with the possibility of settlement. Before the introduction of the codified Shariah in 2000, similar issues such as pregnancy out of wedlock were often resolved in the Chief's Court (*fadan Sarki*), and in most cases the man at fault was identified and asked to take responsibility in the local community.

Most of the time, the men at fault took responsibility and showed good faith. This helped to preserve and strengthen the dignity and good order of the community. After the codification of the Shariah in 2000, some officials, especially the *hisbah/da'awah* (religious police), felt that they needed to demonstrate the implementation of the Shariah and provide examples of violators of the law. Women (accompanied by members of *hisbah* or *da'awah*) began to find themselves in Shariah courts sentenced to flogging or stoning for adultery because they became pregnant, while most men remained free from both allegation and social stigma. The same men who earlier acknowledged their guilt now withdrew and denied, "knowing the woman" with whom they were involved. As soon as the religious police (*hisbah/da'awah*) became involved, if they admitted to knowing the woman, they would also put themselves at risk of being stoned.

---

396. F. Williams and Miles, *Hausaland Divided*, 147.

It is clear that when planning defense strategies, it is to the lawyer's advantage to work within social structures. Reach out to the *Sarki*, members of his council, and the society where the accused resides to try to get them involved with an out-of-court settlement process; or when the case is in the courts, to keep the chief and members of the society involved. This will help legitimize the lawyer's intervention in court should that be necessary. Although, rural societies do apply a collective approach to justice, adjudication remains a possibility for which a lawyer must be prepared. This is illustrated by the case of Amina Lawal.

The Case of Amina Lawal: The Necessity of Planning

Amina Lawal, a Nigerian woman who gave birth to a child out of wedlock, was charged and convicted with *zina* under the Shariah penal code of Katsina State in Northern Nigeria.[397] The trial court had based its conviction on Ms. Lawal's alleged confession and the fact that she was pregnant out of wedlock, two grounds upon which *zina* can be proven under Shariah penal code in Katsina State (assuming that the procedures for establishing the validity of the grounds have been properly adhered to). We, appealed her case to the Shariah court in Funtua, Katsina State, but failed in the attempt to have her discharged and acquitted. Subsequently, we appealed her case to the Katsina State Shariah Court of Appeal (the last court of state appeal for Shariah cases) and won.

The Penal Code of Northern Nigeria (PC), which had been in force since soon after Nigeria's independence from Great Britain in 1960, was repealed in most of the states that introduced the Shariah penal code in 2000. Unlike the criminal code of Southern Nigeria, which had no provision for adultery/fornication, the PC contained a provision against the offense of adultery/fornication. Sections 387 and 388 of the PC provide and define the offense of adultery as, "Whoever being a man/woman subject to any

---

397. Case No. KTS/SCA/FT/86/2002, Amina Lawal v. The State. (In the Shariah Court of Appeal Katsina State of Nigeria.) The Hausa Version, certified true copy of case file, July 22, 2008.

native law or custom in which extra-marital intercourse is recognized as a criminal offense has sexual intercourse not amounting to rape, with a person, who is not and whom he/she knows or has reason to believe is not his/her wife/husband, shall be punished with imprisonment which may extend to two years or with fine or with both."[398]

However, with the codification of the "new Shariah" in Katsina State, Section 124 of the Shariah Penal Code Law (Katsina State), 2001, provides for the offense of *zina* and its punishment thus:

> Whoever, being a man or a woman fully responsible, has sexual intercourse through the genital of a person over whom he has no sexual rights and in circumstances in which no doubt exists as to the illegality of the act, is guilty of the offence of zina.

And, Section 125 stipulates the punishment:

> Whoever, commits the offence of zina shall be punished:
>
> > a. with caning of one hundred lashes if unmarried and shall also be liable to imprisonment for a term of one year; or
> > b. if married, with stoning to death (*rajm*[399]).

It was on these sections that Amina Lawal was first arraigned before the Shariah court in Bakori, on January 15, 2002, with case number 9/2002 (unreported) and was convicted on the two charges that she was pregnant and had a child out of wedlock and she had confessed to adultery. On appeal to the Upper Shariah Court in Funtua, after arguments, the presiding judge, Alh. Aliyu Abdullahi and three other members of the court confirmed the sentence of the Bakori trial court, that Ms. Lawal should be stoned to death

---

398. Gledhill, *Penal Codes of Northern Nigeria*, 675–77. Note that rape does not appear and is not considered in the case of women. Also note the explanation on page 675, which says that Shariah regards "all such intercourse as zina" and punishable as criminal offense.
399. Also written as "rajam."

after she weaned her child.[400] Unsatisfied with the court's judgment, our legal team appealed Amina Lawal's case to the Shariah Court of Appeal, Katsina in Katsina State.[401]

On September 25, 2003, the Shariah Court of Appeal, Katsina State, rendered a judgment for Amina Lawal that set a precedent for a number of fundamental issues in the fair application of Shariah law. The Honorable Khadi of the Court, Aminu Ibrahim Katsina, reading the concurring judgment of four of the five members of the court, ruled that the police should not have charged Ms. Lawal with the offense of *zina* because it was not within their constitutional authority. The court also decided:[402]

1. For an offense of *zina* to be proved, both accused persons must be seen performing the act of *zina* openly, to be seen by at least four responsible Muslim male adults, otherwise the person so alleged should be flogged. Furthermore, where the four witnesses have not been established, the accused must be discharged and acquitted.

2. Discharging the man accused of being with Ms. Lawal for want of evidence or proof (establishing that four eye witnesses had seen the act of *zina*), while convicting Ms. Lawal was an error and could not be sustained before the court.

3. An abuse of law for a judge to sit alone at the trial when the Shariah penal code of Katsina State provides that a judge and two members should sit at the trial court.[403]

4. The confession of the appellant was not valid since it was not repeated multiple times and since the law states undoubtedly that an accused can withdraw a confession at any time before

---

400. Upper Shariah Court No. 1/2002 dated March 15, 2002. Worthy of note is that one of the judges dissented.
401. No. KTS/SCA/FT/86/2002 (unreported).
402. Amina Lawal v. The State as recorded in court in Hausa and translated by the author.
403. Amina Lawal v. The State. See p. 27 where the court referred to Katsina State Shariah Penal Code Law, 2001.

judgment and the trial court should accept such withdrawal of confession.[404]

5. Because the trial court failed to give Ms. Lawal the opportunity to withdraw or recant her confession at least four times, the judgment is vitiated and null *ab-initio* (from the beginning) and the withdrawal or recantation of a confession is not punishable.

6. An accused person cannot swear by the Qur'an but can only take an oath in the name of Allah سبحانه و تعالى (God).

7. Trial court record concerning Ms. Lawal's confession was unclear and raised a lot of doubts. Quoting repeatedly from Hadith the judges said doubts must be resolved in favor of the accused person.[405] The court recounted the entire story of Ma'iz (a person who had allegedly committed *zina* during the time of the Holy Prophet [ﷺ]), to buttress this point.

8. The burden of proof of *zina* must be borne by the prosecutor and not the accused.

9. Ms. Lawal's pregnancy and childbirth could have been the product of her former husband, thereby accepting the "sleeping embryo theory" as accreted by Imam Maliki.[406]

---

404. The Pakistani court supports this position, where it states: "once confession is made, it can be retracted before execution of punishment—the case is then sent for retrial." See Jahangir and Jilani, *Hudood Ordinances*, 50.

405. Fikhul Alal-Mazahibul Arba'a of Imam Malik, Bulugul Maram 1234, Fikhul Sunnah Mujalladi, Jawahirul Ikilil, from the certified true copy of Amina Lawal v. The State, 20, 27, 30, and 32.

406. A woman can be pregnant for a minimum of six months and a maximum of five years, seven years, or twelve years. Al-Muwatta' of Imam Malik, 37 Hadith, found in "The Mudabbar" of Maliki's Muwatta: "Mothers suckle their children for two full years for whoever wishes to complete the suckling" (Sura 2:233). Where pregnancy is within this period of six months to five years, a woman does not deserve to be stoned. Opinions are based on conclusions from empirical evidence (or *Istiqra'*) and the knowledge of embryology at that time, which was also influenced by a widespread belief in the "sleeping fetus." Al-Darqutni reports that "Maliki often said: 'This our slave-girl, the wife of Muhammad Ibn 'Ajlan, is a truthful woman. Her husband is also a truthful man. She had three pregnancies in twelve years. Each pregnancy lasted four years.'" Based on this, Malik placed a bar of four years on gestation; later, most Maliki scholars placed the limit at five

The judgment of the Shariah Court of Appeal of Katsina State is not only explicit and well reasoned, but a tremendous tool to be studied and used. Looking at some of the details in the judgment, one can relate it to cardinal principles of law that may be useful to further knowledge and scholarship.

A Cardinal Principle

There are numerous cardinal principles in Islam.[407] In defending an accused in a case, one such principles is that it is better to release a guilty person than to punish an innocent person.[408] The Prophet was heard to say, "Avert the *hudud* from Muslims as much as you can. So if there is a way out for him, let him off; for verily, it is better for the Imam to error in pardon than to error in punishment."[409] Indeed, an underlying principle of criminal prosecution is that "the innocent shall not be punished."[410] This principle has long been acknowledged as an "essential element of a system for the administration of justice," and is founded upon a belief in the dignity and worth of the human person and upon the rule of law—*actus non-facit reum nisi mens sit rea* (the act itself does not constitute guilt unless done with a guilty intent).[411] The theory that "the intent and the act must concur to constitute a crime" is not only a principle of law, but also of natural justice.[412] The Holy Qur'an has a specific provision addressing *mens rea* (a

---

years. Some of them, particularly in the Maghreb, place it at seven years (and this is what applies today in Morocco). According to Imam Ibn al-Qayyim, there is even a view that places gestation at twelve years.

407. Cardinal principles of Islam include the articles of faith (unity in God, belief in angels, holy books, prophets, the day of resurrection, pre-measure of good and evil, hereafter or life after death, ritual purity, five daily prayers, fasting, *zakat* [giving to charity], and pilgrimage to Mecca). See Doi, *Cardinal Principles of Islam*, 17–156; see also Bah, *Glimpses of Life After Death*.

408. Salama, *Islamic Criminal Jurisdiction System*, 109.

409. Vogel, *Islamic Law and Legal System*, 243.

410. Qur'an 5:32: "Whoever kills a person except for murder or for spreading mischief in the land (through law), it is as if he has killed all mankind! And if a person saves a life it is as if he has saved all mankind."

411. Gledhill, *Penal Codes of Northern Nigeria*, 6.

412. Ibid., 7.

guilty mind): " . . . And there is no blame upon you for that in which you have erred but [only for] what your hearts intended. And ever is Allah Forgiving and Merciful" (33:5).

The Intricacies of Trial

Consequent upon the cardinal principles is the trial of an accused person in court. Generally speaking, counsel for the prosecution usually opens the trial with an oral statement summarizing the facts that he or she intends to prove against the accused. The prosecuting counsel then calls his witnesses, examining them one by one. At the end of each examination, the witness in question can be cross-examined by counsel for the defense. During cross-examination, defense counsel questions the witness in an adversarial manner and is often attempting to discredit the witness. After the cross-examination, the prosecutor may reexamine the witness. The defense then begins its argument, opening with its own statement and introducing witnesses. Again, the witnesses for the defense may be cross-examined by the prosecution and then reexamined by the defense counsel. Following this there are closing arguments. The judge may then set aside the case for further consideration before making his ruling, or he may immediately issue a ruling or judgment.

One should be mindful of important complexities in the general proceedings in the Shariah court, as courts do not strictly adopt the above procedures. In Shariah courts, information to be submitted must be verified by more than a single source, and one must also be attentive to the veracity of information presented as certainty. A lawyer needs to glean these details, so as to avoid having evidence classified as speculation, especially where the Shariah courts employ rules of evidence. Sections 162, 163, and 164 of the Nigerian Evidence Act detail, *inter alia,* rules governing the examination of witnesses.[413] For example, the Shariah court may test the credibility of any witness, summon any witness independently, and can ask any witness any

---

413. For more on the examination of witnesses see G. Zalman, "Confessions," 433–509. See also Mwalimu, *Nigerian Legal System,* 151–75.

question it deems fit with respect to the issues before it.[414] The court must make its finding based upon the evidence before it and then announce that finding.[415] Additionally, the court can compel production of evidence, examine witnesses, and make its finding in writing.[416] Section 167 provides clear mandates with regards to court records in criminal cases:

> In the trial of a criminal matter, a Shariah court shall record the proceeding in a prescribed form: the serial number of the case; the name, tribe or nationality, residence, occupation and age of the accused; the name, tribe, or nationality, occupation and age of the plaintiff; the offense complained of and the offense proven, if any; the date and place of commission of the offense and the date of arrest; the date of the complaint or first information report; the names of the witnesses for the prosecution and for the defense and a record of their evidence in narrative form; the plea of the accused and his examination; the finding, and in the case of conviction, reasons thereof with a reference to the Shariah penal code or other act or law; the sentence or other final order and the date on which the proceedings terminated. The judge of the Shariah court shall sign or seal the record of proceedings.[417]

After a plea has been taken—which in an adversarial jurisdiction usually involves a "not guilty" plea—defense counsel should deny the charges as read against the accused. This places the prosecution in the position of having to establish their case through the use of evidence, such as police report(s), First Information Report (FIR), recorded statements, exhibits, and

---

414. Sokoto State Shariah Criminal Procedure Code Law, 2000, Section 154(2).
415. Ibid., Section 155(1).
416. Ibid., Sections 159 and 162.
417. Ibid., Section 167(2).

witnesses—including eyewitness testimony. From the beginning, prepare the defense as if a trial is inevitable.

The question is not simply whether the client is guilty, but whether the prosecution can prove guilt. A strong defense must be laid out, addressing issues such as questions of fact, law, procedure, and technicalities. Being able to mount a successful defense also requires anticipating prosecutorial responses and formulating answers to those responses. By viewing the case from the prosecution's angle, the defense team is able to see their strategy and weaken their case through pointed questions and cross-examination.

Under common law, there are two broad categories of criminal law: substantive law and procedural law. Procedural law focuses on an individual's rights and due process while substantive law is concerned with offenses and their punishments or sentences. There are generally held to be seven elements of the criminal substantive law: legality, harm, *mens rea* (a guilty mind), *actus reus* (wrongful or guilty acts), concurrence, punishment, and conviction.[418] Trite law is when judges take into account *mens rea* when apportioning blame or rendering a criminal conviction.[419] Trite law does not necessarily exist under Shariah law.

Preparing a defense for a criminal action is a huge undertaking, even more so when it has to do with new areas of law, such as evidentiary proof of *zina* under the Shariah penal code. This difficulty is further compounded when emotions are running high on both sides of the aisle. Such circumstances require a clear, pre-set strategy that is inclusive of legal and nonlegal argument and cognizant that local dynamics could play a role in preparing the case for the defense. The construction of a solid defense includes ideas of "local counsel," Islamic legal scholars and teachers within

---

418. Under substantive law, criminal law is further divided into offenses and punishment. The term concurrence denotes that a crime must match the codification (existing legislation) of the offense within criminal law. Note that Muslim jurists explain that there are three requirements for the application of legal punishment—the offender had to commit the act (*qudra*); know that the act was an offense (*yiml*); and act with intent (*qasd*)—which feels like the theory of *mens rea* and *actus reus*. See Peters, *Crime and Punishment*; see also Gledhill, *Penal Codes of Northern Nigeria*.
419. Trite law refers to principles that are so obvious they do not need to be explained.

the given jurisdiction, and ideas from members of the local bar association, which usually combine knowledge of the law with the acute understanding of the cultural milieu and nuances of a particular society.

Another issue to note is that the clients are generally uneducated and unaware of their offenses and the reasons they are taken to court. The accused are usually shy and not very forthcoming with information. The thoughts of the accused's extended families, including any additional information they can provide, will help the defense team a lot. The defense will at times need to decipher the issues of the case from other sources. For example, in the case of Amina Lawal, I came to know some of the details only much later, after we filed the appeal, through a discussion between Ms. Lawal and Ahmadu Ibrahim (another of our clients who was also accused and sentenced to death by stoning). It was when the two were sharing experiences that I heard details of Ms. Lawal's case that she had not shared with the defense team, but which could have been helpful in putting together the defense case before the appellate court.

There is the need to be careful and consider the ramifications of each action when first taking on a case. In one instance, we met with the family of a woman who had been sentenced to death by stoning after having become pregnant out of wedlock. Upon meeting the family of the accused, we explained that the reason we wished to defend their daughter was not because we believed that what she did was right, but instead because we strongly believed that she had not received *adalchi* (something akin to justice). Such statements devoid of moral judgment can go a long way toward earning the respect and trust of the villagers, regardless of whether we personally share beliefs on such matters. In such circumstances, it helps no one to directly challenge the moral values that hold the society together, and could likely alienate the community.

When defending a client, we do not assume that a present case will play out like previous ones. In fact, we rarely assume anything in relation to a case, as it will often result in unpreparedness. Each case must be handled on its own merits. Attempts should be made to obtain as many pertinent resources as possible (materials on Islamic law, books and decided cases) in order to provide the courts with ample knowledge and perspective so that they may make an informed decision.

Questions of Fact

Questions of fact are issues that involve the resolution of a factual dispute, such as when the accused became pregnant, or controversy with regard to the jurisdiction of a court that is to adjudicate over an offense of *zina*. These questions may be resolved by tiers of facts or by a panel of judges responsible for deciding the factual issues in a trial, but most often by a judge. A court, especially a court of appeal, rarely overturns factual findings.[420] Arguments relating to the accuracy of conclusions of law will be more readily reconsidered by a court of law in criminal proceedings.[421]

"A question of fact may also be raised in a motion for summary judgment (a motion that asks the court to determine whether there are any questions of fact to be tried), which would allow a judge to dismiss the case without a trial."[422] Questions of fact are different from questions of law; a judge can only decide the latter. An example of a question of fact would be two conflicting stories regarding the question of whether the accused and co-accused committed *zina* together or not. The determination of which testimony to accept as fact would be left up to the trier of fact; for example the evidence of the four witnesses to prove adultery under the Shariah law as additional triers of facts, to assert firmly and unequivocally that together they have witnessed the accused committing *zina*.

We can better understand a question of fact by examining some key questions of facts in Ms. Lawal's case:

1. She was charged with an offense, but the charge did not disclose the date on which the offense was committed, the

---

420. Clinton and Matasar, *Casenote Legal Briefs*, 40.
421. Maryland Court of Appeals, *Reports of Cases Argued*, 301.
422. Digest of the decisions of the Supreme Court of the state of New York, Volume 3, By Oliver Lorenzo Barbour, New York (State). Supreme Court (1880), Albany, Weare C. Little & Co., Library of Congress, Washington D.C.; see also the legal dictionary.

place where the offense was committed, or the time and the circumstances under which the offense was committed.

2. At trial, she was not given the opportunity to call witnesses.

3. There was no record of whether or not Ms. Lawal was married at the time of the alleged *zina*.

4. It was clear that Ms. Lawal was pregnant during this time. (This fact is relevant because at that time the law was unclear regarding whether pregnancy could be used as conclusive proof of *zina*.)

5. A determination had yet to be made if the child born to Ms. Lawal was the child of her former husband, who had divorced her eleven months prior to the delivery of the child in question. Further, it had not been determined if the embryo could be considered to be a sleeping fetus.[423]

6. The record was not clear as to whether Ms. Lawal had been given a chance to rebut the accusation against her.

7. Ms. Lawal was arrested and charged with *zina* by the Nigerian Police. (This raises both questions of law and questions of fact because it is unclear whether this arrest was allowed under the Nigerian Constitution and also whether Ms. Lawal had committed an actual offense under the law.)

This case involved many further questions of law and fact: How was Ms. Lawal's alleged offense committed? Did anyone witness the alleged crime? Where and with whom was the alleged offense committed? Was the alleged offense committed in a state of slumber or unsound mind? Did Ms. Lawal willingly confess and utter the said confession repeatedly? The court is called upon to adjudicate these questions.

It should be carefully noted that in law, facts might be considered either immaterial or material. Immaterial facts are facts that are not essential to a

---

423. Amina Lawal v. The State, ceritfied Hausa copy (Nigeria, 2008). The concept of the sleeping embryo has also been documented for Shariah courts in Libya. See Layish, *Shariah and Customs*, vii.

case, and do not constitute part of the *ratio decidendi* (the rationale for the decision) of the case and therefore do not need to be proved. On the other hand, material facts are vital to the legal decision; they are part of the theory of identification of the rationale and are essential to the right of action and must always be proved.

Questions of Law and Procedure

A question of law is an issue that arises before, during, or after a trial and pertains to the interpretation of the law. In jurisprudence, a question of law, known as a point of law, is a question that must be answered by applying relevant legal presumptions through an interpretation of the law.[424] Questions of law are generally expressed in terms of broad legal principles and are capable of being applied to multifarious positions or sets of facts, rather than being dependent on particular circumstances or factual situations. An answer to a question of law as applied to the particular facts of a case is often referred to as a "conclusion of law." A judge, who must weigh the available information and consider it in light of his or her knowledge of the law before issuing a ruling, decides questions of law. Judges also establish whether a question brought up in the course of a trial is a question of law or a question of fact.[425]

In Ms. Lawal's case, one of the questions of law was the provision in Katsina state law that said a trial must be heard by an *Alkali* (judge) and two members, not one, as was the case in her trial.[426] Clearly the judge sitting alone at trial was outside the ambit of the law and thus raised a question of law. Another question of law that arose concerning the trial was at what date Katsina Shariah Penal Code Law of 2001 became legally effective. As provided for by the law itself, "the law shall be deemed to have come into

---

424. See Inbau et al., *Criminal Law*, 549.
425. Hall and Andrews, *American Law and Procedure*, 110.
426. Section 4(1), Chapter 173 ("A law to make provisions for the establishment of Shariah courts and related matters"), Katsina State, 2000, which reads: "A Shariah Court shall be properly constituted if presided over by an Alkali (judge) and two members."

operation on June 20th 2001."[427] If the law had been applied *ex post facto*, then clearly the accused would not have committed any offense at all on the grounds that there can be no crime and no punishment without a previous penal law—"*Nullum crimen, nulla poena sine praevia lege poenali.*"[428] There are also questions of procedure regarding what due process a case deserves. For example, consider the charge of *zina* and the proof thereof. The procedural question here regards the step-by-step sequence of events to which the courts must adhere in order to ensure a just trial for defendants.[429] This then leads us to consider components of an offense of *zina*, which has to be proven to secure conviction.

Proof of Zina

Confession

One can still be convicted of *zina* without the act being witnessed.[430] Freely given confessions of guilt, repeated four times in court, is acceptable proof of *zina* in place of the four witnesses.[431] Similar to the many conditions that must be met for a witness's testimony to be used before a court, a confession from an accused also has many strict requirements surrounding its admissibility in court. One such requirement is that a confession must not be coerced. Because confessions obtained under duress are inadmissible according to Islamic law, judges are encouraged to ensure that confessions have not been forcibly extracted from an accused. If there is any doubt, the confession should not be allowed to be admitted into evidence.[432]

---

427. Chapter 179 ("A law to establish the Shariah Penal Code Law for Katsina State of Nigeria and to make provisions for other related matters"), 2001.

428. Karibi-Whyte, *History and Sources*, 223.

429. Sokoto State Shariah Penal Code Law, Sections 151–168.

430. Doi, *Sharīah*, 236; see also Husni et al., *Muslim Women*, 53. The elements for proof of *zina* are still a controversial topic. While some maintain that any one of the three proofs is conclusive on its own, current thinking suggests that all three elements of proof are required to convict a person of *zina*.

431. B. Williams et al., *One World Many Issues*, 63.

432. Khadduri and Ramazani, *Islamic Conception of Justice*, 152. Jurists have reached a consensus on ḥudūd that for the avoidance of doubt, the Prophet's instructions to avoid

Furthermore, the confessor should be an adult who is of sound mind without fear of harm, and who fully comprehends the consequences of such a confession. The confession must also be uttered repeatedly: at least four times, on four different occasions.[433]

A narrative is told of the fourth Caliph of Islam who came upon an insane woman who had confessed to *zina* and was about to be stoned. He quickly brought a halt to the punishment and declared:

> Do you not know that there are three people whose actions
> are not recorded against them, a lunatic till he (or she) is
> restored to reason, a person who is asleep until he (or she)
> awakens and a boy (or girl) until he (or she) becomes *baligh*
> (mature) . . . Why [then] is it that this woman is being
> stoned?[434]

It should be noted that there is no religious requirement for a Muslim to come forward to confess his or her sin. In fact, he or she is encouraged to hide it and not reveal it. This is in accordance with the Hadiths of the Holy Prophets (and other textual proofs as well).[435]

The person who confesses to having committed *zina* is encouraged to simply repent of the sin, as "God is Most Forgiving." In a tradition narrated in the Hadith compilation of Saḥīḥ al-Bukhari, Number 6439 narrates that "a man confessed the sin of adultery/fornication to the prophet Muhammad (ﷺ).[436] However, the latter kept turning his face away from the confessor, wishing not to hear it. Such was the reluctance of the prophet

---

hudud punishments in cases of doubts or ambiguities: Judicial knowledge is insufficient evidence to establish a crime, he said; and with no direct or corroborating evidence (i.e., a confession or four eyewitnesses to the act), the matter is sufficiently doubtful to avoid the sanction (p. 152). See Whitman, *Origins of Reasonable Doubt*, 10.

433. Kadish, *Encyclopedia of Crime and Justice*, 193. See also O'Kane and Radtke, *Concept of Sainthood*.

434. Ramadan, *Understanding Islamic Law*, 63; see also Kamali, *Textbook of Hadīth Studies*.

435. Owens et al., *Religion and the Death Penalty*.

436. Caner and Caner, *Unveiling Islam*.

Muhammad (ﷺ), when it came to enforcing such harsh punishments."[437]
This event demonstrates the emphasis the Prophet placed on trying to avert
legal punishment as much as possible. The man came and confessed to the
Messenger of Allah سبحانه و تعالى that because "he had engaged in culpable
sexual relationship, the Messenger of Allah سبحانه و تعالى discountenanced
him, in order that he might alter his mind."[438] The custom of affirming the
iniquity of infidelity or illegal sexual intercourse is discouraged, so as to
avoid the need to implement these stringent retributions.

It is believed that God covers up a person's sins in the same way that
clothing covers up a person's nudity and private parts. For instance, in the
story above, God concealed this man's transgression, but the man refused to
leave the matter alone, choosing to be stoned like a dog.[439] It was narrated
in a Hadith that "repentance is a matter between a person and his Lord, it
is better for the person than confessing his sin before a *Khadi* (judge)."[440]
It is recommended that one who commits *zina* suppress his blunder and
let no one know of it, choosing instead to turn to Allah سبحانه و تعالى in
sincere repentance. For instance, when the *hadd* (prescribed punishment)
was enforced on Ma'iz for committing *zina*, a member of the community
pursed him in order to punish him as he contemplated running away. When
the Prophet heard of this, he disapproved and said, "Why didn't you let him
go? Perhaps he would have made repentance and Allah سبحانه و تعالى would
have accepted his repentance."[441] The Prophet of Islam was full of mercy and
compassion and never rushed to judgment, always giving a second chance
and an opportunity for repentance. Just as he said, "Whoever commits any
of these awful sins (*qadhurat*), let him conceal himself with the concealment

---

437. Ponomareff and Bryson, *Curve of the Sacred*, 21.
438. Ramadan, *Understanding Islamic Law*, 64. See also Saḥīḥ al-Bukhari, no. 6439, narrated
by Abu Huraira.
439. Saḥīḥ al-Bukhari, bk. 38, no. 4414, narrated by Abu Huraira: "A man of the tribe
of Aslam came . . . " (Hallaq, *Shari'a*, 132). See also Yust, *Nourishing Child and Adolescent
Spirituality*, 355; and Abdul-Rahman, *Jurisprudence and Islamic Ruling*, 197.
440. Abdul-Rahman, *Islamic History and Biography*, 32.
441. Ibid.

of Allah سبحانه و تعالى, for verily, whoever exposes his action to us (*man abda lana safhatahu*), we will impose the *hadd* punishment upon him."[442]

Four Witnesses

The Golden Rule of proof in Islamic law procedure is that the onus of proof is on the person who makes the assertion. Proof in *zina* cases is even more stringent concerning the requirement that four adult males witness the act of *zina* at the same time. However, Woerlee suggests that the difficulty of attaining this requirement means, "Four witnesses will be impossible to get for conviction."[443]

Regarding the necessity of four eye witnesses, some have argued that stoning was a common form of execution at the time of the Prophet, and that it was rooted in Rabbinic/Jewish tradition.[444] Those who support this assertion cite Deuteronomy 21:18–21 and 17:1–7, Numbers 35, and Revelation 11:3–13, which state that a man shall be put to death on the testimony of two or three witnesses, but no one shall be put to death on the testimony of only one witness.[445] In order to be found guilty of adultery, according to the Old Testament, there had to be two witnesses of good character who would testify against the adulterers. In the Old Testament, the book of Leviticus likewise states that the adulterer and the adulteress are to be put to death.[446] Subsequently, through the Prophet, God made the evidentiary requirements for *zina* even more stringent, as the burden of proof was raised from two to four witnesses. In this manner, the people were shielded from severe punishments.

It has been suggested that the extension of the witnesses, from two to four, took place at a time when women were frequently alleged to have

---

442. Hallaq, *Introduction to Islamic Law*.
443. Woerlee, *Unholy Legacy of Abraham*, 235. Doi also opined that from the beginning of the Islamic predication, and during the life of the Prophet, not one single case of adultery was established by the evidence of four eyewitnesses (*Women in Shariah*, 122). See also Mir-Hosseini, *Marriage and Trial*, 32.
444. Burton, "Origin of the Islamic Penalty," 26.
445. The Holy Bible, New International Version.
446. Ibid., Lev. 24:6–10.

committed fornication, adultery, and harlotry.[447] Even if a woman could not be convicted of the charges, her reputation (and life) would be impaired forever. To prevent this from happening, the Qur'an stipulated that not only was the burden of proof being raised to four witnesses, but if a man accused a woman of sexual immorality with anything less than this, the man would be punished for *qadhf* (slander), as based on verses 24:4–5 of the Qur'an:[448]

> And those who accuse chaste women and then do not produce four witnesses lash them with eighty lashes and do not accept from them testimony ever after. And those are the defiantly disobedient, except for those who repent thereafter and reform, for indeed, Allah is Forgiving and Merciful.

Where there has been an allegation of *zina*, not only must the accuser substantiate the allegation by way of four unimpeachable eyewitnesses, but also each witness must swear to Allah سبحانه و تعالى that he witnessed the act and must call down the torment of Allah سبحانه و تعالى upon himself if he is not stating the actual facts of the matter. Furthermore, the four witnesses must describe the offense in no uncertain terms, such as explicitly stating: "I saw his penis in her vagina."[449] There is no alternative interpretation to this statement. Contrarily, if they say, "We saw him on top of her and they were naked," that is not acceptable. Even if they say, "We saw him doing with her what a man does with his wife," that is not sufficient testimony. They must say explicitly, "We bear witness that his penis was in her vagina."[450]

Needless to say, this is quite a difficult thing to witness. When a man attempted to testify against someone in the days of the second Caliph Umar, the Caliph had this to say: If you were among the (four) thighs (the two

---

447. Shah, *Women, the Koran*, 130; see also Masters and Lee, *Anti-Sex*.
448. Peters, *Crime and Punishment*, 63.
449. Dāwūd, *Abū Dādūd Sulaymān*, 59; see also Hadith of Hanafi: al-Ikhtiyar li talil al-Mukhtar, 2/312–313.
450. Dāwūd, *Abū Dādūd Sulaymān ibn al-Ashdath al-Sijistānī: Third Correct Tradition of the Prophetic Sunna*, 59.

thighs of the accused) you would never be able to give this testimony.[451] The renowned Islamic scholar Shaykh al-Islam Ibn Taymiyah mentioned that no case of *zina* was proven by means of testimony from the time of the Prophet until his own time many centuries later.[452] According to one interpretation, because no case was proven in earlier times, there is then no known case of adultery proven by testimony.

The stringent requirement that these four witnesses be male, Muslim, and of good character hardly seems attainable, according to one argument. Being able to give such detailed and explicit witness to the act of *zina* immediately calls into question that person's character. What person of good character stares at the private parts of others? After all, if the four witnesses were voyeuristically gazing upon the private parts of others in sexual embrace without averting their gaze, then they might not be considered to be people of good character.[453] Concealing the weakness of another is a prominent theme of the moral teachings of Qur'an and Sunnah. Islam puts emphasis on the honor and dignity of the individual and his or her rights to privacy from the encroachment of others. Thus, the Hadith states: "if a person conceals the weakness of another in this world, God will conceal their weakness in the Hereafter."[454]

In the same manner, a Muslim should help another to uphold honor and dignity in the path of good character and, where necessary, admonish sinners to cease and desist from sinning. Rigorous evidentiary requirements sometimes create a heavy burden of proof; it is in actuality quite difficult for anyone to be brought forth for the crime of *zina* that requires the evidence of four witnesses with unimpeachable character. This is especially true when upon examination a Muslim, by the wisdom of the Holy Prophet understands that

---

451. Akbar, *Authenticity of Quran*, 120; see also Browning et al., *Sex, Marriage, and Family*, 209.
452. Salahi, *Muhammad*, 200.
453. "Tell the believing men to lower their gaze and be modest. . . . " (Qur'an 24:30–31).
454. Kamali, *Freedom of Expression*, 123–24.

He who removes from a believer one of his difficulties of this world, Allah سبحانه و تعالى will remove one of his troubles on the Day of Resurrection; and he who finds relief for a hard-pressed person, Allah سبحانه و تعالى will make things easy for him on the Day of Resurrection; he who covers up (the faults and sins) of a Muslim, Allah سبحانه و تعالى will cover up (his faults and sins) in this world and in the Hereafter. Allah سبحانه و تعالى supports His slave as long as the slave is supportive of his brother . . .[455]

It is instructive that the Qur'an unambiguously states:

O you, who have believed, avoid much [negative] assumption. Indeed, some assumption is sin. And do not spy or backbite each other. Would one of you like to eat the flesh of his brother when dead? You would detest it. And fear Allah; indeed, Allah is accepting of repentance and Merciful. (49:12)

What goes on in the privacy of one's own bedroom between two consenting adults by cover of night is not the business of the state or another person. As the holy prophet Muhammad (صلى الله عليه وسلم) declared,

All of my community will be fine except for those who commit sin openly. Part of committing sin openly is when a man does something at night and God conceals it, but in the morning he says, 'O So-and-so, last night I did such and such.' His Lord had covered his sin all night, but in the morning he removed the cover of God.[456]

A similar tale exists from the time of the second Caliph of Islam: a man came to the Prophet and said, "O Apostle of God! I have mingled

---

455. Iqbal, *General Takaful Practice*, 64; and M. Z. Khan, *Gardens of the Righteous*, 60.
456. Eaton, *Islam and the Destiny*, 177; see also Al-Mubarakpuri et al., *Tafsir ibn Kathir*, 204; and Ibn al-Hajjaj, *Sahih Muslim*, 84.

with a woman in the outskirts of Medina . . . So, here am I; judge me according to what you decide." Umar bin Khattab replied: "God had kept your secret! Why then didn't you?"[457] Intruding into the private realm of a person is both inappropriate and incongruous. Islam values one's private space and forbids any authority from spying on its populace. Accordingly, the privacy of any and all person's homes must be reverenced by all others and is sacred, such that even looking through windows to view the activities of others inside a household or elsewhere is forbidden. In addition to the words of the Caliph (leader) of the Muslims, the Qur'an says sanctity of the private life is untouchable (49:12; 24:27).

Another story is told of the second Caliph, Umar ibn al-Khattab, who was once walking on the streets of Medina at night. Suddenly he heard noise coming from one of the houses, a noise suggesting that somebody was drunk and singing loudly. Umar climbed over the wall, entered the house, and witnessed a very disappointing situation. He complained of the situation to the man inside, and said,

> "Did you think that God would allow you to hide this fault of yours?" The man replied, "O Caliph of the Muslims, stop and don't rush. I committed one sin in the eyes of God; however, you have made three mistakes here. First of all, God says, do not spy on one another, Qur'an 49:12, but you spied on me. Second, God says, come to dwellings (in the normal way) by their doors, Qur'an 2:189, but you climbed over my wall. Finally, God says, O you who believe! Do not enter dwellings other than your own until you have ascertained the permission of their residents and have greeted them with peace, Qur'an 24:27, but you entered my house without getting my permission and you did not greet me with peace."[458]

---

457. Abdul-Rahman, *Jurisprudence and Islamic Ruling*, 201; Hashimi, *Ideal Muslim*, 230; see also Hadith 40 by Ṣaḥīḥ al-Bukhari and Ṣaḥīḥ al-Muslim.
458. Campo, *Other Sides of Paradise*, 65. Umar ibn al-Khattab is one of the great

Umar was very upset with himself and replied, "If I forgive you, will you forgive me?" The man said, "Yes." Then Umar said, "I forgive you," and left the house. "And God is most forgiving, most Merciful."[459] These stories illustrate the right to privacy that one should enjoy within one's home. According to the teachings of the Qur'an and these various other sources, it seems to be nearly impossible that one could bear witness to the crime of *zina* (by observing the act of penetration) and still be considered a Muslim of good character.

Pregnancy

Some jurists have mentioned pregnancy as a proof of *zina* in the case of an unmarried woman. However, pregnancy alone cannot be used to prove the crime of *zina* and justify its punishment of death by stoning. *Zina* is also commonly defined as follows:

> Union or insertion of the male sexual organ into the female sexual organs between those who are not legally married, or sexual intercourse of a man with a woman who is not his wife, and whereon valid reason exists to believe that the sexual act was committed under the misapprehension that she was his wife.[460]

Whichever definition is adopted, the key word, especially in light of modern means of insemination, is *penetration*. In our modern era of advanced technology, pregnancy may occur in different ways, even though sexual contact may not involve actual penetration. For instance, women today can become pregnant apart from any direct contact with the opposite

---

Companions of the Prophet and second Caliph of Islam. He was so firm in his practice of Islam that he usually could sense what was right or wrong before the Prophet had informed others of it.

459. *Journal of the Research Society of Pakistan*, 25; see also Kanzu'l-Ummal, 3/808 Hadith no. 8827.

460. El-Rouayheb, *Before Homosexuality*, 137; see also Shahnaz Khan, *Zina, Transnational Feminism*, 137.

sex. Artificial insemination has become an attractive option for women who cannot conceive naturally or, for women who would like to have a child but may not want a "union" or committed relationship with a man. A woman experiencing related declines in her fertility—the proverbial biological clock—may want to enjoy motherhood, even if she does not have a partner. One such woman was Anne-Marie, who through artificial insemination "conceived her first son, Pierre, and gave birth to him in November 2002."[461] Should she be punished or even accused of misconduct simply because of her strong desire to have children?

Many "knowledgeable Muslims" would answer "no" to this question and others like it. In his book *al-Mughnî*, Ibn Qudamah writes, "If a woman becomes pregnant without having a husband or a master, she may not be punished, but instead, she should be asked about it. If she claims that she was coerced into it or that she committed adultery unaware, *under dubious circumstances*, or if she simply does not confess to adultery, then she should not be punished."[462] Abu Hanîfah and al-Shâfi'î concur with Ibn Qudamah in his statement above.

Additional alternative methods of insemination without penetration exist. For instance, a woman could engage in impermissible sexual conduct short of vaginal penetration, which is sometimes referred to as "digital penetration," during which the man might ejaculate on her upper thighs, causing some semen to enter into her private parts.[463] Even though there has been no penetration, she could still become pregnant. However, she still could not rightly fall under the punishment for stoning, since without any actual penetration having occurred, her situation would fall outside the ambit of the legal provision for *zina*. Instances also abound where a woman may have been raped or had sexual relations while temporarily insane or even asleep. Some of the clients I have represented tell of experiences of this nature. Where such *shubha* (doubts) exist as to the circumstances of a

---

461. See Meyer, *Wandering Uterus*, 12.
462. Vogel, *Islamic Law and Legal System*, 245.
463. Turner v. State, 710 So.2d 688 (1998).

pregnancy, the court should not be shy in settling the case in favor of the accused. This doctrine of *shubha* is based on a saying of the Prophet: God's sanction will not be applied in cases where there is room for doubt; such as punishment fixed in the Qur'an and Hadith for crimes considered being against the rights of God.[464] *Hadd* is suspended in cases where there is any ambiguity as to facts and proofs.[465] As Prophet Muhammad (ﷺ) teaches: "Abandon doubt in favor of that which is not doubtful" and "whoever abandons the shubha purifies his faith and his honor."[466]

With respect to pregnancy as proof of adultery, one scholar succinctly described the situation thusly: "If pregnancy is allowed as proof, the woman-affirming spirit of the Qur'an verses is lost."[467] Further, "the protective nature of the Qur'an toward women is also lost if circumstantial evidence is permitted to be admitted for conviction of crimes with such severe punishments."[468] Punishment should be abandoned in cases where doubt exists. As briefly discussed above, it is well known that a woman can become pregnant without engaging in true intercourse (involving penetration). It has also been suggested that the *hadd* is to be administered in the lands of Islam, under the auspices of the Imam or Caliph of the Muslims.[469]

While the Qur'an condemns illegitimate sexual bonds, it promotes individual privacy and the rights of women. To bridge this gap and link these Qur'anic doctrines, it is important to recognize the moral point that *zina* is an unacceptable crime, but one can only be punished if the crime can be proven. For the most part, the issue of *zina* should be dealt with between a person and God, in repentance.[470] The law is meant to serve as a deterrent to prevent people from committing unlawful actions and

---

464. Schabas and Hodgkinson, *Capital Punishment*, 180.

465. Ikkaracan, *Deconstructing Sexuality*, 26.

466. Kamali, *Freedom of Expression*, 11; see also Ibn al-Qayyim, 1983. Note also that upholding the truth is protection from doubt (Qur'an 103:3).

467. Quraishi, "Her Honor," 116.

468. Ibid.

469. Abdul-Rahman, *Meaning and Explanation*, 434.

470. Harris, "Reading the Signs," 192; see also Abdul-Rahman, *Meaning and Explanation*, 434.

corrupting society.[471] While punishment is often credited with making deterrence effective, societies should strive to protect people from severe punishments as much as possible without compromising the law. In the preservation of justice, it is preferable for a judge to be inaccurate in law, in favor of exoneration, than in favor of conviction.[472] "The Islamic state does not encourage the persecution of every sin by the implementation of strict Shariah punishments. Based on the traditions of the prophet Muhammad (ﷺ), neither Muslims nor the Islamic state should actively seek to enforce criminal penalties."[473]

The sacredness of human life is central in Islam.[474] The murder of an innocent person is deemed to be a crime against the entire human race. Conversely, when a life is saved, it is as though the life of all mankind is saved. In this way, the Qur'an places an immense importance on the value of human life (5:32). The Islamic culture promotes an understanding of the need to respect the dignity of all human life. While different cultures and religions may have widely differing views pertaining to morality, fairness, and justice, there are also large areas in which these religions overlap. Allah سبحانه و تعالى Most High told us in the Qur'an:

> Say, O my servants who have wronged themselves: despair
> not of Allah's mercy; surely Allah forgives all sins; surely, He
> is most merciful and compassionate. (39:53).

This verse is often recognized as the most hope inspiring verse in the Qur'an (arja ayatin fi kitabi llah). It affirms that no matter how great our sin, the door of repentance is always open; Allah سبحانه و تعالى loves to forgive. Through this forgiveness, the one who repents from his sin is like the one who did not sin in the first place.[475] Instead of immediately turning to the harshest punishments, sincere repentance should first be explored.

---

471. Kamali, *Principles of Islamic Jurisprudence*, 431.
472. Bouhidiba and Dawālībī, *Different Aspects of Islamic Culture*, 66.
473. Daniels et al., *Criminal Justice in Islam*, 63.
474. Abu-Nimer, *Nonviolence and Peace Building*, 59.
475. Qur'an 39:53; Abdul-Rahman, *Jurisprudence and Islamic Ruling*, 207; see also

Defense Counsel's Role at Trial

Shariah courts in Nigeria are still considered to be in their infancy, with the legal procedural process having not been established in an entirely clear manner. Often, this results in procedural mistakes made by prosecutors and defense attorneys alike. When defending clients, always verify the prosecutor's filing of the case to ensure that certain standards were adhered to. Check to make certain that the charges include the required information: the name and address of the accused, a description and gender of the accused, the exact nature of the charges, where and when the alleged offense was said to have occurred, how the offense was committed, and with whom the offense was committed. Where these are absent, raise objections with regard to due process and thus weaken the prosecution's case.

Among first steps in the preparation of any case is to familiarize oneself with all the issues raised in your case, and compare them to the prosecution. Looking at the charges filed against the accused can assist the defense attorney. What law did the accused break? What elements of the offense were proven at trial and what issues were not addressed at trial that will be issues raised in the appeal? At the outset of each case, identify the strengths of your case and recognize the broad range of arguments the prosecution may have posited against it. For example, if the prosecution did not state when the offense was committed and with whom the offense was committed, and failed to submit a record or evidence indicating whether the accused was married or not (as in Ms. Lawal's case), you have a good starting point for the appeal.

"al-Tirmidhi (3540) narrated that Anas ibn Maalik (may Allah be pleased with him) said: I heard the Messenger of Allah سبحانه و تعالى (peace and blessings of Allah be upon him) say: 'Allah سبحانه و تعالى, may He be blessed and exalted, said: O son of Adam, so long as you call upon Me and ask of Me, I shall forgive you for what you have done, and I shall not mind. O son of Adam, were your sins to reach the clouds of the sky and were you then to ask forgiveness of Me, I would forgive you and I would not mind.'" Classed as saheeh by al-Albaani in Saheeh al-Tirmidhi Also: "Ibn Maajah narrated that Abd-Allah ibn Mas'ood (may Allah be pleased with him) said: The Messenger of Allah (peace and blessings of Allah be upon him) said: 'The one who repents from sin is like one who did not sin.' Classed as hasan by al-Albaani in Saheeh Ibn Maajah."

In preparation for a defense case, a lawyer should consider laying out the four issues—fact, law, procedure, and technicalities—clearly. For example:

> Fact: Did Ms. Lawal commit *zina* as alleged? When, with whom, and how?

> Law: Did she break any law? Which law?

> Procedure: Was Ms. Lawal supposed to report her "transgression" to the court? To a judge? Who should prosecute her?

> Technicalities: At the time she committed the offense, was there a law in place that criminalizes an act of pregnancy without an alleged husband?

Become familiar with the facts of the case, both known and unknown. This is where team input becomes relevant. Research into the case will provide answers to the questions: Who? What? When? Where? How? Ask who is in the panel adjudicating the case on appeal, and who are the other members of the court of appeal? How much of the Shariah law are they familiar with? It is pertinent that the arguments not be formulated with a convoluted language and boring analysis; you do not want to lose the attention of the judges in the middle of an important appeal. Striking a balance between too little and too much presentation is always a challenge. Working from the familiar to the less familiar and back to the familiar when arguing cases is always useful. Avoid as much as possible abstract concepts or too much assay; at times it may be considered a sort of "show off" and judges' attentiveness may be limited in this respect.

When a court is tense or circumstances surrounding a particular hearing are stretched tight, strive to defamiliarize the subject matter by introducing persuasive arguments that do not necessarily argue points of law. Utilizing nonlegal arguments will help smooth moments that strain upon nerves in court. Endeavor to express the intensity of your ideas and feelings and establish a bond of understanding between disputants that is otherwise hard to attain. When in harm's way, think and prepare for an exit strategy readily available prior to adjudication in the event that the situation or environment becomes unfriendly. This general *modus operandi* will allow lawyers to be well prepared in the successful defense of clients.

In applying a firm understanding of the above-mentioned legal concepts, it is important for defense counsel to open its case with a strong witness who will make a lasting impression upon those present. Take full advantage of the "doctrines of primacy," which avers that people are inclined to believe what they learn first and gravitate toward what they hear last.[476] Place witnesses with weaker testimonies between two strong "bookend witnesses." Where required, use visual aids with witnesses that are unable to read or write; but do not overdo it. Try to keep the court's attention by using illustrative images and narratives from a familiar context. Generally, avoid calling the accused as a witness; in *zina* cases the fundamental requirement of four witnesses should acquit or convict the accused once the four witnesses present themselves as they are typically required to do.

Avoid giving the prosecution opportunities to cross-examine the accused in the same manner as any other defense witness, as this can lead to a situation where the accused could potentially damage their own case. According to the Shariah penal code, the judge may intervene at any stage to question a witness.[477] Since the accused are often illiterate and unfamiliar with the proceedings and techniques of the courtroom, they may unintentionally incriminate themselves, whether guilty or not. Finally, try to anchor key points in a common theme and, where useful, you may wish to spring exhibits admitted into evidence on your opponents at the last minute to maximize their effectiveness.

In addressing any apparent weaknesses in the case, endeavor to demonstrate to the court how these weaknesses are immaterial. In the hopes of further influencing their decision, comment on the applicable law relating to issues the court may wish to consider. Conclude by returning to

---

476. Lubet, *Modern Trial Advocacy*, 17.
477. Sokoto State Shariah Criminal Procedure Code Law, 2000, Section 162.

the substance of the case and the client's exigency; you may wish to abide by the ten commandments of argumentation:[478]

1. Thou shall argue your case before the judge, not at him.
2. Thou shall use a logical outline and logical reasoning.
3. With dignity, thou shall speak the truth at all times.[479]
4. Thou shall create crafty engaging arguments: don't beat a dead horse by excessively repeating the same words and pushing the limits.
5. Thou shall lean on the law always.
6. Thou shall use evidence, witnesses, and exhibits to enhance your arguments and increase clarity.
7. Thou shall undermine the opposition for the common good.
8. Thou shall tell stories and use analogies where needed.
9. Thou shall listen to the judge.
10. Thou shall be yourself.

Producing a thorough record of events surrounding the criminal charge is crucial. This record should explain incriminating evidence, motivations, timelines, and any other statement their client plans to make regarding the case. Most important, however, is open communication and collaborative effort between the accused and their attorneys. Without full candor between the two, a comprehensive and effective defense cannot be constructed. These considerations, among others, all enter into a defense attorney's overall strategy. Strategies may be supplemented, altered, or changed during the course of a trial as necessary.

A particularly difficult aspect of the role of defense counsel involves confessions of the accused. The Sokoto State Shariah Criminal Procedure Code Law (SSSCPCL) of 2000 provides guidance regarding the procedure to be adopted in Shariah courts, stating *inter alia:* Where a case is set for

---

478. These commandments were culled from Moses's "Ten Commandments." This author added some of them.

479. Truth is an attribute of Allah سبحانه و نتعالى (God). See S. H. Nasr, *Philosophy, Literature and Fine Arts,* 39.

trial and the accused is present in court, the particulars of the offense shall be stated to the accused and the accused shall be asked if he or she has any cause to show why he or she should not be convicted; if the accused admits a commission of the offense . . . the court may convict him.[480]

However, prior to conviction the court must satisfy itself that the accused understood the details and essentials of the offense.[481] The court must further inform the accused of his or her right to retract his or her admission.[482] This section of the law outlines the court's ability to convict the accused based on a confession if they have not exercised their right to retract such a confession. It allows the lawyers to make the case for acquittal or discharge based on evidence before it. Meanwhile, Section 154 provides for the ability of the court to call witnesses. When an accused states that he/she intends to show cause as to why he/she should not be convicted, the court must proceed to hear the complainant.

The court should also take into account all such evidence as may be produced in support of the prosecution. The court must then ascertain from the complainant or otherwise the names of any persons likely to be acquainted with the facts of that case; the prosecution must do likewise and the court must summon any such witnesses that it deems necessary to give evidence before the court. The accused should be at liberty to cross-examine any witnesses for the prosecution; if he does so, then the prosecutor may re-examine them.[483] Commonly, the burden of proof in criminal cases rests solely with the prosecution; it is not the responsibility of the accused to prove his or her innocence or guilt.[484]

In the event that a case actually goes to trial before a Shariah court, before a plea is taken and recorded, the law provides for the reading of the drafted charge in court to the accused in a language the accused can

---

480. SSSCPCL, Section 152.
481. Ibid., Sections 152 and 153.
482. Ibid., Section 157(3).
483. SSSCPCL.
484. R. McMahon, *Practical Handbook*, 183.

easily understand.[485] The Shariah court may, at its discretion, convict the accused upon a plea of guilty[486] after the court has satisfied itself that the accused has understood the details of the charge and the consequences of the plea.[487] In those instances where the case needs to proceed after the plea, the processes for the examination and cross-examination of witnesses as well as evidentiary procedures is outlined in Section 158 of the Sokoto Code. If it is found that no substantial case can be made against the accused after examination of all the evidence, the court shall order an acquittal that prevents the accused from ever being tried for the same offense again. Note, however, that if the court only orders a discharge, then the accused can be subsequently arraigned and tried all over again.

Also noteworthy are Sections 169 and 170 of the SSSCPCL, which prescribe that the criminal charges must be laid out in a set form; charges must contain a statement of the offense complaint, and the date and place of the offense.

Furthermore, all trials in Shariah courts must be held in open court, where the public has full access to the proceedings.[488] Also, Section 191 of the SSSCPCL provides that "a legal practitioner shall have the right to practice in the Shariah court in accordance with the provision of the Legal Practitioner's Act of 1990." This section is of much significance or consequence in light of the challenges colleagues from Southern Nigeria faced when they came to support the legal team in a case being heard in a Shariah court. They were turned away on the excuse that their appearance was not in compliance with Shariah. In light of both spoken and unspoken complexities, lawyers will do well to show sensitivity and decorum to courts and abide by professional etiquette. However, as lawyers we are entitled to practice in all courts in Nigeria as provided for by law.

---

485. SSSCPCL, 2000, Section 153.
486. Ibid., Section 157(2). See also, Kamali, *Freedom of Expression*, 210.
487. SSSCPCL, Section 160.
488. Ibid., Section 190.

Another section of particular interest for the defense counsel(s) is Section 193 of the SSSCPCL, which includes the accused taking the Islamic oath as provided for also in the Qur'an.[489] This oath, which is distinct from oaths under the common law system, is to be taken only by a person of the Muslim faith and is to be administered in a prescribed way as stated in the case of *Ummah v. Bafullace*.[490] The oath has to be taken in Allah's name or in his attributes and the one taking the oath must be capable and well disposed. The benefit of taking the oath is that in doing so the accused is released of all charges. In most cases a woman is not given the opportunity to take the oath.

Section 128 of SSSCPCL allows for issues to be raised on point of law, with the leave of the Attorney General of the state, and referred to the Shariah Court of Appeal for advisement. For example, where a woman denies an allegation of *zina*, she should be administered the same oath as the man. It is worthy of note that in Ms. Lawal's case, the co-accused denied the allegation of *zina* and was administered the oath and later discharged. Ms. Lawal, and indeed almost all of our female clients, were never given the same opportunity to take the oath. Javed Ahmad Ghamidi suggests, in addition, that oaths be sworn four times, for each person taking the oath.[491] Section 226 of SSSCPCL, 2000, provides that in every trial judgment shall be delivered in writing and pronounced in a language understood by the

---

489. Qur'an 2:224–226: "And do not make [your oath by] Allah an excuse against being righteous and fearing Allah and making peace among people. And Allah is Hearing and Knowing; Allah does not impose blame upon you for what is unintentional in your oaths, but He imposes blame upon you for what your hearts have earned. And Allah is Forgiving and Forbearing. For those who swear not to have sexual relations with their wives is a waiting time of four months, but if they return [to normal relations]—then indeed, Allah is Forgiving and Merciful." Qur'an 3:77: "Indeed, those who exchange the covenant of Allah and their [own] oaths for a small price will have no share in the Hereafter, and Allah will not speak to them or look at them on the Day of Resurrection, nor will He purify them; and they will have a painful punishment."

490. (1997) 11 NWLR (pt. 529) 363 CA.

491. Ghamidi, *Oaths and Their Atonement*, 6. See Ṣaḥīḥ al-Bukhari, bk. 18, no. 4245, where Abdullah Ibn Abbas reported that Allah's Messenger (may peace be upon him) pronounced judgment on the basis of oath by the defendant. See also Lippman et al., *Islamic Criminal Law and Procedure*, 71.

accused in open court; and Section 227 speaks to what a judgment should contain. This becomes especially important, of course, for a lawyer taking a case to the appellate court.

Other sections of the Shariah penal code law address the carrying out of sentences. Section 228 states that *hudud* (capital punishment) and *qiyas* (retaliation) penalties shall not be imposed on an underage person (age of *taklif*).[492] Section 231 addresses the death sentence, including beheading and *lex talionis*, requiring that the accused die in the same manner by which he caused his victim to die. Also legislated is death by stoning in the case of *zina* and death by crucifixion in the case of *hirabah* (robbery/terrorism) where death was caused and property seized.[493] Section 246 also deals with issues surrounding executions, while Section 248 offers an affirmation of the sentence of death, speaking to other areas of focus where planning involves issues of technicalities.

Technicalities of Shariah Law

A "technicality" refers to the quality or condition of being technical. It represents something meaningful or relevant predominantly to a specialist. The term can also denote an obscure point of law. Often the legal doctrine that prevails here is the "fruit of the poisonous tree," which means that anything obtained from a tainted source is also tainted itself. The rule is that evidence that has been obtained in violation of the Constitution or other laws and regulations must be kept out of the trial.

Ms. Lawal's case was settled primarily on legal technicalities. First, there was no law against *zina* in existence when she allegedly committed the offense; second, the trial court record did not indicate the time, place, and date the offense occurred as required by law; and third, the fact that the trial court record did not indicate that Ms. Lawal was married.[494] General

---

492. See Lippman et al., *Islamic Criminal Law and Procedure*, 45. Worthy of note is that there are seven offenses that carry hudud punishments, including stoning, flogging, amputation, cross amputation, crucifixion, beheading, and life imprisonment.

493. SSSCPCL, Section 155(d).

494. See The State v. Amina Lawal. See also Salama, *Islamic Criminal Jurisdiction System*,

principles of law require that in order to charge an individual with an offense, the alleged violation of law must be "on the books" prior to the commission of the alleged offense.

The Shariah penal code of Katsina (which provided for *zina* as a criminal offense) came into law on June 20, 2001, after Ms. Lawal allegedly committed her offense. Procedural technicalities must be strictly adhered to in courts of law, otherwise evidence may be barred from being introduced, or the case may even be thrown out. At trial, all of these technicalities ultimately worked in Ms. Lawal's favor. While the technicalities listed above served as the main errors on which the trial was focused, attention should be paid to other technicalities that may arise during the course of trial. Court errors, such as failure to provide an interpreter, or someone giving evidence that had not been duly sworn in by the court, should be noted. Circumstances in which evidence/documents were admitted into evidence that were from an unverifiable source or that had not been maintained within a proper chain of custody (which could result in a reversal of a conviction on appeal), should also be noted.

However, in rendering decisions on several other cases, the Supreme Court of Nigeria has stood by its stated principle that "mere legal technicalities must be done away with, with a view to dispensing justice to all parties in dispute and most importantly, to the larger society."[495] This principle expresses the idea that mere technicalities should not become an occasion for throwing out the plain demands of justice. Justice can only be done if the substance of a matter is examined. Reliance on procedural technicalities alone to prevent the examination of the substantive merits of a case can quickly lead to injustice. Therefore, courts now insist on the attainment of substantial justice where it is within their discretion to so determine.[496] The case of *Shell Petroleum Development Company Nigeria Limited v. Udi*, states that discretion must be exercised judicially and judiciously; it must be patently

---

where similar opinions on technicalities were expressed.
495. Kamaruzaman, *Understanding Islam*, 293.
496. Chief Jonathan Dosunmu v. Alimi Akanbi Dada (2002) 13 NWLR (pt. 783) 1 at 23.

clear from the record where the discretion of the court is called for one way or the other, and the court should bear in mind the requirement that justice be secured for both parties, and also that it is in the interest of justice that the hearing of a case not be unduly delayed.[497]

This sentiment of the court decision is also reflected in its statements surrounding *A.G. Lagos v. A.G. Federation*[498] per Uwais (Chief Justice of Nigeria at the time):

> Be that as it may, it should be borne in mind that we are in this case concerned with the interpretation of the Constitution. The inconsistency and confusion notwithstanding, this Court has since laid down the principle that in interpreting the Constitution we should not allow mere technicalities to overrule the manifest demands of justice.[499]

Additionally, in the case of *Egolum v. Obasanjo*,[500] Achike JSC held that "the heydays of technicality are now over because the weight of judicial authorities has shifted from undue reliance on technicalities to rendering substantial justice evenhandedly to all parties."[501]

Working Within

An important aspect of handling Shariah cases is how one reconciles a potential dichotomy between personal beliefs and the principles of law. When handling potentially capital cases, we made conscious efforts to engage the other side in friendly dialogue. Through approaching conversations in a nonconfrontational manner, we were able to proceed peacefully and keep the attention on the issues of the case, and circumvent any nonproductive confrontation between legal advocates that might have arisen. We purposefully engaged in this manner with as many individuals

---

497. (Nig) Ltd. v. Udi (1996) 6 NWLR (pt. 8 455) 483 at 496–97.
498. (2004) 18 NWLR (pt. 904) 1 at 75–76, para. F–C.
499. SC 70/2004.
500. Appeal No. CA/L/EPT/LAS/NA/001/2007.
501. Per, Monica Bolna'an Dongban-Mensem JCA, JP.

who opposed our position as possible, even those who thought our work was anti-Islam or anti-Shariah. This allowed us to identify common ground between both sides and to foster a positive atmosphere during face-to-face meetings. As a result, these friendly discussions added value to our case and benefited our clients by helping to reduce tensions.

People who disagreed with us on issues of the law were not necessarily our adversaries. In fact, we operated on the premise that we had no adversaries. It was our position that anyone who disagreed with us had a right to so do. Instead of ignoring these individuals, we tried to make allies out of people who were willing to hear us out, knowing that we all share a common destiny and have many shared values. We also sought out intermediaries who could help extend the hand of fellowship by initiating discussions with people who disagreed with us. We assumed humble postures and avoided being disrespectful, especially when we were granted an audience with the elders of a community. After all, our culture has taught us that a child cannot see what an elder has seen, nor could he even imagine that which the elder has witnessed with his own two eyes. As the Hausa proverb states: *Abunda babba yagani yaro koya hau bene bazai gani ba*—If an elderly person could stand on the flattest surface to view an object, a young adult, even if he climbed the tallest building, will not be able to see.

When planning strategically, it is essential not to lose sight of general societal perceptions. In many societies, women symbolize honor and chastity and are the custodians of a culture's tradition and values. Such perceptions were said to be a motivating factor behind the introduction of the new Shariah: the protection of women. Unfortunately, such protection has in some ways resulted in degrading and reducing the status of women. It is important that religious structures, leaders, and the entire society remain on the path of creating harmony, recognize the value of the woman in society, and emphasize those things that unite us across religions. While this may be a slow, gradual process, it represents the future.

Although defense plans may be executed individually, I believe that they should be executed collectively. A team approach has generally resulted in stronger and more positive outcomes for clients. In our initial cases, lawyers and nongovernmental organizations (NGOs) collaborated. The "strategic team" put together by Baobab, the group that gave the most legal assistance and support, especially in the case of Safiya Hussaini Tugar Tudu, got to see her later discharged and acquitted. Without the team, her story would have been different.

Conclusion

Preparation and planning are essential elements to the successful defense of any case, and especially Shariah cases. As ministers in the temple of justice, our responsibility to our clients is to make sure that we as lawyers have done everything possible in our attempt to ensure that our client receives a just trial. By studying our cases comprehensively from the point of view of the prosecution as well as the defense, we could anticipate possible challenges and plan for them. This enabled us to be as prepared as possible. However, we were always ready for our failures. As a fallback plan, we tried to prepare certain points of law that we would need to raise on appeal should the court initially rule against us. This strategy served us well multiple times, and also allowed us to introduce concepts in court that framed the issues in new ways, enabling the judge to see the case from a new angle. Finally, the presence of an exit strategy is always necessary, especially when working within challenging terrain. Through establishing a plan, we were able to account for virtually most things we encountered and could help to minimize any potential controversy or social discontent after our cases had been ruled upon. This methodology of planning and thorough preparation allowed us to provide our clients with a responsible and determined pursuit of justice.

CHAPTER SEVEN

Think Globally and Act Locally

MAKING DELIBERATE EFFORTS TO THINK globally while acting locally cannot be stressed enough, especially within the context of a continuously evolving Shariah legal system such as in Northern Nigeria. The ability to legally influence the court while setting precedent is a rare opportunity. Given that there is no known precedent where Muslims have been sentenced with capital punishment of stoning or amputation in local Shariah courts, before the introduction of "new Shariah" in 1999, it is appropriate to look to other jurisdictions. Other jurisdictions should be countries in the African subregion or beyond; keeping in mind the similarity of the Shariah laws. This ultimately will help lawyers to articulate the framework of their case, present the case in a cogent manner, and help the court to reach a just decision. The "new Shariah" as practiced in Northern Nigeria since 2000 is still considered to be in its inception when compared to other systems of law. Global thinking must be incorporated to help shape and build the new Shariah law into a comprehensive and equitable system of laws.

A Brief Examination of International Law and its Role in Shariah Courts

Lawyers' ability to keep arguments rooted in the Qur'an and Hadith while incorporating the values of Shariah, the Nigerian Constitution, regional and international human rights treaties, and conventions and protocols (signed by Nigeria) will allow arguments to conform to the expectations of the court.[502] The Shariah courts in both Safiya Hussaini Tungar Tudu and Amina Lawal's cases had shown tendency toward citing cases from other jurisdictions to buttress an issue before them, such as citing the case of Ma'iz, whose act of *zina* was committed in the Middle East. Ultimately, this empowers lawyers to move beyond prescribed jurisdictional limits and demonstrate the merits of a case to the presiding judge. By consulting rulings in cases from other countries that practice Shariah law or have large Muslim populations, lawyers will be able to present compelling arguments before the court. To this end, consulting cases in Turkey, India, Pakistan, Sudan, and Mauritania, as well as human rights cases decided before the United Nations human rights bodies, the European Union human rights commissions, and the inter-American court of human rights, among others, may prove useful in seeking to deconstruct otherwise inflexible legal boundaries. In this way, local jurisdictions may be persuaded.

An example of this approach is the case of Amina Lawal. After our team lost the initial appeal in Ms. Lawal's case, Lawyers Without Borders (LWB) joined our team and added value to our appeal. They provided us with copies of international conventions to which Nigeria was a signatory, and pointed out what sections in the convention might be relevant to the case on further appeal. We explored similar principles expressed in the Qur'an and Hadith, as Shariah judges and lawyers are better acquainted with these sources than with international conventions, the latter being

---

502. Nisrine Abiad contends that the use of Shariah could lead to harmonization between international standards of human rights and those in application in Muslim countries (*Sharia, Muslim States*, 112). He further opined that the inherent flexibility of Shariah could create room for interpretation and for adaption to changes of context and circumstance.

largely unknown in local courts. Together with LWB, we were able to establish an argument that helped us "speak the language of the court." We kept international legal provisions close at hand while speaking and acting in socially prescribed ways. Thinking globally and acting locally requires understanding the application of laws, and learning how to communicate complex legal theory into understandable local context. Take, for example, the concept of *jus cogens* (compelling law) or *jus ad bellum* (right to wage war) alluded to previously. These concepts, of which Nigeria had previously signed international human rights instruments, bind Nigeria and compel it to abide to these "higher laws" and not to violate its commitment to the international conventions.

When thinking globally and acting locally, it is helpful to take into consideration the various principles of the Shariah Penal Code Law (SPCL) in the many diverse jurisdictions in which it has been implemented. This immediately raises questions about some of the global challenges that the Shariah code faces today. Should there be a universal, uniform application of Shariah law? Or should its application be up to each local jurisdiction? Has modern technology rendered the global community borderless so that one universal Shariah code is to be expected?

The idea that Shariah law should govern the life of all Muslims, as some maintain, seems to require that its rule and application be consistent from jurisdiction to jurisdiction. Consistent global jurisdiction and interpretation would certainly aid both lawyers and the courts. In addition, consistency would seem to follow Islamic teaching: the Qur'an and Hadith affirm belief in the equality of origins and rights, and because all human beings are born with the knowledge of good and evil, the essential solidarity of all people is certain. Universality is a central tenet of being a Muslim and humanity is God's vicegerent on earth.[503] The Qur'an states, "Behold, thy Lord said to the angels: I will create a vicegerent [Khalifah] on earth . . . " (2:30).

---

503. Abu-Nimer, *Nonviolence and Peace Building*, 57.

In any case, universal jurisdiction and the approach to the rule of law can be viewed from the standpoint of international law, which derives most of its authority from agreement among nation states. Virtually all countries have acceded to The Universal Declaration of Human Rights (UDHR) and the Charter of the United Nations (UN).[504] As an instrument of international law itself, this charter commits the United Nations to promoting and encouraging respect for human rights and fundamental freedoms for all, without distinction to gender, creed, race, sex, language, and religion. Nearly 150 countries are parties to the International Covenant, and 145 are parties to the International Covenant on Economic, Social, and Cultural Rights.[505] These human rights standards have also been incorporated into the constitutions of many states that were formed after 1945.[506]

Most African countries have ratified the major UN treaties, regional human rights treaties, conventions, protocols, optional protocols, etc. However, some of these countries, including Nigeria, have not fully incorporated these treaty provisions into their domestic law, making it difficult to guarantee that those rights provided for in the treaties will be recognized and protected in the national courts. Nevertheless, when interpreting national constitutional provisions, those provisions of treaties (both UN and regional) that have been domesticated are at least partly relied on by lawyers and judges, along with the findings of human rights commissions.

Nigerian courts are by and large accepting of lawyers who seek to invoke provisions of law, legal practices, and conventions that are generally accepted and applied in other jurisdictions, whether the matters are Shariah or non-Shariah. When practicing before the Shariah courts, our legal team cited cases from many Hadith, and the court used these cases to buttress

---

504. The United Nations charter was ratified Dec. 10, 1948.
505. A multilateral treaty adopted by the United Nations General Assembly on Dec. 16, 1966 and made fully effective on Jan. 3, 1976. The treaty commits its parties to work toward the granting of economic, social, and cultural rights (ESCR) to individuals, including labor rights and rights to health, education, and an adequate standard of living.
506. Widner, *Building the Rule of Law*, 30.

its judgment. In some cases, the Shariah courts based their judgments upon Hadith and similar legislation *suo motu* (of their own motion). In this same vein, courts sometimes cite cases relying on international human rights documents to which Nigeria is a signatory. In Nigeria there are a myriad of court decisions that reference such international human rights instruments.

In the case of *Asika v. Atuanya*, for example, the Court of Appeals upheld the principle of universal protection for all women, declaring any discrimination against women in any law or custom unconstitutional.[507] The court further held that by virtue of Article 2(7) of the United Nations 1979 Convention on the Elimination of all Forms of Discrimination Against Women, the government shall take all appropriate measures, including legislation, to modify or abolish all existing laws, customs, or practices that constitute discrimination against women. This convention, which has universal jurisdiction, is applicable to Nigeria because Nigeria is a party to the convention. Moreover, according to Article 16 of the 1948 Universal Declaration of Human Rights, men and women are entitled to equal protection under the law.

In the case of *Abiodun v. A. G. Federation,*[508] which ruled on the question of the status of the African Charter on Human and Peoples' Rights vis-à-vis other municipal statutes, the court held that where there is a conflict between a statute and the provisions of the African Charter on Peoples' Rights (Ratification and Enforcement) Act (ACPRA), which quotes the Universal Declaration of Human Rights verbatim, the provisions of the charter will prevail over those of the other statutes.[509] The reason for this holding is the presumption that the legislature does not intend to breach

---

507. (2008) 17 NWLR (pt. 1057) 359 CA.
508. (2007) 15 NWLR (pt. 1057) 359 CA.
509. The court was referring to the commitment of states members of the charter, in the Preamble of the African Charter on Human and Peoples' Rights (Ratification and Enforcement) Act Chapter A9 (Chapter 10 LFN 1990) (No. 2 of 1983) Laws of the Federation of Nigeria, 1990.

an international obligation. Furthermore, in *I.G.P. v. ANPP,*[510] *Ration 9,*[511] which contemplated the purpose and validity of the ACPRA, the court held that the "African Charter is an understanding between concerned African States to protect the human rights of their citizens within the territorial jurisdiction of their countries."[512] The African Charter is now part of the domestic laws of Nigeria, and like all other laws, the court should uphold it.

These cases illustrate how international human rights instruments are often cited in the adjudication of cases in front of national courts. However, such citations may not prove relevant in Shariah cases as Shariah courts do not strictly adhere to international legal precedent as the basis for ruling and sentencing. For this reason, there is great value in understanding and sometimes quoting previous Shariah rulings of Shariah courts to another Shariah court because they could have a persuasive effect. Decisions from other jurisdictions, such as Pakistani, Sudanese, or Indian Shariah courts, are instructive.[513] In the stoning cases of both Safiya Hussaini[514] and Amina

---

510. (2007) 18 NWLR (pt. 1066) 457 CA.

511. Ration in this sense means point 9 as held.

512. (2007) 18 NWLR (pt. 1066) 457 CA.

513. In the case of Ms. Safia Bibi v. The State, PLD 1985 FSC 120, Safia Bibi was alleged to have committed *zina-bil-jabr* (another word for *zina*). The trial court acquitted the male accused for want of evidence, and Safia was convicted under Section 10(2) of the 1979 Ordinance on the grounds that the pregnancy was sufficient for conviction. On appeal it was held that she should not have been convicted for *zina* because she pleaded her pregnancy as a result of rape. The court held *inter alia* that "The principle of fiqh is that . . . if unmarried woman delivering a child pleads that the birth was the result of commission of the offence to rape on her, she cannot be punished." Based upon the Hadith from the Prophet who said it, it means: My people are excused for mistakes, forgetfulness and for anything done under compulsion. In another case, Ms. Siani v. The State, PLD 1984 FSC 121, the judge, Muhammad Siddiq, took the view that where no direct positive evidence was laid by the prosecution to substantiate a charge of *zina* under Section 10 of the 1979 Ordinance, the expert evidence of a doctor alone was not sufficient to base such a conviction. At best the said medical evidence could only serve as a piece of corroborative testimony but the same by itself could not be made the foundation of conviction of *zina*. The court further observed that mere pregnancy of an illegitimate child by an unmarried widow or a girl or a woman whose husband had no access to her during the relevant period was not sufficient to hold her guilty under Section 10(2) of the 1979 Ordinance.

514. Appeal No. SCA/GW/28/2001, certified true copy of the judgment.

Lawal, the Shariah court did quote examples/decisions in Ma'iz (an incident that occurred in the Arabian Peninsula and was recorded in the Hadith of Ṣaḥīḥ al-Bukhari) to buttress their decision, giving the cases a universal dimension. This prompts the question: If cases from other jurisdictions can be useful in helping the court reach an informed decision, might not the use of international human rights instruments prove useful as well, especially the Universal Islamic Declaration of Human Rights?

Application of International Human Rights Instruments

The international community has developed many instruments to help ensure protection of an individual's human rights. Of special interest is the Universal Islamic Declaration of Human Rights (the full provisions of which are reproduced in Appendix F of the "Compendium of Laws and Authorities"). The Universal Islamic Declaration of Human Rights (UIDHR), ratified by the Organization of Islamic Countries (OIC) on the 21st of Dhul Qaidah, 1401 (September 19, 1981), was designated as a declaration for mankind and as a guide and instruction manual for those who fear God (Qur'an 3:13).[515] The UIDHR affirms that "Islam gave to mankind an ideal code of human rights fourteen centuries ago aimed at conferring honor and dignity upon, and eliminating the exploitation, oppression and unjust treatment of all of mankind."[516] It further declares,

> Human rights in Islam are firmly rooted in the belief that God, and God alone, is the Law Giver and the Source of all human rights, and that human rights are an integral part of the overall Islamic order giving powerful impetus to the Muslim to stand firm and defend resolutely and courageously the rights conferred on all people by God.

---

515. The dates noted are those with the Islamic lunar calendar and the Gregorian calendar. The Islamic calendar commenced from the migration of the Prophet from Mecca to Medina.
516. Universal Islamic Declaration of Human Rights, Preamble, 21 Dhul Qaidah 1401, Sept. 19, 1981.

The UIDHR is based on the Qur'an and the Sunnah and has been compiled by eminent Muslim scholars, jurists, and representatives of Islamic movements and thought whose membership cuts across the world.[517] The UIDHR represents divine mandates: "Allah (God) سبحانه و تعالى has given mankind through His revelations in the Holy Qur'an and the Sunnah of His Blessed Prophet Muhammad (صلى الله عليه وسلم) an abiding legal and moral framework within which to establish and regulate human institutions and relationships."[518] The UIDHR affirms as an age-old human aspiration: the longing for a just world order where people can live, develop, and prosper in an environment free from fear, oppression, exploitation, and deprivation.

This moral and legal framework provides for many basic rights, including the right to life; right to freedom; right to equality and the prohibition against impermissible discrimination; right to justice; right to a fair trial; right to protection against the abuse of power; right to protection from torture; right to protection of one's honor and reputation; right to asylum; rights of minorities; right and obligation to participate in the conduct and management of public affairs; right to freedom of belief, thought, and speech; right to freedom of religion; right to associate freely; rights related to economic order and society; right to protection of private property; protection of the status and dignity of workers; right to social security; right to found a family and related matters; rights of married women; right to education; right of privacy; and right to freedom of movement and residence.[519]

It is worth noting that according to the Qur'an, women partake in all of the above-mentioned rights, and are also the subject of particular concern in ensuring that such rights are given. The Qur'an liberates women from the status of chattel or inferior creatures and makes them free and equal human

---

517. "O men! Behold, We have created you all out of a male and a female, and have made you into nations and tribes, so that you might come to know one another. Verily, the noblest of you in the sight of God is the one who is most deeply conscious of Him. Behold, God is all-knowing, all aware" (Qur'an 49:13).
518. Culled from the Universal Islamic Universal Declaration of Human Rights, Preamble.
519. Ibid.

beings. The Qur'an also protects all of the downtrodden and oppressed classes of people, stipulating restitution of human beings from every kind of bondage. Acknowledging the human tendency towards dictatorship and oppression, verse 3:79 of the Qur'an states with clarity:

> It is not (possible) that a man, to whom is given the Book, and Wisdom, And the Prophetic Office, should say to people: "Be ye my worshippers rather than Allah's." On the contrary He would say; "Be ye worshippers of Him who is truly The Cherisher of all."[520]

Notwithstanding, at times some of the relevant teachings of our local Muslim clerics appear to be more concerned with trying to control women's bodies and their sexuality than encouraging the teaching of what is due to women, their position and glory before the Almighty Allah سبحانه و تعالى, and their fundamental human rights in Islam. Unfortunately, women are sometimes the target of unspeakable violations of human rights as a result of a persistent inability to define their challenges and issues.

In some societies, female children are discriminated against from the moment of birth and throughout their lifetimes. Generally, a woman cannot claim equality with her husband. The husband is regarded as his wife's gateway to heaven or hell, the arbiter of her final destiny. However, some people view the idea that a woman requires absolute obedience to her husband to reach heaven (*aljannna mace mijinta*) as contradicting the Islamic doctrine that there is no intermediary between the believer and God. Respect for husband and parent, which is a sign of obedience, should not qualify as an intermediary act between a woman and God. Furthermore, the Hadith states: "The paradise lies at the feet of your mother."[521]

A narrative of Hazrat Abu Hurairah that relates this Hadith was told thus: A man asked the Prophet of Allah سبحانه و تعالى—"upon whom lies my polite behavior," the Prophet answered "Your mother." The man asked the

---

520. Ibid.; see also the Qur'an.
521. Culled from Qasmi, *International Encyclopedia of Islam*, 11.

same question a second time, the Prophet again answered—"Your mother." The man will not let go, he asked again a third time the same question, the Prophet answered again the third time—"Your mother." It is only the fourth time the man asked that the Prophet answered—"Your father."[522] There is consensus of opinion by Islamic scholars and clerics that the Prophet's emphasis on the mother underscores the righteous position of women in Islam. It therefore presents a conundrum for those who still hold to the view that may contradict the above stated words of the Holy Prophet and fundamental tenets of respect and appreciation for Muslim women.

As mentioned earlier, the African Charter on Human and Peoples' Rights (Banjul Charter), which was adopted by the Assembly of the Heads of State and Government of the Organization of African Unity (OAU) on June 27, 1981, and came into force on October 21, 1986, is another important human rights document worthy of note.[523] The African Charter stipulates that "freedom, equality, justice and dignity are essential objectives for the achievement of the legitimate aspirations of the African peoples."[524] It further pledges to coordinate and intensify the African peoples' cooperation and efforts to achieve a better life for the peoples of Africa, and to promote international cooperation while giving due regard to the Charter of the United Nations on the Universal Declaration of Human Rights.

The African Charter marked the beginning of a formal structure for the defense of human rights by establishing the African Commission on Human and Peoples' Rights and its twofold mandate for the promotion and protection of human rights.[525] As part of its protective mandate, the commission considers individual communications whose main functions are:

---

522. Shujaat Khan, *Family Life Under Islam*, 57.
523. All 54 OAU states have now ratified the African Charter. OAU officially became the African Union on July 9, 2002, essentially keeping the same structures and documentations.
524. Umozurike, *African Charter*, 145.
525. The African Commission is established under Article 30 of the African Charter and its mandate is set out in Article 45. The African Commission held its first session in Addis Ababa, Ethiopia, in November 1987. See also Eze, *Human Rights in Africa,* 147.

1. To promote Human and Peoples' Rights and in particular:

    a. to collect documents, undertake studies and researches
        on African problems in the field of human and peoples'
        rights, . . . give its views or make recommendations to
        Governments.

    b. to formulate and lay down, principles and rules aimed
        at solving legal problems relating to human and peoples'
        rights and fundamental freedoms upon which African
        Governments may base their legislations.

    c. to co-operate with other African and international
        institutions concerned with the promotion and protection
        of human and peoples' rights.

2. Ensure the protection of human and peoples' rights under
    conditions laid down by the Charter. . . . [526]

From 1988 to the present, it has become apparent that the commission
frequently (in terms of Articles 60 and 61 of the African Charter[527]) refers
to the texts of various UN human rights treaties as well as to the findings
of UN human rights treaty bodies.[528] Using the positive principles and
techniques of the Charter and other similar regional and international
human rights mechanisms will enhance local, religious, and traditional legal

---

526. Ouguergouz, *African Charter*, 519.
527. "The Commission shall draw inspiration from international law on human and
peoples' rights, particularly from the provisions of various African instruments on Human
and Peoples' Rights, the Charter of the United Nations, the Charter of the Organization of
African Unity, the Universal Declaration of Human Rights, other instruments adopted by
the United Nations and by African countries in the field of Human and Peoples' Rights,
as well as from the provisions of various instruments adopted within the Specialized
Agencies of the United Nations of which the Parties to the present Charter are members.
The Commission shall also take into consideration, as subsidiary measures to determine
the principles of law, other general or special international conventions, laying down rules
expressly recognized by Member States of the Organization of African Unity, African
practices consistent with international norms on Human and Peoples' Rights, customs
generally accepted as law, general principles of law recognized by African States as well as
legal precedents and doctrine."
528. Olowu, *Integrative Rights-Based Approach*, 75.

systems. The deployment of multiple instruments of human rights can best reflect the varied cultural outlooks of justice.

International Treaties as Human Rights Instruments

The purposes and principles of the Universal Islamic Declaration of Human Rights, the Charter of the United Nations, and the African Charter are becoming increasingly important in the global sphere. Not only do these charters and declarations promote the sovereign equality of states, they also uphold the fundamental role treaties play in the history of international relations. As a source of law, treaties seek to develop peaceful cooperation among nations for the maintenance of international peace and security.

Treaties seek to promote friendly relations between countries that desire to strengthen ties in consenting to an international convention on diplomatic networking. Such treaties promote principles of free consent, good faith, and the Latin *pacta sunt servanda* ("agreements must be kept").[529] These networks, which should be taken into consideration when dealing with local issues in a global setting, are to provide privileges and immunities that contribute to the development of amicable associations among nations, irrespective of their differing constitutional and social systems. Suffice to recognize that skepticism, distrust, and apprehension will arise. Guilty of sounding like a broken record, there also exist lots of possibilities for common ground and collaboration.

Article 14 of the Vienna Convention on the Law of Treaties, to which Nigeria is a signatory, declares that once international treaties have been ratified, a state is bound to carry out its international obligations and may not invoke its domestic law as a justification for non-implementation.[530] Thus, the federal government of Nigeria has the ultimate responsibility for ensuring that human rights are respected in its territories in accordance with its prior international human rights obligations. Subsequent state-declared Shariah law may need to recognize its commitment to signed

---

529. Kaczorowska, *Public International Law*, 91.
530. Civil Liberties Organization, *Islam and Human Rights*, 27.

treaties and seek to invoke its reason for noncompliance with regard to those obligations.

In order to think globally, lawyers can consider using the concept of *jus cogens* and its peremptory principles of international law. The concept of *jus cogens* originated in the nineteenth century, and thus there are relatively early paradigms of its use in judicial process. Some commentators argue that treaty law validates *jus cogens,* while others argue that the universal and non-derogating nature of *jus cogens* means that it exists regardless of any treaties. However, most states accept it as a fundamental principle of law and justice. In effect, *jus cogens* may represent fundamental norms of international law in a universal and non-derogatory manner that allows lawyers to address international human rights instruments. *Jus cogens* are closely related to universal jurisdiction. For example, the International Criminal Tribunal for the former Yugoslavia (ICTY) determined in *Prosecutor v. Furundžija* that there is a *jus cogens* for the prohibition of torture.[531] It also stated that universal jurisdiction applies to torture as "the torturer has become like the pirate and the slave trader before him, *hostis humani generis,* 'an enemy of all mankind.'"[532]

The Nigerian Constitution as a Human Rights Instrument

While international law plays a large role with regard to human rights issues in Nigerian courts, the Nigerian Constitution also provides for the protection of fundamental human rights and ensures due process and a fair hearing (*see especially* Chapter IV of the 1999 Constitution). Acquainting ourselves with provisions of Chapter IV is indispensable. These provisions represent the pinnacle of human rights for all Nigerian citizens, and counsel may find the following sections quoted useful in court.

---

531. Case No. IT-95-17/1-T, http://www.unhcr.org/cgi-bin/texis/vtx/refworld/rwmain?docid=40276a8a4.
532. Ibid.

Section 33

1. Every person has a right to life, and no one shall be deprived intentionally of his life, save in execution of the sentence of a court in respect of a criminal offense of which he has been found guilty in Nigeria.

Section 34

1. Every individual is entitled to respect for the dignity of his person, and accordingly
    a. no person shall be subject to torture or to inhuman or degrading treatment; ...

Section 35

1. Every person shall be entitled to his personal liberty and no person shall be deprived of such liberty save ... in accordance with a procedure permitted by law ...

Section 36

1. In the determination of his/her civil rights and obligations, including any question or determination by or against any government or authority, a person shall be entitled to a fair hearing within a *reasonable time* by a *court or other tribunal established by law* and constituted in such manner as to secure its *independence and impartiality* (emphasis mine) ...

3. The proceedings of a court or the proceedings of any tribunal relating to the matters mentioned in subsection (1) of this section (including the announcement of the decisions of the court or tribunal) shall be held in public ...

4. Whenever any person is charged with a criminal offense he shall, unless the charge is withdrawn, be entitled to a fair hearing in public within a reasonable time by a court or tribunal ...

5. Every person who is charged with a criminal offense shall be presumed to be innocent until he is proved guilty; Provided that nothing in this section shall invalidate any law by reason only that the law imposes upon any such person the burden of proving particular facts.

6. Every person who is charged with a criminal offense shall be entitled to:
    a. be informed promptly in the language that he understands and in detail as to the nature of the offense;
    b. be given adequate time and facilities for the preparation of his defense;
    c. defend himself in person or by legal practitioners of his own choosing;
    d. examine, in person or by his legal practitioners, the witnesses called by the prosecution before any court or tribunal and obtain the attendance and carry out the examination of witnesses to testify on his behalf before the court or tribunal on the same conditions as those applying to the witnesses called by the prosecution; and
    e. have, without payment, the assistance of an interpreter if he cannot understand the language used at the trial of the offense. . .

8. No person shall be held to be guilty of a criminal offense on account of any act or omission that did not, at the time it took place, constitute such an offense, and no penalty shall be imposed for any criminal offense heavier than the penalty in force at the time the offense was committed . . .

Section 38

1. Every person shall be entitled to freedom of thought, conscience and religion, including freedom to change his religion or belief, and freedom (either alone or in community

with others, and in public or in private) to manifest and
propagate his religion or belief in worship, teaching, practice
and observance . . .

Section 39

1. Every person shall be entitled to freedom of expression,
    including freedom to hold opinions and to receive and impart
    ideas and information without interference . . .

Section 42

1. A citizen of Nigeria of a particular community, ethnic group,
    place of origin, sex, religion or political opinion shall not,
    by reason only that he is such a person, be discriminated
    against . . .

The position of the Nigerian Constitution on human rights echoes
its commitment to certain basic and inalienable rights that require no
defense because their truth is self-evident. Their virtue beyond question,
such rights include the right to life, dignity of human persons, freedom
from discrimination, and restriction on and derogation from fundamental
human rights, among others. Mindful of the added benefits of other human
rights instruments, Nigeria has sought to promote and protect such rights
through its commitment to regional and international human rights
mediums, including the Universal Declaration of Human Rights, which,
as discussed above, was signed, ratified, and domesticated by Nigeria. The
UDHR also allows for subsequent visits by the Special Rapporteur to work
with individuals and organizations at local and regional bases to investigate,
monitor, and recommend solutions with regard to specific human rights
challenges.[533]

In fact, during one of his visits to Nigeria, the United Nations Special
Rapporteur to Nigeria remarked that the Shariah legal system adopted

---

533. The Special Rapporteur is a specially appointed ambassador of the Secretary General
of the United Nations.

by the twelve Northern states in Nigeria contains provisions that raise concerns in terms of human rights. He remarked that certain forms of punishment contained in the codes, such as amputation or stoning of Muslims, constituted treatment contrary to universally recognized norms. Norms that prohibit torture and other degrading and inhumane treatment or punishment are included in some of the international conventions to which Nigeria subscribes.[534]

Section 19 of the Constitution further stipulates that the foreign policy objectives of Nigeria includes," ... promotion of international co-operation for the consolidation of universal peace and mutual respect among all nations and elimination of discrimination in all its manifestations; respect for international law and treaty obligations. . . . " And the Second Schedule, Part I, item 31 states that the government will implement treaties relating to matters on the exclusive legislative list where such treaty is between the federation and any other country when such treaty has been enacted into law by the National Assembly.[535]

Practice of some Shariah Courts appears to contradict the principle of *nulla poena sine lege* (no penalty without law). When some of our clients were convicted, for example, there was no offense in place criminalizing *zina*. The *nulla poena sine lege* principle of legality is a core value, a human right, and also an underlying defense in criminal prosecution—no crime or punishment can exist without a legal ground. A guarantee of human liberty, on the other hand, protects individuals from state abuse and unjust intervention as it secures fairness and clarity of the judicial power. It is a fundamental principle of free societies. The principle is often associated with the attempts to constrain states, governments, and judicial and legislative bodies from enacting retroactive legislation. Section 36(8) states:

---

534. *Office of the United Nations High Commissioner for Human Rights, Framework for Communications*. E/CN.4/2002/73/Add.2, para. 168 and 228.
535. Constitution of the Federal Republic of Nigeria, 1999, Section 1.

No person shall be held to be guilty of a criminal offense
on account of any act or omission that did not, at the time
it took place, constitute such an offense, and no penalty
shall be imposed for any criminal offense heavier than the
penalty in force at the time the offense was committed.

This position that only a law can define a crime and prescribe a
punishment in the Nigerian Constitution,[536] is also impliedly validated
under the first known written constitution in the world, the Constitution
of Medina, where Article 56 states that

. . . an individual goes out to fight (in accordance with
the terms of this Pact) or remains in his home, he will be
safe unless he has committed a crime or is a sinner (i.e.,
No one will be punished in his individual capacity for not
having gone out to fight in accordance with the terms of
this Pact).[537]

Also known as the Charter of Medina, this constitution was drafted by
the prophet Muhammad (صلى الله عليه وسلم) as a formal agreement between himself and
all the significant tribes and families of Yathrib (Medina), which included not
only Muslims, but also Jews and Pagans.[538] The charter instituted a number
of rights and responsibilities for the community and brought them all within
one actual, organized community, the *ummah*. The Constitution of Medina
provided for the security of the community (and for women in particular),
for religious freedom, for the role of Medina as a sacred place (including a
ban on all violence and weaponry), and for stable tribal relations.[539]

---

536. Ibid., Section 36(12).
537. Ashraf, *First Written Constitution*, 140. See Compendium for the full text.
538. Rejwan, *Many Faces of Islam*, 96.
539. Toorawa and Allen, *Islam*, 7.

Justice in Islam

Justice is a basic principle of Islam since it has its roots in God Himself.[540] Islam considers justice to be a supreme virtue.[541] It is the basic objective of Islam that justice stands next in order of priority to belief in God's exclusive right to worship and the truth of Prophet Muhammad's (ﷺ) prophethood.[542] The very fact that two of the attributes of Allah سبحانه و تعالى are closely linked to justice apparently underscores the significance of imparting justice to all. The two attributes of Allah سبحانه و تعالى are the Just (al-Adil) and the Dispenser of Justice (al-Muqsit).[543] The Holy Qur'an states, "Allah commands justice, the doing of good, and liberality ... " (16:90). In Islam, justice is also a moral virtue and an attribute of human personality. Justice is close to equality in the sense that it creates a state of equilibrium in the distribution of rights and duties, but they are not identical. Prophet Muhammad (ﷺ) underscored the importance of rulers being just in one of his famous sayings: "There are seven categories of people whom Allah سبحانه و تعالى will shelter under His shade on the day when there will be no shade except His. (One will be) a just leader" (Saḥīḥ al-Muslim).

Justice is a principle reflected in the divine, universal word of God, even though many philosophers have opined on the notion of justice.[544] In particular, justice and cumulative justice find their basis in the Stoics and Roman natural law,[545] Thomas Aquinas's theory of natural law and natural rights,[546] as well as in Immanuel Kant's concept that law is the most just moral form;[547] that there is no unjust or immoral rule.[548] Jeremy Bentham further maintained that the most right and just action is that action that

---

540. Shujaat, *Social Justice in Islam*, 44.
541. Cornell, *Voices of Islam*, 174.
542. Rane, *Reconstructing Jihad*, 193.
543. Lichtenstrader, *Islam and the Modern Age*, 83.
544. Kamrava, *New Voices of Islam*, 154.
545. Friedrich, *Philosophy of Law*, 27.
546. Goyette et al., *St. Thomas Aquinas and the Natural Law Tradition*, 244.
547. Sullivan, *Immanuel Kant's Moral Theory*, 167.
548. Bentham, *Introduction to the Principles of Morals*, xxxiv.

brings the most good to the greatest number of people.[549] In addition, John Austin surmised that a just law was a rule laid down for an intelligent being by an intelligent being superior to him. For Austin, the law is trickily divorced from justice and is based on ideas of morality and immorality, which is arguably the position of law and justice in Islam.[550]

Explaining the relationship between law, justice, and morality, Maulana Mufti Muhammad Shafi says:

> One of the distinctions of Islam is that looked at from a wider perspective, its moral instructions are also legal injunctions, since it is on their basis that the record and the punishment of the Hereafter are to be decided, which is of fundamental importance in the life of Muslim . . . If you think over the style of the Quran, you will find that with every legal and moral injunctions, are associated with reminders of concepts of fear of God and provisions for life Hereafter.[551]

On the other hand, Dean Roscoe Pound's theory of justice considers justice as the end of law.[552]

The concept and theory of justice is interconnected both legally and politically. Law, religion, morality, and rights are all intertwined when considered in accordance with justice, and can be difficult to separate. While justice can be relative or universal, the administration of justice requires consistency. The concept of justice can be written for different societies with different customs, values, and traditions. In Islam, the concept of

---

549. Parekh, *Jeremy Bentham Critical Assessment*, 743.
550. Lampe, *Justice and Human Rights*, 26.
551. Shujaat, *Social Justice in Islam*, 125.
552. Stone, *Human Law and Human Justice*, 263; see also his *Province and Function of Law*. Pound worked at Harvard from 1910–1937 and served as dean of Harvard Law School from 1916–1936. After World War II he helped reorganize the judicial system of Taiwan. He wrote "Spurious Interpretation" in 1907, *Outlines of Lectures on Jurisprudence* in 1914, *The Spirit of the Common Law* in 1921, *Law and Morals* in 1924, and *Criminal Justice in America* in 1930. See also Keller, *Generous Justice*, 11.

justice is given the highest status, because not only does humanity define justice, but also the Creator himself, Allah سبحانه و تعالى. Justice in Islam is a command of Allah سبحانه و تعالى (God) and whoever violates it faces grievous punishment.[553] The concept of justice in Islam encapsulates equality before the law, equity, and adaptability within an Islamic jurisprudence that may change over time.[554] Meanwhile, Kumar suggests that Allah سبحانه و تعالى is just.[555] Furthermore, "And the Word of your Lord has been fulfilled in truth and in justice. None can change His Words" (Q. 6:115); " . . . Be just, for it is closest to God-consciousness . . . " (Q. 5:8); and "Say: 'My Lord has commanded justice . . .'" (Q. 7:29).

In Islam, Allah سبحانه و تعالى is the Almighty who is the supreme lawgiver. Allah سبحانه و تعالى has unlimited knowledge and wisdom. Only Allah سبحانه و تعالى has knowledge and knows all.[556] Justice must be administered through the correct guidelines and standards set by divine revelation.[557] True justice places a high value on social and individual justice alike. Hans-Georg Gadamer refers to this dual focus of laws, or law as an internal morality, suggesting that laws should be general, promulgated, and not retroactive.[558] Rulemaking and the application of rules should be minimal, and laws should be understandable, non-contradictory, achievable, realistic, and constant through time.[559] There must also be congruence between the laws as announced and as applied; social justice is inconceivable without individual justice.[560]

It is worth noting that in Nigeria, under the indirect rule of the British in the twentieth century, Islamic law was preserved to a certain extent.

---

553. Doi, Sharīah, 3.
554. Abu-Nimer, Nonviolence and Peace Building in Islam, 57–58.
555. Kumar, Encyclopedia of Human Rights, 184.
556. Abdul-Rahman, Meaning and Explanation, 33.
557. Hanif, Islamic Concept of Crime, 137.
558. Gadamer, Truth and Method, 126; see also Franco, Political Philosophy of Michael Oakeshott, 119; and Fuller, Morality of Law, 153.
559. Benditt, Law as Rule and Principle, 97.
560. Patterson, Companion to Philosophy of Law, 220; see also Lampe, Justice and Human Rights (2010), 24.

However, during this period, Islamic law was confined to laws that were not considered repugnant to natural justice.[561] For instance, the practice of polygamy was preserved throughout this time, and while this might have caused problems among some Muslims, it also demonstrated that some aspects of Shariah could still be administered effectively within the confines of a constitution. However, it seems that the latest interpretation and establishment of the new Shariah Penal Code Law with regards to the administration of punishments, fails to comply with basic human freedoms. Such rights include unintentionally extended punishments to non-Muslims, such as the mode of dress for women, the sale and consumption of alcohol, and other related vices.

Whether in the global sphere or in a local setting, everyone wants to feel justly treated with respect and dignity; this is true even more so in Islam. Justice is seen as a bond that holds a society together and transforms society into one big brotherhood or sisterhood. Islamic justice requires that all people be regarded and treated equally before all courts, the noble and not so noble, the wealthy and the not so wealthy.[562] In the case of Northern Nigeria, in states with the codified Shariah penal code, all Muslims should be treated equally before the Shariah courts. No one, by reason of his or her status, should ever despair for justice before a Shariah court. It also requires that the burden of proof always lie with the accuser and not the accused.

Shariah law safeguards freedoms and has sufficient provisions to lead the outcome of each case toward the road for justice and fairness, as evidenced especially well in the case of Amina Lawal, and specifically concerning the argument of the sleeping fetus.[563] The need exists to balance these freedoms

---

561. Within the context that at times Islamic law is referred to as "customary law," see Matson, "Common Law Abroad," 753–79, specifically p. 767. Natural justice refers to a procedural fairness as a legal philosophy, mostly used in the UK and Australian common law jurisdiction, which is used to determine just, or fair processes in legal proceedings. This concept is closely related to natural law. See also Yadudu, "Islamic Law and Reform Discourse."

562. Rosen, *Anthropology of Justice*, 75.

563. Somini Sengupta, "Facing Death for Adultery, Nigerian Woman Is Acquitted," *New York Times*, Sept. 26, 2003.

with the respect for law and its rule, as well as other fundamental human rights provisions. This is a responsibility and obligation to each one of us, and thereby to all of us. In Shariah, the rule of law is meant to be inseparable from moral rules. Just laws are merely the proper application of moral values, and moral values are supreme.

The Gift of Freedom

Muslims maintain that Allah's gift of human freedom gave us the ability to hear His call, to know His will, and to decide our response. It is a freedom that the law cannot create within us. Divine grace, working in all human hearts, is the source of this freedom. Allah سبحانه و تعالى risked everything in giving us the gift of human freedom, for only in that way could He have ended up with a meaningful and glorifying creation (Qur'an 21:107; 3:85; 2:256–257).[564] Moreover, it is the only way we could be held accountable for our actions; this freedom renders judgment not so much as a matter of reward and punishment, but of consequences that result from free choices made by "response-able" men and women.

The right to freedom of belief is endorsed by the Qur'an, which also affirms that "God will judge human beings not on the basis of what they profess, but on the basis of their belief and righteous conduct" (18:29).[565] In this context, it is important to mention the Qur'anic dictum, "Let there be no compulsion in religion" (Surah 2:256).

In thinking globally and acting locally, the common denominator is freedom, or liberty. Freedom of religion is a matter of individual conscience, and implies the freedom to practice one's religion privately or publicly, alone or in community with others, and within the circle of those whose faith one shares. It has been suggested that secularism, the idea that no one religion should be established by the state, is one of the indispensable

---

564. Ghanea, *Minorities, Peoples and Self-determination*, 229.
565. This verse is part of the religious human rights in the Qur'an. See also Witte and van der Vyver, *Religions Human Rights*, 376.

conditions of democracy.[566] The Constitutional Court of Turkey reflected such thinking in one of its rulings, stating that the Turkish Constitution safeguarded the principles of secularism and religious freedom against any notions of religious discrimination or intolerance.[567] The court emphasized this especially in the light of Turkey's own experience with how specific features of Islam and rules of Shariah may, at times, conflict with democratic principles. The court further suggested that the principle of secularism prohibits the state of Turkey from manifesting a preference for one particular religion or belief over another. Since the state is called to be the guarantor of the freedom of conscience and of equality for all citizens before the law, it must remain neutral in these matters.

Moreover, in democratic societies in which several religions may coexist side by side within the same population, to place certain limits may be necessary in order to protect the interests of the various groups and ensure that everyone's beliefs are respected. The state's role is to be a neutral and impartial arbiter in the free exercise of various religions or belief systems and in ways that will prove conducive to public order, religious harmony, and tolerance in a democratic society. The Turkish Constitutional Court also considers it the duty of the state to remain neutral and impartial.[568] The Turkish Constitutional Court ruled,

> ... freedom of thought, conscience and religion is one of
> the foundations of a democratic society. It is not only a
> most precious possession for people of faith, but also for
> atheists, agnostics, sceptics and the unconcerned as well.
> That freedom entails *inter alia*, the freedom to hold or not

---

566. See Refah Partisi (the Welfare Party) and Others v. Turkey (1998) 26 EHRR. See also Taylor, *Freedom of Religion*, 314.
567. Turkish Constitution, 1982, Preamble. See also Ansay and D. Wallace, *Introduction to Turkish Law*, 34; Ghanea, *Minorities, Peoples, and Self-determination*, 229; Turkish Constitution of 1921; and Turkish Constitution of 1961.
568. Refah Partisi (the Welfare Party) and Others v. Turkey.

to hold religious beliefs and to practice or not to practice
a religion.[569]

This certainly is beyond the letters of the law; it is wisdom embodied.

Thinking globally and acting locally allows lawyers to approach cases
resourcefully. Through the use of international human rights instruments,
adjudication can be used to impact and shape the law of local jurisdictions
in a manner that will seek to protect fundamental rights in accordance
with accepted principles of international law. By keeping an open mind
and always looking for new and innovate ways to achieve goals, lawyers can
accomplish much in the way of ensuring justice for all.

Summary

Nigeria is a diverse and a pluralistic society, which presents religious,
ethnic, and political challenges; however, this is no excuse for complacency
within the system. With its commonwealth scattered among all its people
and states, each containing vast deposits of natural resources and immense
human capital, Nigeria should be poised to realize its dreams, even if only
on a small scale. It may only be one issue, one time, one day, and one person,
but our opportunity is now. It is up to the leadership and people of this
land to fulfill Nigeria's potential and ensure that all can dwell in peace and
safety while renewing trust in our government and fostering individual and
communal rejuvenation. The public yearns for peace, security, and freedom,
which can only be accomplished by a unified effort to take the country to
new and greater heights.

Certainly, the Qur'an did not leave us without guidance, morally and
otherwise, as it states, "yet it is not right for all to go out (in search of
Knowledge) together; out of each community, a group should go out to
study the religion, so that they can teach when they return . . ." (9:122). It
went on in chapter 47:17 to say, "Allah has increased the guidance of those
who follow the right path and given them, their awareness [of Him]." And

---

569. Ibid.

surely, "Allah loves those who seek to purify themselves (both morally and physically)" (2:222). Lastly, as Draz shared from the Qur'an, that Allah loves those who do good (2:195; 3:134, 148; 5:93), those who are just (5:42), those who are patient (3:146), those who are pious (3:31; 9:108), those who repent of their sins and try to become pure (2:222; 9:108), those who put their trust in Him (3:159), and those who follow His Messenger (3:31).[570]

Finally, our vision may be different, our mission far apart, but hopefully our destination is the same. Keep in mind that "recognition of the inherent dignity and of the equal and inalienable rights of all members of the human family is the foundation of freedom, justice, and peace in the world."[571] The pursuit of equality will have to come from a multidimensional approach; thinking creatively, identifying and using international norms, and developing common relationships in global advocacy to suit local needs. As John Stoltenberg voiced,

> Historically, when people have not had justice or freedom, they have had only the material reality of injustice and non-freedom. When freedom and justice don't exist, they are but a dream, an abstract idea longed for. One can't really know what justice is or what liberty feels like. We can only recognize their absence and what it feels like to hope and yearn for their presence, to imagine them, and to desire them with a passion. Equality of the sexes is a freedom, which has not been recognized in many societies, and cannot be until there is justice. And justice is incompatible with a definition of freedom that is based on the subordination of women. Equality is still a radical idea, which inspires an array of emotions in various cultures. When the time for equality has come, perhaps then we will know justice, passion with compassion, and dignity and

---

570. Draz, *Moral World of the Quran*, 155.
571. United Nations, 1948, Universal Declaration of Human Rights.

humanity with honor. Until that time, when the integrity within each person is celebrated, we will not truly know the freedom of a world of real equality and opportunity, where freedom reigns! Some of us want to go there! Some of us want to be there! We know that the struggle will be long and arduous, but we know that the passion for justice cannot be denied. Someday—SOMEDAY—there will be both justice and freedom for each person—and thereby for us all.[572]

Conclusion

While the temple of justice is a natural, transparent and all-inclusive space, the network of paths that lead to it could be difficult and beset with obstacles. The seven strategies discussed in this book are part of a dialogue for learning the terrain and how best to work around the disparities in the new Shariah. While a lawyer's ability to remain focused, to be aware of the cultural dynamics surrounding a case and to know the details in the application and interpretation of the law are ways that lead closer to justice, there are important external factors that should not go unnoticed. In every case, institutional, intellectual, structural, and social environments can affect a lawyer's work toward promoting justice, more broadly, as a people's cultural frame of reference.

Both the influence and shortcomings of the court system are crucial to understand. The registry is a powerful institution within the Shariah court; it functions not only as the administrative unit of the court, but usually as the first point of contact for litigants. Because most of the litigants are illiterate and have never been to court, the registry plays an essential role in guiding and assisting them; at times serving as a liaison between judges, lawyers, and other participants in a case. It is important to note that internal limitations can upset the efficient functioning of the registry. A number of

---

572. Stoltenberg, *Refusing to Be a Man*, 118.

factors, including the registry's own bureaucratic practices, often result in delays in the litigation process, with cases pending before the court for years. Litigants, for example, have complained about the lack of available receipts for funds that they have paid to the registry for court fees. The new Shariah was meant to assist in closing this loophole. Also important to note is the registry staff's lack of training or necessary skills as to how the new Shariah is to be implemented. At times, these shortcomings may affect an innocent litigant's case.

No less important is the issue of language. While Shariah law is codified in English, the courts, including the judges and staff, use Hausa; the regional language of Northern Nigeria. This is of concern as English is inaccessible to most judges, clerks, and staff in the rural courts, let alone the people at the grassroots level whom the law is meant to assist. Language can be the greatest of barriers. Where there is no common language, there is no effective communication. It is an overwhelming task for lawyers to have to read the law in English, and then to have to provide not only a Hausa translation of the English text, but in some instances, also a translation in Arabic. As a result, the substance of Shariah law has been difficult to fully grasp within the context of these courts—its meaning can be lost in translation. If we are to ever see the law fully and justly applied in these areas we will need to give the people access to the law in their own language and, at the very least, to make them aware of the law's existence.

One of the purposes for the codification of the Shariah penal code in 2000 was to ensure that Muslims in Nigeria would have the benefit of being governed by the law of their choosing. The "new Shariah" was to promote and administer justice. Getting this right is indispensable; otherwise, if the process itself makes justly applying legal theories too difficult, the codified law could be defeated, or stripped of its substance. With all its good intention and good will, the unintended gaps created by its hurried implementation may result in weakening the Shariah laws. A lack of knowledge of the Qur'an and Hadith by some Shariah judges and lawyers is an example of the many challenges that call for attention before the law can be justly administered.

It bears repeating that all these forces can be used as an advantage to support litigants—especially those facing a potential death sentence—to breathe the fresh air of freedom.

There are obstacles to justice from both the practical and structural levels of society. Although it may seem trivial at first, the courthouse can be a real factor in how Shariah cases are adjudicated. For example, in some towns and villages, the courtrooms are very hot, cramped, and poorly maintained. They easily become congested, especially during trials of any notoriety. In a recent (2011) visit to a Shariah court in the town of Bauchi, I saw more than forty people sitting on four benches designed to accommodate about twenty people. Another forty-plus people were seated on the floor of the courtroom, with an additional twenty-plus hanging around the only two windows that supplied ventilation to the room. A lawyer needs to be aware of these factors that could affect his or her performance and thus the outcome of the trial.

In addition, many of the Shariah courtrooms in some towns and rural areas have no electricity, no fan, and no air conditioning. At times, there is no paper, no pen, no water, and often no good roads leading to the courthouse. In fact, it seems in some states there is no deliberate government investment made in court infrastructures. This can sometimes make for a difficult experience, especially as communities have strong feelings about seeing justice done. The conditions in which judges are asked to work are often inadequate as well, not only in terms of the condition of the courtroom, but also in their take-home pay, which does not provide them with a living wage. If the latter is lacking, judges can become vulnerable to other sources that may compromise justice.

Outside the courthouse there are other factors one must consider. The institution of legal aid, which is important especially to people at the grassroots level that are unable to afford a lawyer, lacks the necessary support, including an investment of resources and personnel by the government and the society. As a result, the Nigerian Legal Aid Council's quest for fairness and justice is impeded for a sizeable portion of the village population. For example, in the Gusau prison in Zamfara State, during 2002 and 2003, a number of Muslims were convicted of crimes punishable by amputation. Frustrated by the delay in the actual carrying out of the sentence, one individual, who had been imprisoned for about three years—during which time his wife had left and his family consequently slipped into ever-increasing disarray—decided to help justice along. Using a stone, he attempted to amputate his own wrist! This example vividly illustrates the harm that can result when justice is delayed, which can in turn lead to justice denied.

There were also within the Gusau prison system several women awaiting trial for *zina* (from 2002 to 2005) as well as for culpable homicide, both of which are punishable by death. The latter, punished by hanging, is for allegedly having caused the death of their children. It is thought that women throw away their children, which could be construed as evidence of adultery, to avoid the punishment of stoning for *zina*. While Gusau is a large city, the lawyers working for the Legal Aid Council appeared to have no knowledge of these cases. In fact, there were only four Legal Aid Council lawyers (2003) for a population of about three million people in Zamfara State.[573] Due to understaffing, these victims did not have true access to the justice system that the laws and covenants are supposedly providing for them. These women, and others like them, continue to languish in prison.

Networking with the coalition of civil societies, nongovernmental organizations (NGOs), community-based organizations (CBOs), and others who are willing to assist in these cases is crucial. While those imprisoned have rights under the Nigerian Constitution—the right to a fair hearing, the right to have their cases heard by a court of law in their own language, the right of privacy, etc.—these rights will remain merely words on a piece of paper unless those accused are conscious of these rights and are able to enjoy them. With the high rate of illiteracy and little awareness of the law, the work of the Legal Aid Council becomes even more daunting. These challenges could be addressed through the government's making deliberate

---

573. As of the completion of this work (2012), this statement remains true.

policies at all levels to increase funding in areas such as personnel. NGOs can also contribute a great deal.

Another consideration is the social status of those accused. Generally speaking, affluent people have no trouble finding a lawyer, or even a team of lawyers, to assist them in the rare instance they find themselves in court. The people needing assistance with transportation to the courthouse, paying court fees, and other basic matters are those living in poor rural areas. These are the ones who often make up the majority of the accused. The situation is even more pressing for those convicted of capital offenses and other serious crimes.

The Islamic notion of justice should not be altered or tampered with according to the whims and caprices of those who possess the money and power to do so. NGOs and civil societies should by and large support a clear agenda that is commensurate to the values of the society in which they operate. Some NGOs do not always reflect this, a task made difficult when the perspectives and values of foreign donors drive the organizations' agendas. Like the waves of the sea, they move with the wind. Unfortunately, the programs often attached to well-meant funding may not necessarily be in tune with the realities and needs of the communities they serve.

Although there are complexities and challenges to the defense of an accused person before a Shariah court, as well as broader issues that can cloud the spirit and radiance of the temple of justice, we must be unwavering in our commitment to the lessons drawn from the Qur'an and Hadith, and all its commentaries, while allowing for the respect for an international standard for the rule of law. Human rights and due process cut across cultures and communities—these we should seek to express in our actions and pursue for the divinity of our humanity.

Compendium of Laws and Authorities (Appendices)

THE FOLLOWING APPENDICES PROVIDE some provisions in the Qur'an, Hadith, and other authorities, including relevant statutes and case law, that can be considered while arguing cases before Shariah courts. The concept of Shariah is revealed in the objectives of its practical provisions in the Holy Qur'an and other subsidiary legislations; general rules in contrast to selective, factionalism, or diminution. Tolerance and kindness is the pillar on which justice rests and strengthens the social structure of just communities.[574]

The Qur'an stresses the importance of the right to seek justice and the duty to do justice. Justice encompasses both the concept that all are equal and recognizes the need to help equalize those suffering from a deficiency or loss.[575] Emanating from this right is the right to be treated with justice and equity. Nonetheless, justice is not an absolute equality of treatment, since human beings are not equal as far as their human aptitude or their human condition is concerned.

---

574. Jones, *Some Cases on Criminal Procedure*.
575. Ashrof, *Islam and Gender Justice*, 178.

The Qur'an, the sacred scripture of Islam, considers justice to be a supreme virtue; it is the desire of Islam that justice stands next in order of priority to belief in God and its exclusive right to worship the truth of Muhammad's prophethood.[576] The Qur'an and Hadith lay down the principles of spirituality, faith, and justice. The scriptures demand that justice be met for all, and that it is an inherent right of all human beings under Islamic law.[577] The abiding dedication of the Qur'an to the foundational establishment of justice is found in its declaration, "And the Word of your Lord has been fulfilled in truth and in justice. None can change His Words" (6:115).

To render justice is a trust that God has conferred on the human being and, like all other trusts, its fulfillment must be guided by a sense of responsibility beyond mere conformity to set rules. Thus, the Qur'an states "to render justice, ranks as the most noble of acts of devotion next to belief in God; It is the greatest of all the duties entrusted to the prophets . . . and it is the strongest justification for man's stewardship of earth."[578]

Furthermore, this concise compilation of verses in the Holy Qur'an, Hadiths, and other legislations will hopefully serve as an additional body of knowledge. Over time, principles were elaborated for the study of Hadith by Islamic intellectuals, scholars, and jurists and they are commonly accredited to the science of Hadith study. Evidence that establishes or confirms the accuracy of Hadith as reliable, and the use of Hadith to verify or to disclaim knowledge of Islamic practice, is left to learned men or Islamic scholars who posses a deep understanding of Islamic jurisprudence and history. This Compendium pulls from this fountain of knowledge and wisdom.

Qur'anic provisions are presented here with the English translation, followed by tafsir al-Jalalayn—explanation of the text by approved learned Islamic scholars.[579] The provisions are grouped for easy access. The verses

---

576. Rane, *Reconstructing Jihad*, 193.
577. Cornell, *Voices of Islam*, 174.
578. Khadduri and Liebesny, *Law in the Middle East*, 243.
579. Holy Qur'an online resource, http://quran.com/.

may have been taken "out of context," but the author finds the content fascinating. Readers with access to the Qur'an should read the verses in their *fullness*; however, for readers without access to the Qur'an, I hope the verses will edify and guide you as they did me.

Selected Provisions from the Holy Qur'an and Tafsir[580]

General and Reinforcing Principles

Q. 24:1 We have sent down and made [that within it] obligatory and revealed therein verses of clear evidence that you might remember.

Tafsir al-Jalalayn: *This is, a sūra which We have revealed and prescribed (read faradnāhā, or [the intensive form] farradnāhā, on account of the large number of prescriptions contained in it) and wherein We have revealed manifest signs, [signs] containing clear indications, that perhaps you might remember (tadhakkarūna: the second tā' [of tatadhakkarūna] has been assimilated with the dhāl), that you might be admonished.*

Q. 60:8 Allah does not forbid you from those who do not fight you because of religion and do not expel you from your homes—from being righteous toward them and acting justly toward them. Indeed, Allah loves those who act justly.

---

580. Tafsir, interpretation means exegesis of the Qur'an.

Tafsir al-Jalalayn: God does not forbid you in regard to those who did not wage war against you, from among the disbelievers, on account of religion and did not expel you from your homes, that you should treat them kindly (an tabarrūhum is an inclusive substitution for alladhīna, 'those who') and deal with them justly: this was [revealed] before the command to struggle against them. Assuredly God loves the just . . .

Q. 7:199 Take what is given freely, enjoin what is good, and turn away from the ignorant.

Tafsir al-Jalalayn: Show forgiveness, enjoin what is good, and stay away from the foolish (i.e. don't punish them). And if an evil whisper comes to you from Shaytan (Satan), then seek refuge with Allah. Verily, He is Hearing, Knowing . . .

Q. 67:1–2 Blessed is He in whose hand is dominion, and He is over all things competent—[He] who created death and life to test you [as to] which of you is best in deed—and He is the Exalted in Might, the Forgiving—

Tafsir al-Jalalayn: Blessed, exalted above the attributes of created beings, is He in Whose hand, at Whose disposal, is [all] sovereignty, [all] authority and power, and He has power over all things. [He] Who created death, in this world, and life, in the Hereafter—or both of them in this world, since the sperm-drop is imbued with life, [life being] that [power] by which sensation becomes possible, death being the opposite of this or the non-existence of it—these being two [alternative] opinions; in the case of the latter [life in the Hereafter], 'creation' implies 'ordainment'—that He may try you, that He may test you in [this] life, [to see] which of you is best in conduct, [which of you] is most obedient to God, and He is the Mighty, in His vengeance against those who disobey Him, the Forgiving, to those who repent to Him;

Q. 4:110 And whoever does a wrong or wrongs himself but then seeks forgiveness of Allah will find Allah Forgiving and Merciful.

Tafsir al-Jalalayn: Whoever does evil, [commits] a sin by which another is harmed, as when Tu'ma falsely accused the Jew, or wrongs himself, committing a sin [the consequences of which are] limited to him, and then prays for God's forgiveness, for it, that is to say, [and then] he repents, he shall find God is Forgiving, Merciful, to him.

Right to Basic Necessities of Life

Q. 51:19 And from their properties was [given] the right of the [needy] petitioner and the deprived.

Tafsir al-Jalalayn: and there was a share in their wealth [assigned] for the beggar and the deprived, [the latter being] the one who does not beg, because of his self-restraint.

Q. 2:188 And do not consume one another's wealth unjustly or send it [in bribery] to the rulers in order that [they might aid] you [to] consume a portion of the wealth of the people in sin, while you know [it is unlawful].

Tafsir al-Jalalayn: Consume not your goods between you, that is to say, do not let one consume the goods of the other, in deception, that which is illicit according to the Law, such as theft and extortion; and, do not, proffer them, the regulation of these [goods] or any bribes, to the judges, that you may consume, as a result of any arbitration, a portion of other people's goods, embroiled, in sin while you are aware, that you are in error.

Q. 17:70 And we have certainly honored the children of Adam and carried them on the land and sea and provided for them of the good things and preferred them over much of what We have created, with [definite] preference.

Tafsir al-Jalalayn: And verily We have honored, We have preferred, the Children of Adam, [above other creation], by [giving them] knowledge, speech and [their being] a creation of even proportions amongst other things, including their [means of] purification after death, and carried them over land, on animal-back, and sea, in ships, and provided them with good things and We have preferred them above many of those whom We created, such as livestock and wild animals, with a marked preferment (the min [of mimman, 'of those whom'] has the sense of mā, 'of what', or something close to it, and includes the angels, the purpose being to give preference to the [angelic] genus; there is no requirement to give [explicit] preference to the individuals [of this category of being], since they [angels] are superior to mankind, excepting the prophets).

Q. 95:4 We have certainly created man in the best of stature;

Tafsir al-Jalalayn: Verily We created man (al-insān: the generic) in the best of forms, [in the best] proportioning of his shape.

Human Rights in Islam[581]

Q. 2:171 The example of those who disbelieve is like that of one who shouts at what hears nothing but calls and cries cattle or sheep—deaf, dumb and blind, so they do not understand.

Tafsir al-Jalalayn: The likeness, the attribute, of those who disbelieve, and the one who calls them to guidance, is as the likeness of one who shouts to that which hears nothing, save a call and a cry, only a sound, not understanding its meaning: when they listen to an admonition they are like cattle that hear the cry of their shepherd but do not understand what he is saying; they are deaf, dumb, blind—they do not comprehend, any admonition.

Q. 6:152 And do not approach the orphan's property except in a way that is best until he reaches maturity. And give full measure and weight in justice. We do not charge any soul except [with that within] its capacity. And when you testify, be just, even if [it concerns] a near relative. And the covenant of Allah fulfill. This has He instructed you that you may remember.

Tafsir al-Jalalayn: And that you do not approach the property of the orphan save with that, approach, which is fairer, namely, the one wherein lie his best interests, until he is of age, when he is sexually mature. And give full measure and full weight, in justice, fairly, desisting from any fraud. We do not charge any soul beyond its capacity, what it can bear in such [matters], so that if one makes a mistake in a measure or weight, and God knows that his intention had been well-meaning, then he suffers no blame, as is stated in one hadīth. And if you speak, [to pass] a judgement or otherwise, then be just, by being truthful, even if he, the person receiving the statement or the one being accused in it, should be a kinsman. And fulfill God's

---

581. In Islam, human right has a corresponding duty and obligation. It is based on the idea of human dignity and equality of mankind. The idea of human right in Islam is universal and uniform; it transcends barriers of location and is for all times. See Chaudhry, *Human Rights in Islam*, 12.

covenant. This is what He has charged you with, that perhaps you will remember (read tadhakkarūn or tadhkurūn), you will be admonished.

Q. 17:22 Do not make [as equal] with Allah another deity and [thereby] become censured and forsaken.

Tafsir al-Jalalayn: Do not set up another god besides God, or you will sit blameworthy, forsaken, with no one to assist you.

Q. 17:23 And your Lord has decreed that you not worship except Him, and to parents, good treatment. Whether one or both of them reach old age [while] with you, say not to them [so much as], "uff," and do not repel them but speak to them a noble word.

Tafsir al-Jalalayn: And your Lord has decreed, He has commanded, that you worship none save Him, and, that you show, kindness to parents, by being dutiful to them. If they should reach old age with you, one of them (ahaduhumā is the subject [of the verb]) or both (a variant reading [for yablughanna] has yablughān, 'both [should] reach', in which case ahaduhumā would be substituting for the [dual indicator] alif [of yablughān]) then do not say to them 'Fie' (read uffan or uffin, uffa or uffi, a verbal noun meaning tabban, 'perish!' or qubhan, 'evil!') nor repulse them, but speak to them gracious words, fair and gentle [words].

Q. 17:24 And lower to them the wing of humility out of mercy and say, "My Lord, have mercy upon them as they brought me up [when I was] small."

Tafsir al-Jalalayn: And lower to them the wing of humility, show them your submissive side, out of mercy, that is, on account of your affection for them, and say, 'My Lord, have mercy on them, just as they, had mercy on me when [they], reared me when I was little.'

Q. 17:25 Your Lord is most knowing of what is within yourselves. If you should be righteous [in intention]—then indeed He is ever, to the often returning [to Him], Forgiving.

Tafsir al-Jalalayn: Your Lord knows best what is in your hearts, [in the way] of what may be concealed of dutifulness or disobedience [to parents]. If you are righteous, obedient to God, then truly, to those who are penitent, those who return to obedience of Him, He is Forgiving, of any slip that might have issued on their part regarding their duty to the parents, so long as they do not conceal [within themselves] any disrespect [towards them].

Q. 17:26 And give the relative his right, and [also] the poor and the traveler, and do not spend wastefully.

Tafsir al-Jalalayn: And give the kinsman his due, of dutifulness and kindness, and the needy and the traveller [as well]; and do not squander, by expending for [any purpose] other than in obedience to God.

Q. 17:28 And if you [must] turn away from the needy awaiting mercy from your Lord which you expect, then speak to them a gentle word.

Tafsir al-Jalalayn: But if you [have to] overlook them, that is, the kinsmen and the others mentioned, and do not give to them, seeking mercy from your Lord, [a mercy] which you expect [in the future], that is, [you do not give to them] because of a request for provision which you are waiting to come to you [from your Lord], before you give to them, then speak to them gentle words, pleasant and reasonable [words], promising them that you will give to them when the provision [from God] arrives.

Q. 17:29 And do not make your hand [as] chained to your neck or extend it completely and [thereby] become blamed and insolvent.

Tafsir al-Jalalayn: And do not keep your hand chained to your neck, in other words, do not withhold it completely from expending, nor open it, in order to expend, completely, or you will sit blameworthy—this refers to the first case—and denuded, cut off, having nothing—this refers to the latter case.

Q. 17:30 Indeed, your Lord extends provision for whom He wills and restricts [it]. Indeed He is ever, concerning His servants, Acquainted and Seeing.

Tafsir al-Jalalayn: Truly your Lord expands provision, He makes it abundant, for whomever He will and He straitens, He restricts it for whomever He will. Indeed He is ever Aware and Seer of His servants, Knower of what they hide and what they manifest, giving them provision in accordance with their welfare.

Do Not Kill

Q. 17:33 And do not kill the soul which Allah has forbidden, except by right. And whoever is killed unjustly—We have given his heir authority, but let him not exceed limits in [the matter of] taking life. Indeed, he has been supported [by the law].

Tafsir al-Jalalayn:And do not slay the soul [whose life] God has made inviolable, except with due cause. Whoever is slain wrongfully, We have certainly given his heir, the one inheriting from him, a warrant, a sanction [to retaliate] against the slayer; but let him not commit excess, [let him not] overstep the bounds, in slaying, by slaying other than the killer [of the one slain], or by other than that [instrument] with which he [the slain] was killed; for he is supported [by the Law].

Q. 4:93 But whoever kills a believer intentionally—his recompense is Hell, wherein he will abide eternally, and Allah has become angry with him and has cursed him and has prepared for him a great punishment.

Tafsir al-Jalalayn: And whoever slays a believer deliberately, intending to kill him, with something that is lethal, aware of the fact that he [the slain] is a believer, his requital is Hell, abiding therein, and God is wroth with him and has cursed him, He has removed him from His mercy, and has prepared for him a mighty chastisement, in the Fire: this may be explained as [referring to] the person that deems such [killing] licit, or as being his requital if he were to be requited, but it would not be anything new if this threat [of punishment] were to be forgone, because of what He says: Other than that [that is, idolatry] He forgives whomever He will [Q. 4:48]. It is reported from Ibn 'Abbās that it [the verse] should be understood as it stands, abrogating other verses of 'forgiveness'. The verse in [sū rat] al-Baqara [Q. 2:178] clearly indicates that the one who kills deliberately should be killed in return, or if he is pardoned then he has to pay the blood-money, the value of which has already been mentioned. It is made clear in the Sunna that between the intentional and the unintentional, there is a type of killing that is identified as [being with] quasi-deliberate intent (shibh al-'amd), where the killer has slain with what in most cases is not lethal [implement]. In such a case, there is no [right to] retaliation and blood-money is paid instead, so that it [this type of killing] is described as intentional, but [considered] unintentional in [that there applies] the fixing of the period [for payment] and the sharing of the burden [by the killer's clan]; in this [case] and that of intentional killing redemption is more urgent than in unintentional killing.

Q. 17:31 And do not kill your children for fear of poverty. We provide for them and for you. Indeed, their killing is ever a great sin.

Tafsir al-Jalalayn: And do not slay your children, by burying them alive, fearing penury, poverty. We shall provide for them and for you. Slaying them is truly a great sin.

Q. 6:151 Say, "Come, I will recite what your Lord has prohibited to you. [He commands] that you not associate anything with Him, and to parents, good treatment, and do not kill your children out of poverty; We will provide for you and them. And do not approach immoralities—what is apparent of them and what is concealed. And do not kill the soul which Allah has forbidden [to be killed] except by [legal] right. This has He instructed you that you may use reason."

Tafsir al-Jalalayn: Say: 'Come, I will recite that which your Lord has made a sacred duty for you: that (allā: [consisting of an-lā] and being explicative) you associate nothing with Him, that you be dutiful to parents, and that you do not slay your children, by burying them alive, because of poverty, destitution, that you may fear—We will provide for you and them—and that you do not draw near any acts of lewdness, grave sins, such as fornication, whether it be manifest or concealed, that is, [acts committed] overtly or in secret, and that you do not slay the life which God has made sacred, except rightfully, as in the case of retaliation, or [as] the prescribed punishment for apostasy, and the stoning of an adulterer. This, which is mentioned, is what He has charged you with, that perhaps you will understand, reflect . . . '

Q. 5:32 Because of that, We decreed upon the Children of Israel that whoever kills a soul unless for a soul or for corruption [done] in the land— it is as if he had slain mankind entirely. And whoever saves one—it is as if he had saved mankind entirely. And our messengers had certainly come to them with clear proofs. Then indeed many of them, [even] after that, throughout the land, were transgressors.

Tafsir al-Jalalayn: Whoever does evil, [commits] a sin by which another is harmed, as when Tu'ma falsely accused the Jew, or wrongs himself, committing a sin [the consequences of which are] limited to him, and then prays for God's forgiveness, for it, that is to say, [and then] he repents, he shall find God is Forgiving, Merciful, to him.

Right to Justice

Q. 4:105 Indeed, We have revealed to you, [O Muhammad], the Book in truth so you may judge between the people by that which Allah has shown you. And do not be for the deceitful an advocate.

Tafsir al-Jalalayn: Tu'ma b. Ubayriq stole a coat of mail and hid it with a Jew. When it was discovered with the latter, Tu'ma accused him of having stolen it, and swore by God that he [Tu'ma] had not stolen it, and his clan asked the Prophet (s) to advocate on his behalf and absolve him, whereupon the following was revealed: Surely We have revealed to you the Book, the Qur'ān, with the truth (bi'l-haqq is semantically connected to anzalnā, 'We have revealed') so that you may judge between people by that which God has shown you, what God has taught you. And do not be a disputant for traitors, like Tu'ma, disputing on their behalf.[582]

Q. 4:135 O you, who have believed, be persistently standing firm in justice, witnesses for Allah, even if it be against yourselves or parents and relatives. Whether one is rich or poor, Allah is more worthy of both. So follow not [personal] inclination, lest you not be just. And if you distort [your testimony] or refuse [to give it], then indeed Allah is ever, with what you do, Acquainted.

Tafsir al-Jalalayn: O you who believe, be upright in justice; witnesses, of the truth, for God, even though it, the witnessing, be against yourselves, so be witness against them [yourselves] by affirming the truth and not concealing it; or, against, parents and kinsmen, whether the person, witnessed against, be rich or poor; God is closer to the two, than you and He has better knowledge of what is good for them. So do not follow any whim, in your testimonies by being partial to the rich one, seeking his pleasure, or [by being partial] to the poor one out of compassion for him, lest you swerve, so that you do not incline away from the truth, for if you twist (a variant

---

582. See Roald, *Women In Islam*, 108.

reading [for talwūw] has talū) [if] you distort your testimony, or refrain, from giving
it, surely God is ever aware of what you do, and will requite you accordingly.

Q. 5:8 O you who have believed, be persistently standing firm for
Allah, witnesses in justice, and do not let the hatred of a people prevent
you from being just. Be just; that is nearer to righteousness. And fear Allah;
indeed, Allah is Acquainted with what you do.

Tafsir al-Jalalayn: O you, who believe, be upright before God, in [fulfilling]
what is His due, witnesses in equity, in justice. Let not hatred of a people, namely, the
disbelievers, cause you not to be just, and to harm them on account of their enmity; be
just, towards both friend and foe, that, justice is nearer to God-fearing. And fear God;
surely God is aware of what you do, and will requite you for it.

Q. 5:45 And We ordained for them therein a life for a life, an eye
for an eye, a nose for a nose, an ear for an ear, a tooth for a tooth, and for
wounds is legal retribution. But whoever gives [up his right as] charity, it
is an expiation for him. And whoever does not judge by what Allah has
revealed—then it is those who are the wrongdoers.[583]

Tafsir al-Jalalayn: And therein, in the Torah, We prescribed, We made obligatory,
for them that a life, be slain in return, for a life, if it has slain one; and an eye, should
be gouged out, for an eye, and a nose, is to be cut off, for a nose, and an ear, is to be
amputated, for an ear, and a tooth, should be pulled out, for a tooth (a variant reading
has the last four [nouns] in the nominative); and for wounds (read wa'l-jurūhu or
wa'l-jurūha) retaliation, that is, the person is entitled to retaliate if this is feasible, as
in the case of a hand or a leg; but in cases where one is not able to [retaliate], this is
left to arbitration. Although this stipulation was prescribed for them, it is established
in our Law; but whoever forgoes it, that is, retaliation, out of charity, able to restrain
himself, then that shall be an expiation for him, of what he has done [of other
sins]. Whoever does not judge according to what God has revealed, in the matter of
retaliation and otherwise, those are the evildoers.

Q. 7:29 Say, [O Muhammad], "My Lord has ordered justice and that
you maintain yourselves [in worship of Him] at every place [or time]

---

583. See also Kamrava, *New Voices of Islam*, 155.

of prostration, and invoke Him, sincere to Him in religion." Just as He originated you, you will return [to life]—

Tafsir al-Jalalayn: Say: 'My Lord enjoins justice, fairness. And set (wa-aqīmū is a supplement to the [syntactical] significance of bi'l-qist, 'justice', that is to say, [it is as if] He said, 'Be just and set [your faces]', or read [wa-aqīmū] with an implied fa-aqbilū, 'so turn' towards it) your faces, towards God, in every place of worship, performing your prostrations purely for Him, and call upon Him, worship Him, devoting your religion to Him, [free] of any idolatry. As He brought you into being, [as] He created you, when you were nothing, so you will return, that is, [so] He will bring you back to life on the Day of Resurrection.

Q. 16:90 Indeed, Allah orders justice and good conduct and giving to relatives and forbids immorality and bad conduct and oppression. He admonishes you that perhaps you will be reminded.

Tafsir al-Jalalayn: Indeed God enjoins justice—[that is] affirmation of [His] Oneness, or [actually] being fair, and virtue, performance of the [religious] obligations, or that you should worship God as if you were able to see Him, as [reported] in the hadīth; and giving to kinsfolk—He has singled it [kinship] out for mention by way of [highlighting] its importance—and He forbids lewdness, fornication, and abomination, with regard to the [stipulations of the] Law, [abomination] such as disbelief and acts of disobedience, and aggression, wrongdoing against people—He also singles this out for mention by way of [showing] its importance; just as He began with [the mention of] 'lewdness', in this way, He admonishes you, through commands and prohibitions, so that you might remember, [that you might] be admonished (tadhakkarūna, 'you [might] remember', the original tā' [of tatadhakkarūnu] has been assimilated with the dhāl). In the Mustadrak [of al-Hākim al-Naysābūrī] it is reported from Ibn Masʿūd that [he said]: 'This [verse] is the most comprehensive verse in the Qur'ān in terms of [what is] good and [what is] evil.'

Q. 42:15 So to that [religion of Allah] invite, [O Muhammad], and remain on a right course as you are commanded and do not follow their inclinations but say, "I have believed in what Allah has revealed of the Qur'an, and I have been commanded to do justice among you. Allah is our Lord and your Lord. For us are our deeds, and for you your deeds. There is no [need for] argument between us and you. Allah will bring us together, and to Him is the [final] destination."

Tafsir al-Jalalayn; So to that then, [to that] affirmation of [God's] Oneness, summon, O Muhammad (s), people, and be upright, in [summoning them to] this, just as you have been commanded, and do not follow them in their desires, to abandon it. And say: 'I believe in whatever Book God has revealed. And I have been commanded to be just between you, in passing judgement. God is our Lord and your Lord. Our deeds concern us and your deeds concern you, and so each [one of us] will be requited according to his [own] deeds. There is no argument, [no] dispute, between us and you—this was [revealed] before the command to struggle [against them]. God will bring us together, at the [time of the] Return to decide [definitively] between us, and to Him is the [final] destination', the [ultimate] return.

Q. 57:25 We have already sent Our messengers with clear evidences and sent down with them the Scripture and the balance that the people may maintain [their affairs] in justice. And We sent down iron, wherein is great military might and benefits for the people, and so that Allah may make evident those who support Him and His messengers' unseen. Indeed, Allah is Powerful and Exalted in Might.

Tafsir al-Jalalayn: We have verily sent Our messengers, the angels, to prophets, with clear signs, with the definitive proofs, and We revealed with them the Scripture and the Balance, justice, so that mankind may uphold justice. And We sent down iron, We caused it to be extracted from mineral ores, wherein is great might, with which one may wage battle, and [many] uses for mankind, and so that God may know, a knowledge of direct vision (li-ya 'lama'Llāhu is a supplement to li-yaqūma'l-nāsu, 'so that mankind may uphold') those who help Him, by helping [to uphold] His religion through [the use of] instruments of war made of metal and otherwise, and His messengers through the Unseen (bi'l-ghaybi: a circumstantial qualifier referring to the [suffixed pronoun] hā', 'Him', of yansuruhu, '[who] aid Him'), that is to say, while He [God] is not seen by them in this world. Ibn 'Abbās said: 'They help Him even though they do not see Him' (yansurūnahu wa-lā yubsirūnahu). Assuredly God is Strong, Mighty, without any need of being helped, but such [help] benefits those who proffer it.

Right to Honor

Q. 24:4 And those who accuse chaste women and then do not produce four witnesses—lash them with eighty lashes and do not accept from them testimony ever after. And those are the defiantly disobedient . . . [584]

Tafsir al-Jalalayn: And those who accuse honourable women [in wedlock], who are chaste, of fornication, and then do not bring four witnesses, to testify as eyewitnesses to their fornication, strike them eighty lashes, that is, each one of them, and do not accept any testimony from them ever, in anything; and those, they are the immoral, for committing a grave sin (kabīra) . . .

Q. 33:58 And those who harm believing men and believing women for [something] other than what they have earned have certainly born upon themselves a slander and manifest sin.

Tafsir al-Jalalayn: And those who cause hurt to believing men and believing women without the latter's having done anything, [those who] accuse them of what they have not done, have verily borne [the guilt of] calumny, they have borne lies, and [the burden of] manifest sin.

Right to Freedom of Religion

Q. 2:256 There shall be no compulsion in [acceptance of] the religion. The right course has become clear from the wrong. So whoever disbelieves in Taghut and believes in Allah has grasped the most trustworthy handhold with no break in it. And Allah is Hearing and Knowing.

Tafsir al-Jalalayn: There is no compulsion in, entering into, religion. Rectitude has become clear from error, that is to say, through clear proofs it has become manifest that faith is rectitude and disbelief is error: this was revealed concerning the Ansār [of Medina] who tried to compel their sons to enter into Islam; so whoever disbelieves in the false deity, namely, Satan or idols (tāghūt, 'false deity', is used in a singular and plural sense), and believes in God, has laid hold of the most firm handle, the tight

---

584. Abbas Abdullahi Machika, the former Attorney General of Katsina State, opined that verses 6, 7, 8 and 9 of chapter 24 of the Holy Qur'an, contain an elaborate procedure of Li'an (oath of mutual appreciation between husband and wife) under Islamic Law (*Guide to Advocate*, 79).

knot, unbreaking, that cannot be severed; God is Hearing, of what is said, Knowing, of what is done.

Q. 5:92 And obey Allah and obey the Messenger and beware. And if you turn away—then know that upon Our Messenger is only [the responsibility for] clear notification.

Tafsir al-Jalalayn: *And obey God and obey the Messenger, and beware, of disobedient acts; but if you turn away, from obedience, then know that Our Messenger's duty is only to proclaim plainly, to convey clearly [the Message]—your requital falls on Us.*

Q. 5:99 Not upon the Messenger is [responsibility] except [for] notification. And Allah knows whatever you reveal and whatever you conceal.

Tafsir al-Jalalayn: *The duty of the Messenger is only to convey [the Message], to you; and God knows what you reveal, what deeds you manifest, and what you hide, and what of these you conceal, and He will requite you for it.*

Q. 6:107 But if Allah had willed, they would not have associated. And We have not appointed you over them as a guardian, nor are you a manager over them.

Tafsir al-Jalalayn: *Had God willed, they would not have been idolaters; and We have not set you as a keeper over them, a watcher, so that you might then requite them for their deeds; nor are you a guardian over them, so that you might [be able to] coerce them to faith—this was [revealed] before the command to fight [them].*

Q. 10:99 And had your Lord willed, those on earth would have believed—all of them entirely. Then, [O Muhammad], would you compel the people in order that they become believers?

Tafsir al-Jalalayn: *And if your Lord willed, all who are in the earth would have believed together. Would you then compel people, to do what God did not will that they do, until they are believers? No!*

Q. 10:108 Say, "O mankind, the truth has come to you from your Lord, so whoever is guided is only guided for [the benefit of] his soul, and whoever goes astray only goes astray [in violation] against it. And I am not over you a manager."

Tafsir al-Jalalayn: Say; 'O people, that is, people of Mecca, the Truth has come to you from your Lord. So whoever is guided, is guided only for the sake of his own soul, since the reward of his being guided will be his, and whoever errs, errs only against it, since the evil consequence of his erring shall befall [only] it [his soul]. And I am not a guardian over you', that I might then compel you to [accept] guidance.

Q. 16:82 But if they turn away, [O Muhammad]—then only upon you is [responsibility for] clear notification.

Tafsir al-Jalalayn: But if they turn away, [if] they reject Islam, your duty, O Muhammad (s), is only to convey [the Message] plainly—this was [revealed] before the command to fight [the disbelievers].

Q. 18:29 And say, "The truth is from your Lord, so whoever wills—let him believe; and whoever wills—let him disbelieve." Indeed, We have prepared for the wrongdoers a fire whose walls will surround them. And if they call for relief, they will be relieved with water like murky oil, which scalds [their] faces. Wretched is the drink, and evil is the resting place.

Tafsir al-Jalalayn: And say, to him and to his companions that this Qur'ān is, 'The truth [that comes] from your Lord; so whoever will, let him believe, and whoever will, let him disbelieve'—this is [meant as] a threat to them. Indeed We have prepared for the wrongdoers, that is, the disbelievers, a Fire, and they will be surrounded by its pavilion, [by] that which encloses [the Fire itself]. If they cry out for help, they will be succoured with water like molten copper, like thick [burning] oil, which scalds faces, because of [the intensity of] its heat, if it is brought near them. What an evil drink, that is, and how ill, is the Fire [as], a resting-place! (murtafaqan is a specification derived from the agent of the verb, in other words, vile is the person choosing to rest thereon; and this is in contrast to what He will say next about Paradise: How fair a resting-place [below, verse 31]. For, indeed, what resting-place can there be in the Fire?

Q. 42:48 But if they turn away—then We have not sent you, [O Muhammad], over them as a guardian; upon you is only [the duty of] notification. And indeed, when We let man taste mercy from us, he rejoices in it; but if evil afflicts him for what his hands have put forth, then indeed, man is ungrateful.

Tafsir al-Jalalayn: *But if they are disregardful, of answering [God], We have not sent you as a keeper over them, to keep [track of] their deeds by securing what is demanded of them. Your duty is only to deliver the Message—this was [revealed] before the command to struggle [against them]. And indeed when We let man taste from Us some mercy, some grace, such as wealth and good health, he exults in it; but if some ill, [some] calamity, befalls them (the pronoun here refers to 'man', on the basis of the [plural import of the] generic noun) because of what their [own] hands have sent ahead, [because of what] they have offered [of deeds]—the expression refers to 'the hands' because most actions are effected by them), then lo! man is ungrateful, for the grace.*

Q. 88:21 So remind, [O Muhammad]; you are only a reminder.

Tafsir al-Jalalayn: So remind, them of God's graces and the proofs affirming His Oneness. For you are only admonishers . . .

Q. 88:22 You are not over them a controller.

Tafsir al-Jalalayn: *you are not a taskmaster over them (a variant reading [for musaytir] has musaytir, that is to say, [not one who has been] given authority over them)—this was [revealed] before the command to struggle [against the disbelievers].*

Right to Privacy

Q. 24:27 O you, who have believed, do not enter houses other than your own houses until you ascertain welcome and greet their inhabitants. That is best for you; perhaps you will be reminded.

Tafsir al-Jalalayn: *O you, who believe, do not enter houses other than your houses until you have [first] asked permission and greeted their occupants. So a person must say, 'Peace be upon you, may I enter?', as is stated in one hadīth. That is better for you, than entering without permission, that perhaps you might remember (tadhakkarūna: the second tā [of tatadhakkarūna] has been assimilated with the dhāl) the superiority of such [conduct] and so follow it.*

Q. 24:58 O you who have believed, let those whom your right hands possess and those who have not [yet] reached puberty among you ask permission of you [before entering] at three times: before the dawn prayer and when you put aside your clothing [for rest] at noon and after the night prayer. [These are] three times of privacy for you. There is no blame upon you nor upon them beyond these [periods], for they continually circulate among you—some of you, among others. Thus does Allah make clear to you the verses; and Allah is Knowing and Wise.

Tafsir al-Jalalayn: O you who believe, let those whom your right hands own, of male slaves and female slaves, and those of you who have not reached puberty, from among the free men, and who have not become [sexually] aware of women, ask leave of you three times: at three times [of the day]: before the dawn prayer, and when you put off your garments at noon, and after the night prayer. [These are] three periods of privacy for you (read thalāthu ['awrātin lakum] with nominative inflection as the predicate of an implied subject followed by a genitive annexation, with the annexed term standing in place thereof [of the predicate], in other words [the implied predicate followed by the annexation is] hiya awqāt, 'these are times of …'; or read thalātha ['awrātin lakum] in the accusative, the implication being that awqāta is itself in the accusative as a substitute for the [syntactical] status of what precedes it, in place of which stands the annexed term). It is because clothes are taken off that private parts are revealed during such [periods]. Neither you nor they, namely, slaves and young boys, would be at fault, in entering upon you without asking leave, at other times, that is, after the three times of day [specified]; they frequent you, to provide service, [as] some of you [do] with others (this sentence corroborates the preceding one). So, just as He has clarified what has been mentioned, God clarifies for you the signs, the rulings; and God is Knower, of the affairs of His creatures, Wise, in what He has ordained for them. It is said that the 'permission' verse (āyat al-isti'idhān) was abrogated; but it is also said that it was not [abrogated], but that people thought little of neglecting to seek permission [in such situations].

Q. 49:12 O you, who have believed, avoid much [negative] assumption. Indeed, some assumption is sin. And do not spy or backbite each other. Would one of you like to eat the flesh of his brother when dead? You would detest it. And fear Allah; indeed, Allah is Accepting of repentance and Merciful.

Tafsir al-Jalalayn: O you, who believe, shun much suspicion. Indeed some suspicions are sins; that is to say, it causes one to fall into sin. This [suspicion] may have many forms, such as thinking ill of the good folk from among the believers—and such [good folk] are many—in contrast to the immoral individuals among them in whose case there is no sin, so long as it [the suspicion] is in accordance with their outward behavior. And do not spy (tajassasū: one of the two tā letters [of tatajassasū] has been omitted): do not pursue the imperfections and faults of Muslims by searching them out; nor backbite one another, do not speak of him by [mentioning] something which he is averse to [having mentioned of himself], even if it be true. Would any of you love to eat the flesh of his brother dead? (read maytan or mayyitan). That is to say, it would not be right for him [to do so]. You would abhor it. Thus to backbite him in life would be like eating his flesh when he is dead. This latter [form of behavior] has been suggested to you and you were averse to it, so be averse to the former too. And fear God, that is, His punishment for backbiting, by repenting of it; assuredly God is Relenting, accepting of the penitence of those who repent, Merciful, to them.

Q. 24:28 And if you do not find anyone therein, do not enter them until permission has been given you. And if it is said to you, "Go back," then go back; it is purer for you. And Allah is knowing of what you do.

Tafsir al-Jalalayn:And if you do not find anyone in them, to give you permission, [still] do not enter them until permission has been given to you. And if it is said to you, when you are seeking permission, 'Go away,' then go away, for this, going away, is purer, that is, better, for you, than sitting [and waiting] at the doorstep. And God knows what you do, whether you enter with permission or without it, and He will requite you for it.

Arbitrary Imprisonment

Q. 6:164 Say, "Is it other than Allah I should desire as a lord while He is the Lord of all things? And every soul earns not [blame] except against itself, and no bearer of burdens will bear the burden of another. Then to your Lord is your return and He will inform you concerning that over which you used to differ."

Tafsir al-Jalalayn: Say: 'Shall I seek any other than God for a lord, for a god, in other words, I shall not seek any other than Him, when He is the Lord, the Possessor, of all things?' Every soul earns, of sin, only against itself; and no burdened, [no] sinful, soul shall bear the burden of another, soul. Then to your Lord shall you return, and He will inform you of that over which you differed.

Unlawful Sex

Q. 17:32 And do not approach unlawful sexual intercourse. Indeed, it is ever an immorality and is evil as a way.

Tafsir al-Jalalayn: And do not come [anywhere] near fornication—this [form of expressing it] is more effective than [saying] 'Do not commit it'. It is indeed an indecency, an abomination, and, it is, an evil way . . .

Abstain from Unlawful Sexual Relationship

Q. 24:33—But let them who find not [the means for] marriage abstain [from sexual relations] until Allah enriches them from His bounty. And those who seek a contract [for eventual emancipation] from among whom your right hands possess—then make a contract with them if you know there is within them goodness and give them from the wealth of Allah which He has given you. And do not compel your slave girls to prostitution, if they desire chastity, to seek [thereby] the temporary interests of worldly life. And if someone should compel them, then indeed, Allah is [to them], after their compulsion, Forgiving and Merciful.

Tafsir al-Jalalayn: And let those who cannot find the means to marry be continent, [those who do not have] the bridal money or the means for financial support needed for marriage, [let them restrain themselves] from fornication, until God enriches them, [until] He improves their means, out of His bounty, and they marry. And those who seek a written contract [of emancipation], from among those whom your right hand owns, of male slaves and female slaves, contract with them accordingly, if you know in them any good, such as trustworthiness and the ability to earn [income] in order to fulfill the amount stated in the written contract, which might be worded for example thus: 'I contract you for [the amount of] two thousand *to be paid over a period of two months, at one thousand a month, and if you fulfill this, you are a free man', and the other would say, 'I accept'; and give them — this is a command for the [slaves'] owners—out of the wealth of God which He has given you, in the measure that will help them to fulfill their commitment to you (the action of ītā', 'giving', here suggests that some of the amount to which they have committed themselves should be waived). And do not compel your slave-girls, your handmaidens, to prostitution, fornication, when they desire to be chaste, to abstain therefrom (this 'desire' is the cause of the [act of] 'compulsion', so that the statement is not properly a conditional), that you may seek, through such compulsion, the transient things of the life of this world—this was revealed regarding 'Abd Allāh b. Ubayy, who used to force his slave-girls to earn money through fornication. And should anyone compel them, then surely God, after their compulsion, will be Forgiving, to these [slave-girls], Merciful, to them.*

Q. 42:37 And those who avoid the major sins and immoralities, and when they are angry, they forgive . . .

Tafsir al-Jalalayn: and those who avoid grave sins and indecencies, those [acts] that require [the implementing of] the prescribed legal punishments (hudūd) ([the supplement above is] an example of supplementing the part to the whole) and [who], when they are angry, forgive, they let it pass . . .

Provision for Fornication (*Zina*)

Q. 24:2 The [unmarried] woman or [unmarried] man found guilty of sexual intercourse—lash each one of them with a hundred lashes, and do not be taken by pity for them in the religion of Allah, if you should believe in Allah and the Last Day. And let a group of the believers witness their punishment.

Tafsir al-Jalalayn: As for the fornicatress and the fornicator, that is, of those not in wedlock—because those [in wedlock] are stoned according to the Sunna (the al [in al-zāniya, 'the fornicatress', and al-zānī, 'the fornicator'] according to some mentioned [opinions] is a relative [particle]; the clause [al-zāniyatu wa'l-zānī] is a subject, and because of its similarity to a conditional, the fā has been inserted into the predicate, which is [the following, fa'jlidū]): strike each of them a hundred lashes, [a hundred] strikes (one says jaladahu to mean daraba jildahu, 'he struck him on the skin'). According to the Sunna, in addition to this [punishment] there is also banishment for a whole year.

The slave, however, receives half of the mentioned [punishment]. And do not let any pity for them overcome you in God's religion, that is to say, in [the fulfillment of] His rulings, by disregarding any part of their prescribed punishment, if you believe in God and the Last Day, namely, the Day of Resurrection: in this [statement] there is an incitement to [abide by] what was [mentioned] before the conditional [above] and it also constitutes the response to the latter, or [at least is] an indication of the response to it. And let their punishment, the flogging, be witnessed by a group of the believers—some say [that this should be a group of] three; some say four, as in the number of witnesses testifying to an act of fornication.

Q. 24:5 Except for those who repent thereafter and reform, for indeed, Allah is Forgiving and Merciful.

Tafsir al-Jalalayn: except those who repent thereafter and make amends, in their deeds, for God is indeed Forgiving, of their [unsubstantiated] accusations, Merciful, to them, in inspiring them to make repentance whereby their immorality is curbed and their testimony becomes [once again] acceptable—some say, however, that it can never be accepted [thereafter], if the proviso is taken to refer to the last clause.

Q. 24:6 And those who accuse their wives [of adultery] and have no witnesses except themselves—then the witness of one of them [shall be] four testimonies [swearing] by Allah that indeed, he is of the truthful.

Tafsir al-Jalalayn: And those who accuse their wives, of fornication, but have no witnesses, to [substantiate] this, except themselves—which happened with some Companions—then the testimony of one of them (fa-shahādatu ahadihim, the subject) shall be to testify [swearing] by God four times (araba'a shahādātin, is in the accusative as a verbal noun) that he is indeed being truthful, in accusing his wife of committing fornication,

Q. 24:7 And the fifth [oath will be] that the curse of Allah be upon him if he should be among the liars.

Tafsir al-Jalalayn: and a fifth time that God's wrath shall be upon him if he were lying, in this (the predicate of the subject [fa-shahādatu ahadihim, 'then the testimony of one of them'] is [the implicit] 'will spare him the prescribed [legal] punishment for [false] accusation').

Q. 24:8 But it will prevent punishment from her if she gives four testimonies [swearing] by Allah that indeed, he is of the liars.

Tafsir al-Jalalayn: And the punishment, namely, the prescribed [legal] punishment for fornication that is established upon his testimony, shall be averted from her if she testify [swearing] by God four times that he is indeed lying, in accusing her of having fornicated . . .

Q. 4:58 Indeed, Allah commands you to render trusts to whom they are due and when you judge between people to judge with justice. Excellent is that which Allah instructs you. Indeed, Allah is ever Hearing and Seeing.

Tafsir al-Jalalayn: Verily, God commands you to restore trusts, that is, the rights entrusted [to you by others], back to their owners: this was revealed when 'Alī, may God be pleased with him, took the key of the Ka'ba from its keeper, 'Uthmān b. Talha al-Hajabī, by force, upon the arrival of the Prophet (s) in Mecca in the year of the Conquest, after he ['Uthmān] had tried to prevent him ['Alī from taking it] saying, 'If I had known that he was the Messenger of God, I would not have prevented him'. The Messenger of God (s) then ordered him ['Alī] to give it back to him ['Uthmān] saying to him, 'Here you are, [it is yours] now and always'. He ['Uthmān] was amazed by this, whereupon 'Alī recited to him this verse, and he accepted Islam. Upon his death, he ['Uthmān] gave it [the key] to his brother, Shayba, and thus it remained in [the keep of] his descendants. Although the verse was revealed regarding a specific occasion, it holds true in general on account of the plural person [to which it is addressed]. And when you judge between people, He commands, that you judge with justice. Excellent is (ni'immā, the mīm of ni'ima has been assimilated with the indefinite particle mā, which is the object described, in other words, na'ima shay'an, 'an excellent thing [is]') the admonition God gives you, to restore a trust and to judge with justice. God is ever Hearer, of what is said, Seer, of what is done.

Q. 2:143 Thus, have We made of you an Ummah justly balanced, that ye might be witnesses over the nations and the Messenger a witness over yourselves; and We appointed the Qibla to which thou was used, only to test those who followed the Messenger from those who would turn on their heels (From the Faith). Indeed it was (A change) momentous, except to those guided by Allah. And never would Allah Make your faith of no effect. For Allah is to all people Most surely full of kindness, Most Merciful.

Tafsir al-Jalalayn: Thus, in the same way that We guided you to it, We appointed you, O community of Muhammad (s), a midmost community, excellent and upright, that you might be witnesses to the people, on the Day of Resurrection, that their messengers delivered [the Message] to them; and that the Messenger might be a witness to you, that he delivered [the Message] to you, and We did not appoint, make, the direction, for you now, the direction, you were facing, that is the Ka'ba: the Prophet (s) used to face it in prayer, but when he emigrated he was commanded to face the Holy House [of Jerusalem], [in order to win the hearts of the Jews]. He prayed in this direction for sixteen or seventeen months before he changed direction; except that We might know, [that it become] manifest knowledge, who followed the Messenger, and believed in him, from him who turned on his heels, and returned to unbelief doubting the religion and thinking that the Prophet (s) was confused about this issue; and a number of them apostatized as a result of this—though it, the change of direction, were (wa-in, 'though', is softened, and its noun apocopated, originally being: wa-innahā) a grave thing, troublesome for people, save for those, of them, whom God has guided; but God would never cause your faith, that is, your prayers towards the Holy House [of Jerusalem], to be wasted, but He will reward you for them (the reason that this [verse] was revealed was that some had asked about the status of those that had died before the change of direction [of prayer]); truly, God is Gentle with, believing, people, Merciful, when He does not let their deeds go to waste (al-ra'fa means 'intensity of mercy', and is mentioned first to allow for the end rhyme of the verse [with the preceding one]).

Q. 25:68 Those who invoke not, with Allah, any other god, nor slay such life as Allah has made sacred except for just cause, nor commit fornication;—and any that does this (not only) meets punishment.

Tafsir al-Jalalayn and [those] who do not call on another god along with God, nor slay the soul which God has forbidden, that it be slain, except with due cause, and who do not commit fornication—for whoever does that, namely, [whoever does] one of these three things, shall meet with retribution ...

Q. 49:6 O you, who have believed, if there comes to you a disobedient one with information, investigate, lest you harm a people out of ignorance and become, over what you have done, regretful.

Equality Before the Creator

Q. 49:13 O mankind, indeed We have created you from male and female and made you peoples and tribes that you may know one another. Indeed, the most noble of you in the sight of Allah is the most righteous of you. Indeed, Allah is Knowing and Acquainted.

Tafsir al-Jalalayn: O mankind! We have indeed created you from a male and a female, [from] Adam and Eve, and made you nations (shu ʿūb is the plural of sha ʿb, which is the broadest category of lineage) and tribes (qabā ʾil, which are smaller than nations, and are followed by ʿamā ʾir, 'tribal districts', then butūn, 'tribal sub-districts', then afkhādh, 'sub-tribes', and finally fasā ʾil, 'clans'; for example Khuzayma is the sha ʿb, while Kināna is the qabīla, Quraysh is the ʿimāra, Qusayy is the batn, Hāshim is the fakhdh, and ʿAbbās is the fasīla) that you may come to know one another (ta ʿārafū: one of the two tā letters [of tata ʿārafū] has been omitted), that you may acquire knowledge of [the customs of] one another and not to boast to one another of [whose is the more] noble lineage, for pride lies only in [the extent to which you have] fear of God. Truly the noblest of you in the sight of God is the most God-fearing among you. Truly God is Knower, of you, Aware, of your inner thoughts.

Judge in Truth Without Discrimination

Q. 5:48 And We have revealed to you, [O Muhammad], the Book in truth, confirming that which preceded it of the Scripture and as a criterion over it. So judge between them by what Allah has revealed and do not follow their inclinations away from what has come to you of the truth. To each of you We prescribed a law and a method. Had Allah willed, He would have made you one nation [united in religion], but [He intended] to test you in what He has given you; so race to [all that is] good. To Allah is your return all together and He will [then] inform you concerning that over which you used to differ?

Tafsir al-Jalalayn: *And We have revealed to you, O Muhammad (s), the Book, the Qur'ān, with the truth (bi'l-haqq is semantically connected to anzalnā, 'We have revealed') confirming the Book that was before it and watching over it, testifying [to it] — the 'Book' means the Scriptures. So judge between them, between the People of the Scripture, if they take their cases before you, according to what God has revealed, to you, and do not follow their whims, deviating, away from the truth that has come to you. To every one of you, O communities, We have appointed a divine law and a way, a clear path in religion, for them to proceed along. If God had willed, He would have made you one community, following one Law, but, He separated you one from the other, that He may try you in what He has given to you, of the differing Laws, in order to see who among you is obedient and who is disobedient. So vie with one another in good works, strive hastily thereunto; to God you shall all return, through resurrection, and He will then inform you of that in which you differed, in the matter of religion, and requite each of you according to his deeds.*

Protest Against Tyranny

Q. 4:148 Allah does not like the public mention of evil except by one who has been wronged. And ever is Allah Hearing and Knowing.

Tafsir al-Jalalayn: *God does not like the utterance of evil words out loud, by any person, that is to say, He will punish him for it, unless a person has been wronged, in which case He would not punish him for uttering it out loud, when he is informing [others] of the wrong done to him by the wrong-doer or summoning [them] against him. God is ever Hearer, of what is said, Knower, of what is done.*

Q. 5:32 Because of that, We decreed upon the Children of Israel that whoever kills a soul unless for a soul or for corruption [done] in the land—it is as if he had slain mankind entirely. And whoever saves one—it is as if he had saved mankind entirely. And our messengers had certainly come to them with clear proofs. Then indeed many of them, [even] after that, throughout the land, were transgressors.

Tafsir al-Jalalayn: *Because of that, which Cain did, We decreed for the Children of Israel that whoever slays a soul for other than a soul, slain, or for, other than, corruption, committed, in the land, in the way of unbelief, fornication or waylaying and the like, it shall be as if he had slain mankind altogether; and whoever saves the life of one, by refraining from slaying, it shall be as if he had saved the life of all mankind—Ibn 'Abbās said [that the above is meant] in the sense of violating and protecting its [a soul's] sanctity [respectively]. Our messengers have already come to them, that is, to the Children of Israel, with clear proofs, miracles, but after that many of them still commit excesses in the land, overstepping the bounds through disbelief, killing and the like.*

Arguing for the Powerless

Q. 16:76 Allah sets forth (another) Parable of two men: one of them dumb, with no power of any sort; a wearisome burden is he to his master; whichever way be directs him, he brings no good: is such a man equal with one who commands Justice, and is on a Straight Way?

Tafsir al-Jalalayn: And God strikes a similitude (mathalan, this is substituted by [the following, rajulayn]) two men, one of whom is dumb [from birth], having no power over anything, as he cannot understand nor be understood, and who is a liability, burdensome, to his master:—the [legal] guardian of his affairs—wherever he directs him, he does not bring, therefrom, any good, he does [not] succeed, and this is the similitude of the disbeliever. Is he, that is, the dumb one mentioned, equal to one who enjoins justice, that is, to one who is able to speak, of benefit to people, since he enjoins it [justice] and encourages [others to] it, and follows a path, a way, that is straight?—this being the second [man], the believer—No [he is not equal to him]. It is also said that this [last similitude] is a similitude of God, while the [similitude of the] dumb one is of the idols, so that the preceding [verse] contains the similitude of the disbeliever and the believer.

Q. 6:115 The word of thy Lord doth find its fulfillment in truth and in justice: None can change His words: for He is the one who heareth and knoweth all.

Tafsir al-Jalalayn: Perfected is the word of your Lord, in the way of rulings and appointed terms, in truthfulness and justice (sidqan wa-'adlan is for specification); none can change His words, either by contravening [His rulings] or evading [His appointed terms]. He is the Hearing, of what is said, the Knowing, of what is done.

Thy Lord Forgives and He is Most Merciful

Q. 7:167 Behold! thy Lord did declare that He would send against them, to the Day of Judgment, those who would afflict them with grievous penalty. Thy Lord is quick in retribution, but He is also Oft forgiving, Most Merciful.

Tafsir al-Jalalayn: And when your Lord proclaimed, made it known, that He would send against them, [that is, the Jews,] to the Day of Resurrection, those who would inflict on them grievous torment, through humiliation and the exacting of the jizya-tax [from them]. Thus, God sent Solomon against them, and after him, Nebuchadnezzar, who slaughtered [some of] them and took [others among] them captive, and imposed the jizya-tax on them. They continued to pay this [tax] to the Magians up until the [time of the] sending of our Prophet (s), who [also] imposed it on them. Lo! Verily your Lord is swift in requital, of those who disobey Him. And lo! Verily He is Forgiving, to those who obey Him, Merciful, [in dealing] with them.

Q. 7:170 As to those who hold fast by the Book and establish regular prayer, - never shall We suffer the reward of the righteous to perish.

Tafsir al-Jalalayn: And those who adhere (read yumassikūn or yumsikūn) to the Scripture, from among them, and have established prayer, the likes of 'Abd Allāh b. Salām and his companions, verily We shall not let the wages of reformers go to waste (innā lā nudī 'u ajra l-muslihīn: the sentence is the predicate of alladhīna, 'those who'; also there is here the replacing of the [third person] pronominalisation [alladhīna, 'those who'] with an overt noun [al-muslihīna, 'reformers'], in other words, their wages).

Q. 7:180 The most beautiful names belong to Allah: so call on him by them; but shun such men as use profanity in his names: for what they do, they will soon be requited. (Invoking the names of Allah that depict justice.[585])

---

585. May the beauty of our humanity as expressed in the many names of the Almighty be our desire our fortress as we aspire to practice law, in sometimes challenging circumstances to remember: Allah, The All Beneficent, The Most Merciful in Essence, The Compassionate, The Most Gracious; The Most Merciful, The Most Merciful in Actions; The Owner, The Sovereign, The True and Ultimate King; The Most Holy, The Most Pure, The Most Perfect; The Peace and Blessing, The Source of Peace and Safety, The Most Perfect; The Guarantor, The Self Affirming, The Granter of Security, The Affirmer of Truth; The Guardian,

Q. 7:180 The most beautiful names belong to Allah: so call on him by them; but shun such men as use profanity in his names: for what they do, they will soon be requited. (Invoking the names of Allah that depict justice.)

Tafsir al-Jalalayn: And to God belong the, ninety nine, Most Beautiful Names—mentioned in hadīth—(al-husnā is the feminine for al-ahsan) so invoke, name, Him by them, and leave those who blaspheme His Names (yulhidūn, 'they blaspheme', from [fourth form] alhada or [first form] lahada, meaning 'those who incline away from the truth'), by deriving from them names for their gods, as in the case of al-Lāt, from Allāh ('God'), al-'Uzzā, from al-'Azīz ('Mighty'), and Manāt, from al-Mannān ('Lord of Favors'). They will be requited, in the Hereafter, the requital, for what they did—this was [revealed] before the command to fight [them].

Q. 24:49 But if the right is on their side, they come to him with all submission.

Tafsir al-Jalalayn: But if right be on their side they would come to him willingly, hastening compliantly.

Q. 24:51 The answer of the Believers, when summoned to Allah and His Messenger, in order that He may judge between them, is no other than this: they say, "We hear and we obey": it is such as these that will attain felicity.

Tafsir al-Jalalayn: All that the believers say, when they are summoned to God and His Messenger, that he may judge between them, is that they say, in other words, the saying that befits them is [to say]: 'We hear and we obey', by responding [to the summons]. And those, then, are the successful, the ones who will be saved.

The Preserver, The Overseeing Protector; The Almighty, The Self Sufficient, The Most Honorable; The Powerful, The Irresistible, The Compeller, The Most Lofty, The Restorer/ Improver of Affairs; The Tremendous; The Creator; The Rightful; The Fashioner of Forms; The Ever Forgiving; The All Compelling Subduer; The Bestower; The Ever Providing; The Opener, The Victory Giver; The All Knowing, The Omniscient; The Restrainer, The Straightener; The Expander, The Munificent; The Giver of Honor; The Gentle, The Subtly Kind; The Forbearing, The Indulgent; The Magnificent, The Infinite; The All Forgiving; The Sublimely Exalted; The Bringer of Judgment; The Bountiful, The Generous; The Judge, The Arbitrator; The Utterly Just.

Q. 10:54 Every soul that hath sinned, if it possessed all that is on earth, would fain give it in ransom: They would declare (their) repentance when they see the penalty: but the judgment between them will be with justice, and no wrong will be done unto them.

Tafsir al-Jalalayn: And if each soul that has done wrong, [that] has disbelieved, had all that is in the earth, of riches, it would offer it as ransom, against chastisement on the Day of Resurrection; and they will feel remorse within them, for having neglected faith, when they see the chastisement, their leaders keep it [their remorse] secret from the weak ones whom they had led astray, fearing reproach, but it has been decided justly between them, [between] all creatures, and they are not wronged, in anything.

Q. 10:55 Is it not (the case) that to Allah belongeth whatever is in the heavens and on earth? Is it not (the case) that Allah's promise is assuredly true? Yet most of them understand not.

Tafsir al-Jalalayn: Why, surely to God belongs all that is in the heavens and the earth. Why, surely God's promise, of resurrection and requital, is true, [is] fixed, but most of them, people, do not know, this.

Q. 39:69 And the Earth will shine with the Glory of its Lord: the Record (of Deeds) will be placed (open); the prophets and the witnesses will be brought forward and a just decision pronounced between them; and they will not be wronged in the least.

Tafsir al-Jalalayn: And the earth will shine with the light of its Lord, when God reveals Himself for the passing of judgement, and the Book, of deeds, shall be set in place, for the Reckoning, and the prophets and witnesses, namely, Muhammad (s) and his community, will be brought, to bear witness that the messengers delivered [the Message to their respective communities]. And judgement will be made between them with truth, in other words, justly, and they will not be wronged, in a single thing.

Pardon and Reconciliation

Q. 42:40 And the retribution for an evil act is an evil one like it, but whoever pardons and makes reconciliation—his reward is [due] from Allah. Indeed, He does not like wrongdoers.

Tafsir al-Jalalayn: For the requital of an evil deed is an evil deed like it: the latter is [also] referred to as 'an evil deed' because in [outward] form it resembles the former; this is evident in what concerns retaliation for wounds. Some [scholars] say that even if another were to say, 'May God disgrace you!', then one should respond [equally] with, 'May God disgrace you!' But whoever pardons, his wrongdoer, and reconciles, the amity between himself and the one pardoned, his reward will be with God, that is to say, God will give him his reward without doubt. Truly He does not like wrongdoers, that is, those who initiate acts of wrongdoing and so merit His punishment.

Q. 42:41 And whoever avenges himself after having been wronged—those have not upon them any cause [for blame].

Tafsir al-Jalalayn: And whoever defends himself after he has been wronged, that is to say, after the wrongdoer has wronged him—for such, there will be no course [of action] against them, no blame [on them].

Q. 42:42 The cause is only against the ones who wrong the people and tyrannize upon the earth without right. Those will have a painful punishment.

Tafsir al-Jalalayn: A course [of action] is only [open] against those who wrong people and seek [to commit], [who] commit, in the earth what is not right, [what are] acts of disobedience. For such there will be a painful chastisement.

Q. 49:10 The believers are but brothers, so make settlement between your brothers. And fear Allah that you may receive mercy.

Tafsir al-Jalalayn: The believers are indeed brothers, in religion. Therefore [always] make peace between your brethren, when they fall into dispute with one another (a variant reading [for the dual form akhawaykum, 'your two brethren'] has ikhwatakum, 'your brothers') and fear God, so that perhaps you might receive mercy.

Q. 49:11 O you, who have believed, let not a people ridicule [another] people; perhaps they may be better than them; nor let women ridicule [other] women; perhaps they may be better than them. And do not insult one another and do not call each other by [offensive] nicknames. Wretched is the name of disobedience after [one's] faith. And whoever does not repent—then it is those who are the wrongdoers.

Tafsir al-Jalalayn: *O you who believe, do not let any people, that is, any men among you, deride (yā ayyuhā'lladhī na āmanū lā yaskhar . . . [to the end of] the verse, was revealed regarding the [Banū] Tamīm delegation when they derided the poor among the Muslims, like 'Ammār [b.Yāsir] and Suhayb [al-Rūmī]; al-sukhriya means 'scorn' and 'disdain') another people: who may be better than they are, in God's sight; nor let any women, from among you, deride [other] women who may be better than they are. And do not defame one another, do not cast aspersions [on others] and hence have aspersions cast on you, that is, let none among you denigrate another; nor insult one another by nicknames, do not call another by a nickname which he detests, such as 'O degenerate one!' or 'O disbeliever!'. Evil is the name, mentioned out of mockery, derision and mutual reviling, of immorality after faith! (al-fusūqu ba'da'l-īmāni substitutes for al-ismu, 'the name', to indicate that it [such naming of others] is 'immorality' as it is [an action which is] usually repeated). And whoever does not repent, of such [immorality], those—they are the evildoers.*

Selected Passages from the Qur'an, Hadith, and Other Authorities

ISLAM CONCEPT OF HUMAN RIGHTS is essentially based on human the idea of dignity and equality of mankind.[586]

"O mankind! Be careful of your duty to your Lord who created you from a single soul and from it created its mate and from them twain hath spread abroad a multitude of men and women. Be careful of your duty toward Allah in whom ye claim (your rights) of one another, and toward the wombs (that bare you). Lo! Allah hath been a Watcher over you" (Q. 4:1).

"O ye who believe! Stand out firmly for justice, as witnesses to God, even as against yourselves, or your parents, or your kin, and whether it is (against) rich or poor: for God can best protect both. Follow not the lusts (of your hearts), lest ye swerve, and if ye distort (justice) or decline to do justice, verily God is well-acquainted with all that ye do" (Q. 4:135).

"O mankind! We created you from a single (pair) of a male and a female, and made you into nations and tribes, that ye know each other

---

586. Chaudry, *Human Rights in Islam*, 11.

(not that ye may despise each other). Verily the most honoured of you in the sight of Allah is (he who is) the most righteous of you . . . " (Q. 49:13).

Thus, these verses place all the human beings on an equal level and make the pious and righteous superior to the wicked and evildoers on the basis of virtuous conduct.[587]

In his famous sermon delivered on the occasion of farewell pilgrimage, Prophet Muhammad addressed the people, "O people, be aware: your God is one. No Arab has any superiority over a non-Arab, nor any non-Arab has any superiority over an Arab, and no white one has any superiority over a black one, and no black one any superiority over a white one except on the basis of taqva (piety). The most honourable among you in the sight of Allah is he who is the most pious and righteous of you."[588]

Again, according to another tradition, the Prophet said: "You are all the children of Adam, and Adam was created from the dust. Let the people give up boasting of their ancestors, otherwise they will stand more degraded than a mean insect in the sight of Allah" (Qur'an 49:13). In yet another Hadith: "Allah does not see your outward appearances and your possessions but He sees your hearts and your deeds."[589] What more can we ask for?

Qur'an 5:49 is explicit about Allah's command which provides: "So judge between them by that which Allah hath revealed, and follow not their desires; but beware of them lest they seduce thee from some part of that which Allah hath revealed unto thee. And if they turn away, then know that Allah's Will is to smite them for some sin of theirs. Lo! many of mankind are evil-livers." Abu Aharr in his

---

587. Chaudhry, *Human Rights in Islam*, 32.
588. Ibid., 12.
589. Curtis, *Columbia Sourcebook of Muslims*, 227.

Hadith went further to reveal some of the ill of oppression and the need for justice.[590]

---

590. My servants, I have made oppression unlawful for Me and unlawful for you, so do not commit oppression against one another. My servants, all of you are liable to err except one whom I guide on the right path, so seek right guidance from Me so that I should direct you to the right path. O My servants, all of you are hungry (needy) except one whom I feed, so beg food from Me, so that I may give that to you. O My servants, all of you are naked (need clothes) except one whom I provide garments, so beg clothes from Me, so that I should clothe you. O My servants, you commit error night and day and I am there to pardon your sins, so beg pardon from Me so that I should grant you pardon. O My servants, you can neither do Me any harm nor can you do Me any good. O My servants, even if the first amongst you and the last amongst you and even the whole of human race of yours, and that of jinns even, become (equal in) God-conscious like the heart of a single person amongst you, nothing would add to My Power. O My servants, even if the first amongst you and the last amongst you and the whole human race of yours and that of the jinns too in unison become the most wicked (all beating) like the heart of a single person, it would cause no loss to My Power. O My servants, even if the first amongst you and the last amongst you and the whole human race of yours and that of jinns also all stand in one plain ground and you ask Me and I confer upon every person what he asks for, it would not. in any way, cause any loss to Me (even less) than that which is caused to the ocean by dipping the needle in it. My servants, these for you I shall reward you for them, so he who deeds of yours which I am recording finds good should praise Allah and he who does not find that should not blame anyone but his own self. Sa'id said that when Abu Idris Khaulini narrated this Hadith he knelt upon his knees.

The Constitution of the Federal Republic of Nigeria 1999 (Selected Sections)

Section 1

(1) The Constitution is supreme and its provisions shall have binding force on the authorities and persons throughout the Federal Republic of Nigeria.

(3) If any other law is inconsistent with the provisions of this Constitution, this Constitution shall prevail, and that other law shall, to the extent of the inconsistency, be void.

Section 4

(1) The legislative powers of the Federal Republic of Nigeria shall be vested in a National Assembly for the Federation, which shall consist of a Senate and a House of Representatives.

(2) The National Assembly shall have power to make laws for the peace, order and good government of the Federation or any part thereof with respect to any matter included in

the Exclusive Legislative List set out in Part I of the Second Schedule to this Constitution.

(3) The power of the National Assembly to make laws for the peace, order and good government of the Federation with respect to any matter included in the Exclusive Legislative List shall, save as otherwise provided in this Constitution, be to the exclusion of the Houses of Assembly of States.

(4) In addition and without prejudice to the powers conferred by subsection (2) of this section, the National Assembly shall have power to make laws with respect to the following matters, that is to say:— ...

(5) If any Law enacted by the House of Assembly of a State is inconsistent with any law validly made by the National Assembly, the law made by the National Assembly shall prevail, and that other Law shall, to the extent of the inconsistency, be void.

(6) The legislative powers of a State of the Federation shall be vested in the House of Assembly of the State.

(7) The House of Assembly of a State shall have power to make laws for the peace, order and good government of the State or any part thereof with respect to the following matters, that is to say:— ...

(9) Notwithstanding the foregoing provisions of this section, the National Assembly or a House of Assembly shall not, in relation to any criminal offense whatsoever, have power to make any law which shall have retrospective effect.

Section 10

The Government of the Federation or of a State shall not adopt any religion as State Religion.

Section 14

(1) The Federal Republic of Nigeria shall be a State based on the principles of democracy and social justice.

(2) (a) Sovereignty belongs to the people of Nigeria from whom government through this Constitution derives all its powers and authority;

(b) the security and welfare of the people shall be the primary purpose of government.

Section 15

(1) The motto of the Federal Republic of Nigeria shall be Unity and Faith, Peace and Progress.

(2) accordingly, national integration shall be actively encouraged, whilst discrimination on the grounds of place of origin, sex, religion, status, ethnic or linguistic association or ties shall be prohibited.

Section 17

(1) The State social order is founded on ideals of Freedom, Equality and Justice . . .

(2) (a) every citizen shall have equality of rights, obligations and opportunities before the law;

(b) the sanctity of the human person shall be recognized and human dignity shall be maintained and enhanced;

(c) governmental actions shall be humane . . .

Section 33

(1) Every person has a right to life, and no one shall be deprived intentionally of his life, save in execution of the sentence of a court in respect of a criminal offense of which he has been found guilty in Nigeria . . .

Section 34

(1) Every individual is entitled to respect for the dignity of his
     person, and accordingly

     (a) no person shall be subject to torture or to inhuman or
         degrading treatment;

     (b) no person shall he held in slavery or servitude; . . .

Section 35

(1) Every person shall be entitled to his personal liberty and no
     person shall be deprived of such liberty save in the following
     cases and in accordance with a procedure permitted by
     law— . . .

(2) Any person who is arrested or detained shall have the right
     to remain silent or avoid answering any question until after
     consultation with a legal practitioner or any other person of
     his own choice.

(3) Any person who is arrested or detained shall be informed
     in writing within twenty-four hours (and in a language that
     he understands) of the facts and grounds for his arrest or
     detention . . .

(6) Any person who is unlawfully arrested or detained shall
     be entitled to compensation and public apology from the
     appropriate authority or person; and in this subsection, "the
     appropriate authority or person" means an authority or person
     specified by law.

Section 36

(1) In the determination of his civil rights and obligations,
     including any question or determination by or against any
     government or authority, a person shall be entitled to a fair
     hearing within a reasonable time by a court or other tribunal

established by law and constituted in such manner as to secure its independence and impartiality . . .

(4) Whenever any person is charged with a criminal offense, he shall, unless the charge is withdrawn, be entitled to a fair hearing in public within a reasonable time by a court or tribunal . . .

(5) Every person who is charged with a criminal offense shall be presumed to be innocent until he is proved guilty; Provided that nothing in this section shall invalidate any law by reason only that the law imposes upon any such person the burden of proving particular facts.

(6) Every person who is charged with a criminal offense shall be entitled to

(a) be informed promptly in the language that he understands and in detail of the nature of the offense;

(b) be given adequate time and facilities for the preparation of his defense;

(c) defend himself in person or by legal practitioners of his own choice;

(d) examine, in person or by his legal practitioners, the witnesses called by the prosecution before any court or tribunal and obtain the attendance and carry out the examination of witnesses to testify on his behalf before the court or tribunal on the same conditions as those applying to the witnesses called by the prosecution; and

(e) have, without payment, the assistance of an interpreter if he cannot understand the language used at the trial of the offense.

(7) When any person is tried for any criminal offense, the court or tribunal shall keep a record of the proceedings and the accused person or any persons authorized by him in that behalf shall

be entitled to obtain copies of the judgment in the case within seven days of the conclusion of the case.

(8) No person shall be held to be guilty of a criminal offense on account of any act or omission that did not, at the time it took place, constitute such an offense, and no penalty shall be imposed for any criminal offense heavier than the penalty in force at the time the offense was committed.

(9) No person who shows that he has been tried by any court of competent jurisdiction or tribunal for a criminal offense and either convicted or acquitted shall again be tried for that offense or for a criminal offense having the same ingredients as that offense save upon the order of a superior court.

(10) No person who shows that he has been pardoned for a criminal offense shall again be tried for that offense.

(11) No person who is tried for a criminal offense shall be compelled to give evidence at the trial.

(12) Subject as otherwise provided by this Constitution, a person shall not be convicted of a criminal offense unless that offense is defined and the penalty therefore is prescribed in a written law, and in this subsection, a written law refers to an Act of the National Assembly or a Law of a State, any subsidiary legislation or instrument under the provisions of a law.

Section 37

The privacy of citizens, their homes, correspondence, telephone conversations and telegraphic communications is hereby guaranteed and protected.

Section 38

(1) Every person shall be entitled to freedom of thought, conscience and religion, including freedom to change his religion or belief, and freedom (either alone or in community with others, and in public or in private) to manifest and

propagate his religion or belief in worship, teaching, practice and observance.

(2)   No person attending any place of education shall be required to receive religious instruction or to take part in or attend any religious ceremony or observance if such instruction ceremony or observance relates to a religion other than his own, or religion not approved by his parent or guardian.

(3)   No religious community or denomination shall be prevented from providing religious instruction for pupils of that community or denomination in any place of education maintained wholly by that community or denomination.

(4)   Nothing in this section shall entitle any person to form, take part in the activity or be a member of a secret society.

Section 39

(1)   Every person shall be entitled to freedom of expression, including freedom to hold opinions and to receive and impart ideas and information without interference . . .

Section 41

(1)   Every citizen of Nigeria is entitled to move freely throughout Nigeria and to reside in any part thereof, and no citizen of Nigeria shall be expelled from Nigeria or refused entry thereby or exit therefrom . . .

Section 42

(1)   A citizen of Nigeria of a particular community, ethnic group, place of origin, sex, religion or political opinion shall not, by reason only that he is such a person:

(a) be subjected either expressly by, or in the practical application of, any law in force in Nigeria or any executive or administrative action of the government, to disabilities or restrictions to which citizens of Nigeria of other communities, ethnic groups, places of origin, sex, religions or political opinions are not made subject; or

(b) be accorded either expressly by, or in the practical application of, any law in force in Nigeria or any such executive or administrative action, any privilege or advantage that is not accorded to citizens of Nigeria of other communities, ethnic groups, places of origin, sex, religions or political opinions.

(2) No citizen of Nigeria shall be subjected to any disability or deprivation merely by reason of the circumstances of his birth . . .

Section 46

(1) Any person who alleges that any of the provisions of this Chapter has been, is being, or likely to be contravened in any State in relation to him may apply to a High Court in that State for redress.

(2) Subject to the provisions of this Constitution, a High Court shall have original jurisdiction to hear and determine any application made to it in pursuance of this section and may make such orders, issue such writs and give such directions as it may consider appropriate for the purpose of enforcement or securing the enforcing within that State of any right to which the person who makes the application may be entitled under this Chapter.

(3) The Chief Justice of Nigeria may make rules with respect to the practice and procedure of a High Court for the purposes of this section.

(4) The National Assembly—

(a) may confer upon a High Court such powers in addition to those conferred by this section as may appear to the

National Assembly to be necessary or desirable for the purpose of enabling the court more effectively to exercise the jurisdiction conferred upon it by this section; and

(b) shall make provisions—

    (i)   for the rendering of financial assistance to any indigent citizen of Nigeria where his right under this Chapter has been infringed or with a view to enabling him to engage the services of a legal practitioner to prosecute his claim, and

    (ii) for ensuring that allegations of infringement of such rights are substantial and the requirement or need for financial or legal aid is real.

Section 277

(1) The Shariah Court of Appeal of a State shall, in addition to such other jurisdiction as may be conferred upon it by the law of the State, exercise such appellate and supervisory jurisdiction in civil proceedings involving questions of Islamic personal Law which the court is competent to decide in accordance with the provisions of subsection (2) of this section.

(2) For the purposes of subsection (1) of this section, the Shariah Court of Appeal shall be competent to decide—

    (a) any question of Islamic personal Law regarding a marriage concluded in accordance with that Law, including a question relating to the validity or dissolution of such a marriage or a question that depends on such a marriage and relating to family relationship or the guardianship of an infant;

    (b) where all the parties to the proceedings are Muslims, any question of Islamic personal Law regarding a marriage, including the validity or dissolution of that marriage, or regarding family relationship, a founding or the guarding of an infant;

(c) any question of Islamic personal Law regarding a wakf, gift, will or succession where the endower, donor, testator or deceased person is a Muslim;

(d) any question of Islamic personal Law regarding an infant, prodigal or person of unsound mind who is a Muslim or the maintenance or the guardianship of a Muslim who is physically or mentally infirm; or

(e) where all the parties to the proceedings, being Muslims, have requested the court that hears the case in the first instance to determine that case in accordance with Islamic personal law, any other question.

Sokoto and Zamfara States Shariah Penal Code Law, 2000 (Selected Sections)

Section 128

Whoever, being a man or woman fully responsible, has sexual intercourse through the genital of a person whom he has no sexual rights in the circumstances in which no doubt exist as to the illegality of the act; is guilty of an offense of Zina.

Section 129

Whoever commits the offense of Zina shall be punished:

(a) with caning of one hundred lashes

(b) if unmarried, and shall also be liable to imprisonment for a term of one year. If married with stoning to death (rajam) . . .

Section 130

(1) A man is said to commit rape, who, save in the case referred to in subsection (2), has sexual intercourse with a woman in any of the following circumstance: Against her will; Without

her consent; With her consent, when her consent has been obtained by putting her in the fear of death or of hurt; With her consent, when the man knows that he is not her husband and that her consent is given because she believes that he is another man to whom she is or believes herself to be lawfully married; With or without her consent, when she is under fifteen years of age or of unsound mind . . .

(2) Sexual intercourse by a man with his wife is not rape.

Section 131

Whoever commits rape shall be punished:

(a) with caning of one hundred lashes
(b) if unmarried, and shall also be liable to imprisonment for a term of one year or If married with stoning (rajam);
(c) In addition to either (a) or (b) above shall pay the dower of her equals (sadaq al-mithli) . . .

Section 132

Whoever has a carnal intercourse against the order of nature with any man or woman is said to commit the offense of sodomy, provided that whoever is compelled by the use of force or in fear of death or grievous hurt or fear of any other serious injury or without his consent to commit the act of sodomy upon the person of another or be the subject of sodomy, shall not be deemed to have committed the offense.

Section 133

Whoever commits the offense of sodomy shall be punished:

(a) With stoning;
(b) If the act is committed by a minor on an adult person, the adult person shall be punished by way of ta'azir which may extend to 100 lashes and minor with correctional punishment.

Section 136

Whoever, being a woman, engages another woman in canal intercourse through her sexual organ or by means of stimulation or sexual excitement of one another has committed the offense of lesbianism.

Section 137

Whoever commits the offense of lesbianism shall be punished with caning which may extend to fifty lashes and in addition be sentenced to a term of imprisonment which may extend six months.

Section 141

Whoever by words either spoken or reproduced signs or by mechanical means or intended to be read or by signs or by visible representations makes or publishes any false imputation of zina or sodomy concerning a chaste person (Mushin), or contests the paternity of such person even where such person is dead, is said to commit the offense of qadhf: Provided that a person is deemed to be chaste (Mushin) who has not been convicted of the offense of zina or sodomy . . .

Section 142

Whoever commits the offense of qadhf shall be punished with eighty lashes of the cane; and his testimony shall not be accepted thereafter unless he repents before the court.

Section 404

Whoever by any means publicly insult or seek to incite contempt of any religion in such a manner as to be likely to lead to a breach of the peace, shall be punished with imprisonment for a term which may extend to two years or with fine or with both.

In February 21, 2000, Sokoto State promulgated another law, "A law to establish Shariah courts to apply Shariah law in Sokoto State." Few sections of the law deserve mention:

Section 3

(1) There is hereby established in the state the following courts:
(b) the Upper Shariah Court;
(c) the Shariah Court of Appeal.[591]

(2) There shall be established a lower Shariah Courts and Upper Shariah Courts in such designated areas as the Grand Khadi shall decide by a warrant.

Section 5

(1) A Shariah Court have jurisdiction to hear and determine civil matters and causes, where the two parties are Muslims, and in criminal cases where the suspects or accused person(s) is/a Muslims.

(2) The Upper Shariah Court and the Shariah Court of Appeal shall only have appellate and supervisory jurisdiction over the Lower Shariah Courts. Provided that where the need arises the Grand Khadi shall have power to confer original jurisdiction on the presiding Alkali of the Upper Shariah Court.

(3) For the purpose of subsection 1 ... the Shariah Court shall be competent to decide all civil matters and causes where all the parties are Muslims including any proceedings involving,— Marriage under Islamic law (Al-Nikah),—Guardianship and maintenance (Al-Kafala) and (Nafaqa),—Succession (Mirath) will (Wasiyya) gift (Hiba) Endowment (Waqf), Pre-emption (Shufa) and Trust (Amana); Land law (Hukum Niza'il Aradi); Contract (Al-Aqd); Tort (Al-Diyya); Commercial Law (Ahkahmul Buyu); Company Law and Partnership (Ahkamul Sharikat) and (Al-Musharakah) ...

(4) For the purpose of subsection (2) of this section the Shariah Court shall be competent to try all criminal cases in which

---

591. Note that the Shariah Court of Appeal is actually the creation of the Constitution of Nigeria, 1999, and one wonders how a state can re-create (re-establish) the court?

suspects or accused person(s) is/are Muslims including: Homicide (Qatlun Nafs); Robbery (Al-Muharaba); Theft (As-Sariq); Defamation (Al-qazf); Drunkenness (Shurbul-Khamr); Causing grievous hurt (Al-qisas); Homosexualism (Luwat); Adultery (Az-Zina); Lesbianism (As-sihaq); Bestiality (Wut'ud-dabba); Perjury (At-tawir); Offering and receiving of gratification (Al-Rishwa); Criminal breach of Trust (Al-Khiyanah); Cheating (Al-gish); Mischief (Al-fasaq); Receiving stolen property (Shaira'u mata'is sariqa); Giving false evidence (Shahadatuz-Zur) . . .

(6) The applicable laws in both civil and criminal proceedings shall include: The Holy Qur'an; Sunnah and Hadith; Ijma; Qiyas; Maslahat; Istihsan; Istishab; Al-urf Muzhabul-Sahabi and other subsidiary sources . . . [592]

(7) . . . specified the books to be used by Shariah Courts . . . The reference books to be used by the Shariah Court shall include the following texts and authorities: Al-Risalah; Muhtasar; Tuhfah; Al-Adawi; Al-Fawakih al Dawani; Ibn Ashir; Bidayat at mujtahid; Al-Mudawwanah; Muwattah Malik; Muyyara; Bahjah; Jawahir-al-Iklil; Dasuki; Al-Khirshi; Bulgatil Salik; Mawahibul Hallaq . . .

(8) . . . further provides that a Shariah court shall have jurisdiction and power only over; Civil causes and matters where the two parties are Muslims; Criminal cases where the suspect or accused is a Muslim . . .

(9) . . . defined what it means by suspect of different religion; Where only one or more of several suspects or accused person(s) are Muslims, the Shariah Court shall not have jurisdiction to hear and determine the case, but the court shall have the power to try the Muslims and refer the case of the others to the

---

592. Section 5 (6) is interesting because it set out to provide the civil and criminal laws to be applicable in Shariah Courts.

Area or Magistrate Courts, or such Court with the competent jurisdiction to try the offense(s).

(10) . . . provides for the practice and procedures in the Shariah Courts; it will include Islamic law and procedure contained in the source and text listed above and rules which shall be made by the Grand Khadi. It further provides that the law of evidence to apply shall be the Islamic law of Evidence of the Maliki School. The section further provides that "every person who is charged with criminal offense shall be entitled to defend himself in person or by a legal practitioner of his choice."

Section 26

Provides that this law of Feb. 21, 2000 will only apply to cases and matters committed AFTER its commencement . . .

Section 5(2)(3)

Provide that all offenses against any other law shall be investigated, inquired, tried and otherwise dealt with according to the same provisions, but subject to any law for the time being in force regulating the manner or place of investigation, inquiry into, trying or otherwise dealing with such offenses. In any matter of criminal nature a Shariah court shall be bound by the provisions of this Shariah criminal procedure code.

Section 12

(2) Upper Shariah court shall have the exclusive jurisdiction to try any or all offenses in Appendix A. (Appendix A offenses are: Zina [adultery]; rape; sodomy; incest; theft; robbery; house breaking; homicide; grievous hurt; use of criminal force; buying or selling of minor or unsound-minded person for immoral purpose; kidnapping; abduction; kidnapping or abduction in order to cause death; criminal intimidation; forgery; breach of official trust; joining unlawful assembly armed with deadly weapon; public servant taking gratification in respect of official

act; false evidence; adulteration of drugs; mischief; offenses relating to ordeal, witchcraft and juju.)

However, even when the offenses are not the ones listed above, the Shariah courts can also have the jurisdiction to try any offense where it deems it fit (Section 12(3). The territorial jurisdiction of the Shariah Alkali (Judge) in Sokoto is throughout the State. The Upper Shariah court Alkali may pass any sentence authorized by law, Sections 14 and 15 SSSCPCL.

Section 15

A Shariah court Alkali may pass sentences only of imprisonment not exceeding 10 years and fine not exceeding seven thousand naira. The Alkali have power to imprison in default of security under Section 95 and power to release persons imprisoned for failure to give security under Section 97 of the SSSCPCL.

Section 151–152

Provide that procedures laid down in this chapter shall be observed by Shariah court, which means—when an accused appears or is brought before the court the particulars of the offense of which he is accused shall be stated to him and he shall be asked if he has any cause to show why he should not be convicted.[593]

Other details to note are the different agents of government to assist in the implementation of the Shariah:

The Ulama Council[594] established by Law No. 16 of 2003; Zamfara State of Nigeria Gazette; their responsibility is to screen recommendations and advertise the qualification, competence and fitness of any person, both in character and learning, to be appointed as a Shariah Court Alkali (Judge) under the Shariah Court establishment law 1999. The position is remunerated. The Council is appointed by the Governor.

---

593. Section 152.
594. Zamfara State, Law No. 16 (a law to provide for the establishment of the Council of Ulama in the state), Oct. 3, 2003, No. 3, Vol. 5, Section 4.

The Hisbah Commission,[595] established by Law No. 17 of 2003. Their responsibility is monitoring and ensuring the application and compliance with Shariah Penal Code Law; keep record of all pending Hudud cases; sanitizing society of social vices; take measure to ensure conformity with the teaching of Shariah, such as worship, dress code, business transactions and relationships; ensure that all ceremonies, celebrations and anniversaries are in accordance with the teaching of Shariah; enlighten the public on Shariah and its application and carry out all other functions that the Governor assigned to them. The Chairman and the board of six permanent commissioners are appointed by the Governor, they are also remunerated by government as the Governor may determine.

Shariah Research and Development Commission[596] established by Law No. 18 of 2003 is one such commission to pay attention to. It is a body corporate that will carry out research from theology to advance contemporary social issues; collect data from all other Shariah agencies for purposes of research; publish research findings; organize workshops, symposiums and seminars on development and current trends in Islamic law. They will be remunerated by the government as the governor may determine. They are appointed and dismissed by the governor.

The Public Complaint Commission; the chairman of this commission who shall be a legal practitioner shall be appointed by the Governor; the chairman and the commissioner of the commission will be remunerated by government. The commission may determine the manner by which complaints are lodged; visit and inspect premises subject to Shariah law; investigate special care administrative acts . . .

---

595. Ibid., Section 6(6).
596. Ibid., Section 3.

Cases

Shalla v. The State[597]

This is a case of defaming the Holy Prophet Muhammad's name. It was alleged that Abdullahi Alh. Umaru had defamed the Prophet's name; therefore, the appellant [Shalla] and five others killed him. Thereupon the appellant and the five others were brought to court. The charge against them was that when they heard the rumor that Abdullahi Alh. Umaru had defamed the Holy Prophet's name they brought out the Islamic textbook *Risalah* and read aloud some portion from it that the punishment of any person who insults the Holy Prophet is death. Thereupon the third accused struck the deceased on the neck with a machete. After investigation by the police the appellant along with the five other accused persons were arrested and prosecuted at the court below which convicted all of them for the offenses under Sections 85, 97 and 221(a) of the penal code. They were each sentenced to death accordingly.

---

597. S.C. 245/2004.

Meanwhile, in his judgment, Justice Ibrahim Muhammad Tanko, held inter alia " . . . Islamic religion is not a primitive religion that allows its adherents to take the law into their own hands and to commit jungle justice. Instead there is a judicial system in Islam which hears and determines cases including the trial of criminal offenses and anybody accused of committing an offense against the religion or against a fellow Muslim brother should be taken to the court (either a Sharia or a secular/common law court) for adjudication. . . . Although it is true that there is the provision in Risala which prescribes the punishment of death on any Muslim who insults the Holy Prophet, such punishment can only be imposed by the appropriate authority (i.e., the court) rather than by any member of the society whether a Muslim or otherwise . . . This position was endorsed by the Iranian Constitution when it provides in Article 36(5) that the passing and execution of a sentence must be only by a competent court . . . "[598]

Mohammad Sarwar v. Shahida Parveen[599]

This is a case of alleged void marriage, between Mohammad Sarwar and Shahida Parveen. Shahida had been previously married and claimed to have been divorced before marrying Sarwar. Since Shahida's divorce had not been registered, the court took the view that the divorce stood invalidated. Her marriage was considered void and taken to be a confession of *zina*. The trial court ruled that Shahida and Sarwar's marriage was illegal and awarded them the maximum *hadd* punishment of stoning to death.

On appeal, her defense counsel argued that the statement made by the accused (that they were married) was not intended as a confession, but as a denial of the charge of *zina*. Subsequently, the couple was acquitted on re-trial. The Federal Supreme Court of Pakistan set aside the conviction and

---

598. Ibrahim Muhammad Tanko is Justice of the Supreme Court of Nigeria. Note that the Islamic revolution in Iran was echoed in Nigeria. To read more, see Algar, *Roots of the Islamic Revolution*, 81.
599. NLR 1988 (SD) FSC 188.

held that even if the divorce was invalid, an invalid divorce *per se* could not be taken as a confession for the purposes of *hadd* punishment.

Ubaidullah v. The State[600]

The Pakistani case of Ubaidullah held that to prove the offense of rape, corroborative evidence is generally required.

Zafran Bibi was allegedly raped by a neighbor. Bibi, 28, was convicted of adultery under Islamic laws which many regard as deeply prejudicial. A year after she reported the rape, a judge sentenced her to death by stoning. In Bibi's case, the judge ruled the fact that she changed her statement to name a new attacker was a confession of adultery.

The appellant court accepted Zafran Bibi's testimony; the court was satisfied that "there was nothing on record to presume that she was a woman of easy virtue." The onus of proving lack of consent becomes an even more serious issue in view of the fact that it seems the Pakistani law does not protect a rape victim from attacks on her character. Such an attack may be permitted under the Qanun-e Shahdat Order 1984, which provides that "when a man is prosecuted for rape or an attempt to ravish, it may be shown that the prosecutrix was of generally immoral character."[601] Meanwhile, on May 7, 2002, Seth Mydans of the *New York Times* reported that Zafra was discharged: "Bowing to public outrage, a Pakistani court has freed a rape victim who was sentenced to death by stoning for the crime of having extramarital relations."[602]

Yusuf Amuda Garba & ORS v. University of Maiduguri[603]

The Nigerian supreme court held inter alia that fair hearing constitutes that a person being charged must know the allegation against him/her,

---

600. PLD 1983 FSC 11.
601. See Kumar, *Women and Crime*, 587; and Qanun-e-Shahdat Order, 1984, Article 151(4).
602. Seth Mydans, *New York Times*, "Sentenced to Death, Rape Victim is Freed by Pakistani Court."
603. (1986) 2 NWLR (pt. 18) 559.

the evidence given to substitute the allegation, the various statements made relating thereto, fair opportunity of correcting or contradicting the evidence put forward, and hearing all evidence in the presence of the person charged.

The State v. Suleiman Audu & Ors[604]

An accused person is presumed innocent in a criminal case until proven otherwise. The court held that "a person is presumed to be innocent unless his or her guilt is proved beyond reasonable doubt. The onus of proof is always on the prosecutor. It is not a matter of putting the evidence of both sides on an imaginary scale and see which side is tilting. The accuser must prove his case beyond reasonable doubt or else the accusation falls on the ground, the accused goes away scot free."

Shatacche v. Balaraba[605]

The Nigeria Federal Court of Appeal held unequivocally that "Passing and execution of a sentence must be only by a competent court and in accordance with law."

Alh. Saidu Maje v. Da'u Dillalin Shanu[606]

The Court of Appeal, in determining the input of Section 277 of the 1999 Constitution of Nigeria, held ". . . There is no gainsaying that the above quoted provisions are clear and not nebulous at all. They therefore need no interpretation other than the literal one and the words therein must be given their ordinary meaning. The provisions should therefore serve as guide to Shariah Court of Appeal of the states and indeed the other grades of Area/Shariah Courts. These provisions have limited the jurisdiction of Shariah Court of Appeal of the states to entertain and determine appeals filed before them which subject matter only relates to Islamic personal law.

---

604. Borno Law Reports, 1987–1988.
605. (2002) 10 NWLR (pt. 775) 221 CA.
606. CA/K/142/S/2005.

What Islamic personal law matters relate are also specifically listed or defined in subsection (2) of the section. Again, in entertaining such appeals, efforts must be made by the courts to ascertain whether they have jurisdiction or not . . ."

Shaukat Ali v. The State[607]

The Pakistani Supreme Court held that pregnancy of an unmarried woman is not conclusive proof of adultery.

The Republic of Botswana v. Unity[608]

The issue before the Supreme Court of Botswana was the seeming conflict between cultural practices and the Constitution of Botswana. While a child born to a Botswana man is automatically a citizen of Botswana, a child born from a marriage between a Botswana woman and a foreign man could not have Botswana citizenship. In a progressive judgment for the rule of law, the court held " . . . custom as far as possible be read so as to conform to the Constitution. But where this is impossible, it is the custom and not the Constitution, which must go."

Sudan Government v. Amma Babiker Ahmad[609]

The defendant, a divorcee who bore a child, was sentenced by a criminal court to death by stoning. On appeal, the Supreme Court of Sudan determined that, being a divorcee, the defendant was neither a *muhsan* (liable to stoning penalty) nor a virgin (liable to the 100 lashes penalty), and should therefore be given a discretionary penalty instead.

---

607. PLD 2006, SC81.
608. Civil Appeal No. 4 of 1991, Botswana. See also Seng, "In Conflict between Equal Rights," 543–82.
609. (1985) Sudan Law Journal and Reports, 129–31.

Sudan Government v. Kalthum 'Ajabnna[610]

The Supreme Court of Sudan overturned the *hadd* sentence handed down by the criminal court. The defendant, a divorcée who bore a child by a man with whom she had no marital bond, retracted the "confession" used by the criminal court to convict her of *zina* by testifying to the coercive nature of the sexual relationship. The Supreme Court accordingly remitted the sentence of death by stoning, and the defendant received the discretionary sentence of a two-year prison term, which included her pre-trial detention.

Sudan Government v. Hajjah Suleiman[611]

The defendant, a divorcée, was raped by two men on her family's farm and became pregnant. The defendant was convicted of adultery and sentenced to death by stoning in the criminal court, which disregarded the defendant's allegations of rape, claiming, "It is very difficult if not impossible to have full sexual intercourse with a woman against her will." In a "landmark ruling," the Supreme Court of Sudan upheld the defendant's allegations of rape, overturned the verdict handed down by the criminal court, and ordered the acquittal of the defendant on all charges.

Alhaji Alkamawa v. Alhaji Bello and Another[612]

The Supreme Court in Nigeria, held inter-alia that, "Islamic Law is not the same as customary law as it does not belong to any particular tribe. It is a complete system of universal Law, more certain and permanent and more universal than the English common law."[613] Its adherents further aver that the Shariah provides a complete blueprint for life through its all-encompassing social order, where nothing is superfluous and nothing is lacking.

---

610. (SC/48/1992), The Sudan Law Journal and Reports, 1985, pp. 102.
611. (SC/84/1406AH/1988), The Sudan Law Journal and Reports, 1988, pp. 187–96.
612. 14a. (1998) SCJN, 127 at p. 136.
613. See also Palacio et al., *Law, Equity, and Development*, 153.

Vishaka & Others v. Rajasthan & Others[614]

Ms. Vishaka, an employee of the state's women development program was gang-raped in response to her campaigning against child marriage in the state of Rajastan. Earlier, Ms. Vishaka had complained of sexual harassment to her state employer. The State had no policy on sexual harassment and was unable to follow up on her complaint. Meanwhile, a group of social activists and nongovernmental organizations brought as a class action a petition under Article 32 of the Indian Constitution, citing rights that were being violated by alleged practices of sexual harassment of women in the workplace in India. Article 32 of the Constitution empowered the Supreme Court to issue guidelines for the enforcement of constitutionally guaranteed rights.

The Supreme Court held, that "Gender equality includes protection from sexual harassment and the right to work with dignity, which is a universally recognized basic human right. The common minimum requirement of this right has received global acceptance. The international conventions and norms are, therefore, of great significance in the formulation of the guidelines to achieve this purpose." The court added, "It is now accepted rule of judicial construction that regard must be had to international conventions and norms for construing domestic law when there is no inconsistency between them and there is a void in the domestic law."

---

614. (1997) 6 SCC 241. See also Emerton et al., *International Women's Rights Cases*, 11.

Universal Islamic Declaration of Human Rights[615]

21 Dhul Qaidah 1401 19 September 1981

Contents:

Foreword

Preamble

---

615. Published by the Islamic Council, 16 Grosvenor Crescent, London SW1, and printed here in its entirety. See also Mayer, *Islam and Human Rights*, 217.

This is a declaration for mankind, a guidance and instruction to those who fear God (Al Qur'an, Al-Imran 3:138).

Foreword

Islam gave to mankind an ideal code of human rights fourteen centuries ago. These rights aim at conferring honor and dignity on mankind and eliminating exploitation, oppression and injustice.

Human rights in Islam are firmly rooted in the belief that God, and God alone, is the Law Giver and the Source of all human rights. Due to their Divine origin, no ruler, government, assembly or authority can curtail or violate in any way the human rights conferred by God, nor can they be surrendered.

Human rights in Islam are an integral part of the overall Islamic order and it is obligatory on all Muslim governments and organs of society to implement them in letter and in spirit within the framework of that order.

It is unfortunate that human rights are being trampled upon with impunity in many countries of the world, including some Muslim countries. Such violations are a matter of serious concern and are arousing the conscience of more and more people throughout the world.

I sincerely hope that this *Declaration of Human Rights* will give a powerful impetus to the Muslim peoples to stand firm and defend resolutely and courageously the rights conferred on them by God.

This *Declaration of Human Rights* is the second fundamental document proclaimed by the Islamic Council to mark the beginning of the 15th Century of the Islamic era, the first being the *Universal Islamic Declaration* announced at the International Conference on The prophet Muhammad (peace and blessings be upon him) and his Message, held in London from 12 to 15 April 1980.

The *Universal Islamic Declaration of Human Rights* is based on the Qur'an and the Sunnah and has been compiled by eminent Muslim scholars, jurists and representatives of Islamic movements and thought. May God reward them all for their efforts and guide us along the right path.

Paris 21 Dhul Qaidah 1401 Salem Azzam
19th September 1981 Secretary General

O men! Behold, We have created you all out of a male and a female, and have made you into nations and tribes, so that you might come to know one another. Verily, the noblest of you in the sight of God is the one who is most deeply conscious of Him. Behold, God is all-knowing, all aware (Al Qur'an, Al-Hujurat 49:13).

Preamble

WHEREAS the age-old human aspirations for a just world order, wherein people could live, develop and prosper in an environment free from fear, oppression, exploitation and deprivation, remains largely unfulfilled;

WHEREAS the Divine Mercy unto mankind reflected in its having been endowed with super-abundant economic sustenance is being wasted, or unfairly or unjustly withheld from the inhabitants of the earth;

WHEREAS Allah (God) has given mankind through His revelations in the Holy Qur'an and the Sunnah of His Blessed Prophet Muhammad an abiding legal and moral framework within which to establish and regulate human institutions and relationships;

WHEREAS the human rights decreed by the Divine Law aim at conferring dignity and honor on mankind and are designed to eliminate oppression and injustice;

WHEREAS by virtue of their Divine source and sanction these rights can neither be curtailed, abrogated or disregarded by authorities, assemblies or other institutions, nor can they be surrendered or alienated; . . .

Therefore we, as Muslims, who believe

a) in God, the Beneficent and Merciful, the Creator, the Sustainer, the Sovereign, the sole Guide of mankind and the Source of all Law;

b) in the Vicegerency (Khilafah) of man who has been created to fulfill the Will of God on earth;

c) in the wisdom of Divine guidance brought by the Prophets, whose mission found its culmination in the final Divine message that was conveyed by the prophet Muhammad (Peace be upon him) to all mankind;

d) that rationality by itself without the light of revelation from God can neither be a sure guide in the affairs of mankind nor provide spiritual nourishment to the human soul, and, knowing that the teachings of Islam represent the quintessence of Divine guidance in its final and perfect form, feel duty-bound to remind man of the high status and dignity bestowed on him by God;

e) in inviting all mankind to the message of Islam;

f) that by the terms of our primeval covenant with God our duties and obligations have priority over our rights, and that each one of us is under a bounden duty to spread the teachings of Islam by word, deed, and indeed in all gentle ways, and to make them effective not only in our individual lives but also in the society around us;

g) in our obligation to establish an Islamic order:

i) wherein all human beings shall be equal and none shall enjoy a privilege or suffer a disadvantage or discrimination by reason of race, color, sex, origin or language;

ii) wherein all human beings are born free;

iii) wherein slavery and forced labor are abhorred;

iv) wherein conditions shall be established such that the institution of family shall be preserved, protected and honored as the basis of all social life;

v) wherein the rulers and the ruled alike are subject to, and equal before, the Law;

vi) wherein obedience shall be rendered only to those commands that are in consonance with the Law;

vii) wherein all worldly power shall be considered as a sacred trust, to be exercised within the limits prescribed by the Law and in a manner approved by it, and with due regard for the priorities fixed by it;

viii) wherein all economic resources shall be treated as Divine blessings bestowed upon mankind, to be enjoyed by all in accordance with the rules and the values set out in the Qur'an and the Sunnah;

ix) wherein all public affairs shall be determined and conducted, and the authority to administer them shall be exercised after mutual consultation (*Shura*) between the believers qualified to contribute to a decision which would accord well with the Law and the public good;

x) wherein everyone shall undertake obligations proportionate to his capacity and shall be held responsible pro rata for his deeds;

xi) wherein everyone shall, in case of an infringement of his rights, be assured of appropriate remedial measures in accordance with the Law;

xii) wherein no one shall be deprived of the rights assured to him by the Law except by its authority and to the extent permitted by it;

xiii) wherein every individual shall have the right to bring legal action against anyone who commits a crime against society as a whole or against any of its members;

xiv) wherein every effort shall be made to

(a) secure unto mankind deliverance from every type of exploitation, injustice and oppression,

(b) ensure to everyone security, dignity and liberty in terms set out and by methods approved and within the limits set by the Law;

Do hereby, as servants of Allah and as members of the Universal Brotherhood of Islam, at the beginning of the Fifteenth Century of the Islamic Era, affirm our commitment to uphold the following inviolable and inalienable human rights that we consider are enjoined by Islam.

I.   Right to Life

a) Human life is sacred and inviolable and every effort shall be made to protect it. In particular no one shall be exposed to injury or death, except under the authority of the Law.

b)   Just as in life, so also after death, the sanctity of a person's body shall be inviolable. It is the obligation of believers to see that a deceased person's body is handled with due solemnity.

II.   Right to Freedom

a)   Man is born free. No inroads shall be made on his right to liberty except under the authority and in due process of the Law.

b)   Every individual and every people has the inalienable right to freedom in all its forms: physical, cultural, economic and political—and shall be entitled to struggle by all available means against any infringement or abrogation of this right; and every oppressed individual or people has a legitimate claim to the support of other individuals and/or peoples in such a struggle.

III.   Right to Equality and Prohibition Against Impermissible Discrimination

a)   All persons are equal before the Law and are entitled to equal opportunities and protection of the Law.

b)   All persons shall be entitled to equal wage for equal work.

c)   No person shall be denied the opportunity to work or be discriminated against in any manner or exposed to greater physical risk by reason of religious belief, color, race, origin, sex or language.

IV.   Right to Justice

a)   Every person has the right to be treated in accordance with the Law, and only in accordance with the Law.

b)   Every person has not only the right but also the obligation to protest against injustice; to recourse to remedies provided by the Law in respect of any unwarranted personal injury or loss;

to self-defense against any charges that are preferred against him and to obtain fair adjudication before an independent judicial tribunal in any dispute with public authorities or any other person.

c)   It is the right and duty of every person to defend the rights of any other person and the community in general (Hisbah).

d)   No person shall be discriminated against while seeking to defend private and public rights.

e)   It is the right and duty of every Muslim to refuse to obey any command which is contrary to the Law, no matter by whom it may be issued.

V.   Right to Fair Trial

a)   No person shall be adjudged guilty of an offense and made liable to punishment except after proof of his guilt before an independent judicial tribunal.

b)   No person shall be adjudged guilty except after a fair trial and after reasonable opportunity for defense has been provided to him.

c)   Punishment shall be awarded in accordance with the Law, in proportion to the seriousness of the offense and with due consideration of the circumstances under which it was committed.

d)   No act shall be considered a crime unless it is stipulated as such in the clear wording of the Law.

e)   Every individual is responsible for his actions. Responsibility for a crime cannot be vicariously extended to other members of his family or group, who are not otherwise directly or indirectly involved in the commission of the crime in question.

VI.   Right to Protection Against Abuse of Power

Every person has the right to protection against harassment by official agencies. He is not liable to account for himself except for making a defense to the charges made against him or where he is found in a situation wherein a question regarding suspicion of his involvement in a crime could be reasonably raised.

VII.   Right to Protection Against Torture

No person shall be subjected to torture in mind or body, or degraded, or threatened with injury either to himself or to anyone related to or held dear by him, or forcibly made to confess to the commission of a crime, or forced to consent to an act which is injurious to his interests.

VIII.   Right to Protection of Honor and Reputation

Every person has the right to protect his honor and reputation against calumnies, groundless charges or deliberate attempts at defamation and blackmail.

IX.   Right to Asylum

a)   Every persecuted or oppressed person has the right to seek refuge and asylum. This right is guaranteed to every human being irrespective of race, religion, color and sex.

b)   Al Masjid Al Haram (the sacred house of Allah) in Mecca is a sanctuary for all Muslims.

X.   Rights of Minorities

a)   The Qur'anic principle "There is no compulsion in religion" shall govern the religious rights of non-Muslim minorities.

b)   In a Muslim country religious minorities shall have the choice to be governed in respect of their civil and personal matters by Islamic law, or by their own laws.

XI. Right and Obligation to Participate in the Conduct and Management of Public Affairs

a) Subject to the Law, every individual in the community *(Ummah)* is entitled to assume public office.

b) Process of free consultation *(Shura)* is the basis of the administrative relationship between the government and the people. People also have the right to choose and remove their rulers in accordance with this principle.

XII. Right to Freedom of Belief, Thought and Speech

a) Every person has the right to express his thoughts and beliefs so long as he remains within the limits prescribed by the Law. No one, however, is entitled to disseminate falsehood or to circulate reports which may outrage public decency, or to indulge in slander, innuendo or to cast defamatory aspersions on other persons.

b) Pursuit of knowledge and search after truth is not only a right but a duty of every Muslim.

c) It is the right and duty of every Muslim to protest and strive (within the limits set out by the Law) against oppression even if it involves challenging the highest authority in the state.

d) There shall be no bar on the dissemination of information provided it does not endanger the security of the society or the state and is confined within the limits imposed by the Law.

e) No one shall hold in contempt or ridicule the religious beliefs of others or incite public hostility against them; respect for the religious feelings of others is obligatory on all Muslims.

XIII. Right to Freedom of Religion

Every person has the right to freedom of conscience and worship in accordance with his religious beliefs.

XIV. Right to Free Association

a) Every person is entitled to participate individually and collectively in the religious, social, cultural and political life of his community and to establish institutions and agencies meant to enjoin what is right *(ma'roof)* and to prevent what is wrong *(munkar)*.

b) Every person is entitled to strive for the establishment of institutions whereunder an enjoyment of these rights would be made possible. Collectively, the community is obliged to establish conditions so as to allow its members full development of their personalities.

XV. The Economic Order and the Rights Evolving Therefrom

a) In their economic pursuits, all persons are entitled to the full benefits of nature and all its resources. These are blessings bestowed by God for the benefit of mankind as a whole.

b) All human beings are entitled to earn their living according to the Law.

c) Every person is entitled to own property individually or in association with others. State ownership of certain economic resources in the public interest is legitimate.

d) The poor have the right to a prescribed share in the wealth of the rich, as fixed by Zakah, levied and collected in accordance with the Law.

e) All means of production shall be utilized in the interest of the community *(Ummah)* as a whole, and may not be neglected or misused.

f) In order to promote the development of a balanced economy and to protect society from exploitation, Islamic law forbids monopolies, unreasonable restrictive trade practices, usury, the use of coercion in the making of contracts and the publication of misleading advertisements.

g)   All economic activities are permitted provided they are not detrimental to the interests of the community (*Ummah*) and do not violate Islamic laws and values.

XVI.   Right to Protection of Property

No property may be expropriated except in the public interest and on payment of fair and adequate compensation.

XVII.   Status and Dignity of Workers

Islam honors work and the worker and enjoins Muslims not only to treat the worker justly but also generously. He is not only to be paid his earned wages promptly, but is also entitled to adequate rest and leisure.

XVIII.   Right to Social Security

Every person has the right to food, shelter, clothing, education and medical care consistent with the resources of the community. This obligation of the community extends in particular to all individuals who cannot take care of themselves due to some temporary or permanent disability.

XIX.   Right to Found a Family and Related Matters

a)   Every person is entitled to marry, to found a family and to bring up children in conformity with his religion, traditions and culture. Every spouse is entitled to such rights and privileges and carries such obligations as are stipulated by the Law.

b)   Each of the partners in a marriage is entitled to respect and consideration from the other.

c)   Every husband is obligated to maintain his wife and children according to his means.

d)   Every child has the right to be maintained and properly brought up by its parents, it being forbidden that children are made to work at an early age or that any burden is put on them which would arrest or harm their natural development.

e) If parents are for some reason unable to discharge their obligations towards a child it becomes the responsibility of the community to fulfill these obligations at public expense.

f) Every person is entitled to material support, as well as care and protection, from his family during his childhood, old age or incapacity. Parents are entitled to material support as well as care and protection from their children.

g) Motherhood is entitled to special respect, care and assistance on the part of the family and the public organs of the community (*Ummah*).

h) Within the family, men and women are to share in their obligations and responsibilities according to their sex, their natural endowments, talents and inclinations, bearing in mind their common responsibilities toward their progeny and their relatives.

i) No person may be married against his or her will, or lose or suffer diminution of legal personality on account of marriage.

XX. Rights of Married Women

Every married woman is entitled to:

a) live in the house in which her husband lives;

b) receive the means necessary for maintaining a standard of living which is not inferior to that of her spouse, and, in the event of divorce, receive during the statutory period of waiting (*iddah*) means of maintenance commensurate with her husband's resources, for herself as well as for the children she nurses or keeps, irrespective of her own financial status, earnings, or property that she may hold in her own rights;

c) seek and obtain dissolution of marriage (*Khul'a*) in accordance with the terms of the Law. This right is in addition to her right to seek divorce through the courts.

d) inherit from her husband, her parents, her children and other relatives according to the Law;

e) strict confidentiality from her spouse, or ex-spouse if divorced, with regard to any information that he may have obtained about her, the disclosure of which could prove detrimental to her interests. A similar responsibility rests upon her in respect of her spouse or ex-spouse.

XXI. Right to Education

a) Every person is entitled to receive education in accordance with his natural capabilities.

b) Every person is entitled to a free choice of profession and career and to the opportunity for the full development of his natural endowments.

XXII. Right of Privacy

Every person is entitled to the protection of his privacy.

XXIII. Right to Freedom of Movement and Residence

a) In view of the fact that the World of Islam is veritably Ummah Islamia, every Muslim shall have the right to freely move in and out of any Muslim country.

b) No one shall be forced to leave the country of his residence, or be arbitrarily deported therefrom without recourse to due process of Law.

Treaty of Medina: Prophet Muhammad (ﷺ) Final Farewell Address, Often Cited as a Powerful Reminder of the Essence of Shariah

Full Text of the Madina Charter

This is a document from Muhammad the Prophet (may Allah bless him and grant him peace), governing relations between the Believers i.e. Muslims of Quraysh and Yathrib and those who followed them and worked hard with them. They form one nation—Ummah.

The Quraysh Mohajireen will continue to pay blood money, according to their present custom.

In case of war with any body they will redeem their prisoners with kindness and justice common among Believers. (Not according to pre-Islamic nations where the rich and the poor were treated differently.)

The Bani Awf will decide the blood money, within themselves, according to their existing custom.

In case of war with anybody all parties other than Muslims will redeem their prisoners with kindness and justice according to practice among Believers and not in accordance with pre-Islamic notions.

The Bani Saeeda, the Bani Harith, the Bani Jusham and the Bani Najjar will be governed on the lines of the above (principles).

The Bani Amr, Bani Awf, Bani Al-Nabeet, and Bani Al-Aws will be governed in the same manner.

Believers will not fail to redeem their prisoners they will pay blood money on their behalf. It will be a common responsibility of the Ummah and not of the family of the prisoners to pay blood money.

A Believer will not make the freedman of another Believer as his ally against the wishes of the other Believers.

The Believers, who fear Allah, will oppose the rebellious elements and those that encourage injustice or sin, or enmity or corruption among Believers.

If anyone is guilty of any such act all the Believers will oppose him even if he be the son of any one of them.

A Believer will not kill another Believer, for the sake of an un-Believer (i.e. even though the un-Believer is his close relative).

No Believer will help an un-Believer against a Believer.

Protection (when given) in the Name of Allah will be common. The weakest among Believers may give protection (In the Name of Allah) and it will be binding on all Believers.

Believers are all friends to each other to the exclusion of all others.

Those Jews who follow the Believers will be helped and will be treated with equality. (Social, legal and economic equality is promised to all loyal citizens of the State.)

No Jew will be wronged for being a Jew.

The enemies of the Jews who follow us will not be helped.

The peace of the Believers (of the State of Madina) cannot be divided. (It is either peace or war for all. It cannot be that a part of the population is at war with the outsiders and a part is at peace).

No separate peace will be made by anyone in Madina when Believers are fighting in the Path of Allah.

Conditions of peace and war and the accompanying ease or hardships must be fair and equitable to all citizens alike.

When going out on expeditions a rider must take his fellow member of the Army-share his ride.

The Believers must avenge the blood of one another when fighting in the Path of Allah (This clause was to remind those in front of whom there may be less severe fighting that the cause was common to all. This also meant that although each battle appeared a separate entity it was in fact a part of the War, which affected all Muslims equally).

The Believers (because they fear Allah) are better in showing steadfastness and as a result receive guidance from Allah in this respect. Others must also aspire to come up to the same standard of steadfastness.

No un-Believer will be permitted to take the property of the Quraysh (the enemy) under his protection. Enemy property must be surrendered to the State.

No un-Believer will intervene in favor of a Quraysh, (because the Quraysh has declared war are the enemy).

If any un-believer kills a Believer, without good cause, he shall be killed in return, unless the next of kin are satisfied (as it creates law and order problems and weakens the defense of the State). All Believers shall be against such a wrong-doer. No Believer will be allowed to shelter such a man.

When you differ on anything (regarding this Document) the matter shall be referred to Allah and Muhammad (may Allah bless him and grant him peace).

The Jews will contribute towards the war when fighting alongside the Believers.

The Jews of Bani Awf will be treated as one community with the Believers. The Jews have their religion. This will also apply to their freedmen. The exception will be those who act unjustly and sinfully. By so doing they wrong themselves and their families.

The same applies to Jews of Bani Al-Najjar, Bani Al Harith, Bani Saeeda, Bani Jusham, Bani Al Aws, Thaalba, and the Jaffna, (a clan of the Bani Thaalba) and the Bani Al Shutayba.

Loyalty gives protection against treachery. (Loyal people are protected by their friends against treachery. As long as a person remains loyal to the State he is not likely to succumb to the ideas of being treacherous. He protects himself against weakness.)

The freedmen of Thaalba will be afforded the same status as Thaalba themselves. This status is for fair dealings and full justice as a right and equal responsibility for military service.

Those in alliance with the Jews will be given the same treatment as the Jews.

No one (no tribe which is party to the Pact) shall go to war except with the permission of Muhammed (may Allah bless him and grant him peace). If any wrong has been done to any person or party it may be avenged.

Any one who kills another without warning (there being no just cause for it) amounts to his slaying himself and his household, unless the killing was done due to a wrong being done to him.

The Jews must bear their own expenses (in War) and the Muslims bear their expenses.

If anyone attacks anyone who is a party to this Pact the other must come to his help.

They (parties to this Pact) must seek mutual advice and consultation.

Loyalty gives protection against treachery. Those who avoid mutual consultation do so because of lack of sincerity and loyalty.

A man will not be made liable for misdeeds of his ally.

Anyone (any individual or party) who is wronged must be helped.

The Jews must pay (for war) with the Muslims. (This clause appears to be for occasions when Jews are not taking part in the war. Clause 37 deals with occasions when they are taking part in war.)

Yathrib will be Sanctuary for the people of this Pact.

A stranger (individual) who has been given protection (by anyone party to this Pact) will be treated as his host (who has given him protection) while (he is) doing no harm and is not committing any crime. Those given protection but indulging in anti-state activities will be liable to punishment.

A woman will be given protection only with the consent of her family (Guardian). (A good precaution to avoid inter-tribal conflicts).

In case of any dispute or controversy, which may result in trouble the matter must be referred to Allah and Muhammed (may Allah bless him and grant him peace), The Prophet (may Allah bless him and grant him peace) of Allah will accept anything in this document, which is for (bringing about) piety and goodness.

Quraysh and their allies will not be given protection.

The parties to this Pact are bound to help each other in the event of an attack on Yathrib.

If they (the parties to the Pact other than the Muslims) are called upon to make and maintain peace (within the State) they must do so. If a similar demand (of making and maintaining peace) is made on the Muslims, it must be carried out, except when the Muslims are already engaged in a war in the Path of Allah. (So that no secret ally of the enemy can aid the enemy by calling upon Muslims to end hostilities under this clause.)

Everyone (individual) will have his share (of treatment) in accordance with what party he belongs to. Individuals must benefit or suffer for the good or bad deed of the group they belong to. Without such a rule party affiliations and discipline cannot be maintained.

The Jews of al-Aws, including their freedmen, have the same standing, as other parties to the Pact, as long as they are loyal to the Pact. Loyalty is a protection against treachery.

Anyone who acts loyally or otherwise does it for his own good (or loss).

Allah approves this Document.

This document will not (be employed to) protect one who is unjust or commits a crime (against other parties of the Pact).

Whether an individual goes out to fight (in accordance with the terms of this Pact) or remains in his home, he will be safe unless he has committed a crime or is a sinner. (i.e. No one will be punished in his individual capacity for not having gone out to fight in accordance with the terms of this Pact.)

Allah is the Protector of the good people and those who fear Allah, and Muhammad (may Allah blesses him and grants him peace) is the Messenger of Allah (He guarantees protection for those who are good and fear Allah).[616]

---

616. For in-depth analysis of this covenant see al-Ghunaimi, *Muslim Conception of International Law*, 37.

Glossary of Arabic Terms

SUNNAH—The example or way of life of the Prophet (peace be upon him), embracing what he said, did or agreed to.

KHALIFAH—The vicegerency of man on earth or succession to the Prophet, transliterated into English as the Caliphate.

HISBAH—Public vigilance, an institution of the Islamic State enjoined to observe and facilitate the fulfillment of right norms of public behavior. The "Hisbah" consists in public vigilance as well as an opportunity to private individuals to seek redress through it.

MA'ROOF—Good act.

MUNKAR—Reprehensible deed.

ZAKAH—The 'purifying' tax on wealth, one of the five pillars of Islam obligatory on Muslims.

'IDDAH—The waiting period of a widowed or divorced woman during which she is not to re-marry.

KHUL'A—Divorce a woman obtains at her own request.

UMMAH ISLAMIA—World Muslim community.

SHARI'AH—Islamic law.

Bibliography

Abdallah, Ustaz Yoonus. "Crime, Punishment and Evidence in Islamic Law." In *Understanding Shari'a in Nigeria*, edited by A. M. Yakubu, A. M. Kani, and M. I. Junaid, 37–51. Ibadan, Nigeria: Spectrum Books, 2001.

Abdul-Rahman, Muhammad Saed. *Islam: Questions and Answers—Islamic History and Biography.* Vol. 14. London: MSA Publication, 2003.

———. *Islam: Questions and Answers—Jurisprudence and Islamic Rulings; Transactions, part 8.* Vol. 29. London: MSA Publication, 2004.

———. *Tafsir Ibn Kathir Juz' (Part 26): Al-Ahqaf 1 to Az-Zariyat 30.* London: MSA Publication, 2009.

———. *The Meaning and Explanation of the Glorious Qur'an.* Vol. 9. London: MSA Publication, 2008.

Abiad, Nisrine. *Shariah, Muslim States and International Human Rights Treaty Obligations: A Comparative Study.* London: British Institute of International and Comparative Law, 2008.

Abiodun, J. O. "Remembering Claude Ake: The Social Scientist." In *The Challenge of African Development: Tributes and Essays in Honor of Claude*

Ake, edited by Centre for Advanced Social Science. Port Harcourt, Nigeria: Centre for Advanced Social Science, 1998.

Abu-Nimer, Mohammed. *Nonviolence and Peace Building in Islam:Theory and Practice*. Gainesville, FL: University Press of Florida, 2003.

Adams, Bert N., and Jan Trost. *Handbook on World Families*. London: Sage Publications, 2005.

Adegbite,Abdul-Lateef."Discussion to 'Shari'a in a Multi-Religious Society: The Case of Nigeria' by A. H. Yadudu." In *Understanding Shari'a in Nigeria*, edited by A. M.Yakubu, A. M. Kani, and M. I. Junaid, 145–55. Ibadan, Nigeria: Spectrum Books, 2001.

Adesiyan, David Odunola. *An Accused Person's Rights in Nigerian Criminal Law*. Ibadan, Nigeria: Heinemann Educational Books, 1996.

Ado-Kurawa, Ibrahim. *Shariah and the Press in Nigeria: Islam Versus Western Christian Civilization*. Kano, Nigeria: Kurawa Holdings, 2001.

Aguda, T. Akinola. "The Common Man and the Common Law." In *The Crisis of Justice*, 24–43. Akure, Nigeria: Eresu Hills Publication, 1986.

Ahmad, Ali. "Living with Conflict: Shariah and One Nigeria." Address given at the Sawyer-Mellon Seminar on Sharia and Conflict, Emory University, November 7, 2002.

Ahmed,Akbar S. *Discovering Islam: Making Sense of Muslim History and Society*. London: Routledge, 2002.

Akande, Jadesola O. *Laws and Customs Affecting Women's Status in Nigeria*. Lagos, Nigeria: International Federation of Women Lawyers, Nigeria, 1979.

Akbar, M. M. *Authenticity of Quran*. Vol. 1. Kochi, India: Niche of Truth, 2002.

Algar, Hamid. *Roots of the Islamic Revolution in Iran: Four Lectures by Hamid Algar*. Revised and expanded ed. Oneonta, NY: Islamic Publications International, 2001.

Ali, Abbas J. *Islamic Perspectives on Management and Organization*. Cheltenham, UK: Edward Elgar, 2005.

Ali, Syed Bashir. *Scholars of Hadith*. Skokie, IL: IQRA' International Educational Foundation, 2000.

Amar, Vikram David, and Mark V. Tushnet, eds. *Global Perspectives on Constitutional Law*. New York: Oxford University Press, 2009.

Ambali, M. A. *The Practice of Family Law in Nigeria*. 2nd ed. Zaria, Nigeria: Tamaza Publishing, 2003.

———. *The Practice of Muslim Family Law in Nigeria*. Zaria, Nigeria: Tamaza Publishing, 1998.

American Law Reports. Vol. 4. Lawyers Co-operative Publishing Company, 1919.

An-Na'im, Abdullahi Ahmed. *Islam and the Secular State: Negotiating the Future of Shariah*. Cambridge, MA: Harvard University Press, 2008.

———. *Toward An Islamic Reformation: Civil Liberties, Human Rights, and International Law*. New York: Syracuse University Press, 1990.

Anil, Ela, and C. Arin. *Turkish Civil and Penal Code Reforms from a Gender Perspective: The Success of Two Nationwide Campaigns*. Istanbul, Turkey: Women for Women's Human Rights—New Way, 2005.

Ansay, Tugrul, and Don Wallace, Jr. *Introduction to Turkish Law*. 6th ed. Alphen aan den Rijn, Netherlands: Kluwer Law International, 2011.

Anderson, J. *Islamic Law in Africa*. New York: Frank Cass and Company, 2005.

Aristotle. *Politics.* Edited by William Ellis. Cambridge, MA: Echo Library, 2006.

Aruri, Naseer, and Muhammed A. Shuraydi, eds. *Revising Culture, Reinventing Peace: The Influence of Edward W. Said.* New York: Olive Branch Press, 2001.

Asad, Muhammad. *Islam and Politics.* Geneva: Islamic Centre, 1963.

Asadullah, Abubakr. *Islam Vs. West: Fact or Fiction? A brief Historical, Political, Theological, Philosophical and Psychological Perspective.* iUniverse, 2009.

Ashraf, Muhammad. *The First Written Constitution in the World.* Lahore, Pakistan: Muhammad Ashraf, 1968.

Ashrof, V. A. Mohamad. *Islam and Gender Justice: Questions at the Interface.* Satyawati Nagar, Delhi, India: Kalpaz Publications, 2005.

At-Tahan, Mustafa M. *Perfect Muslim Character: In the Modern World.* Edited by Joanne McEwan and Jeewan Chanicka. Cairo, Egypt: El-Falah Publishing, 1999.

Austin, Frederic. "The Law of Nations." In *Chautauquan* 34 (Oct. 1901– March 1902): 27–33.

Baamir, Abdulrahman Yahya. *Shari'a Law in Commercial and Banking Arbitration: Law and Practice in Saudi Arabia.* Surrey, UK: Ashgate, 2010.

Bah, Alpha Mahmoud. *Glimpses of Life After Death: Revised Edition.* Writer's Club Press, 2003.

Bakhit, M.A. al-, L. Bazin, S. M. Cissoko, M. S. Asimov, and A. Gieysztor, eds. *History of Humanity: Scientific and Cultural Development: From the Seventh to the Sixteenth Century.* Vol. 4. London: Unesco, 2000.

Bambale, Yahaya Yunusa. *Crime and Punishment Under Islamic Law.* 2nd ed. Ibadan, Nigeria: Malthouse Press, 2003.

Barlas, Asma. *"Believing Women" in Islam: Unreading Patriarchal Interpretations of the Qur'an.* Austin, TX: University of Texas Press, 2002.

Bayes, Jane H., and Nayereh Esfahlani Tohidi, eds. *Globalization, Gender, and Religion: The Politics of Women's Rights in Catholic and Muslim Contexts.* New York: Palgrave Macmillan, 2001.

Bayrak, Shaykh Tosun. *The Path of Muhammad: A Book on Islamic Morals and Ethics.* Bloomington, IN: World Wisdom, 2005.

Bello, Mohammed. "Keynote Address." In *Understanding Shari'a in Nigeria*, edited by A. M. Yakubu, A. M. Kani, and M. I. Junaid, 7–14. Ibadan, Nigeria: Spectrum Books, 2001.

Benditt, Theodore M. *Law as Rule and Principle: Problems of Legal Philosophy.* Stanford, CA: Stanford University Press, 1978.

Bennison, Amira K. *Great Caliphs: The Golden Age of the Abbasid Empire.* New Haven, CT: Yale University Press, 2009.

Bentham, Jeremy. *An Introduction to the Principles of Morals and Legislation.* Edited by J. H. Burns and H. L. A. Hart. New York: Oxford University Press, 1996.

Bernstein, Elizabeth, and Laurie Schaffner, eds. *Regulating Sex: Sexual Freedom and the Politics of Intimacy.* New York: Routledge, 2004.

Beyani, Chaloka. "Toward a More Effective Guarantee of Women's Rights in the African Human Rights System." In *Human Rights of Women: National and International Perspectives*, edited by Rebecca J. Cook, 285–306. Philadelphia, PA: University of Pennsylvania Press, 1994.

Bingham, Thomas Henry. *The Rule of Law.* New York: Allen Lane, 2010.

Birt, Barbara. "Let He Who Casts the First Stone." *TimesLive*, December 16, 2009, http://www.timeslive.co.za/opinion/letters/article235375.ece.

Bonner, Michael David. *Jihad in Islamic History: Doctrines and Practice.* Princeton, NJ: Princeton University Press, 2008.

Bouhidiba, Abdelwahab, and Muhammad Ma'rūf Dawālī, eds. *The Different Aspects of Islamic Culture: The Individual and Society in Islam.* Paris: Unesco, 1998.

Bowie, Norman E., and Robert L. Simon. *The Individual and the Political Order: An Introduction to Social and Political Philosophy.* Lanham, MD: Rowman & Littlefield, 1998.

Bradley, John R. *Behind the Veil of Vice: The Business and Culture of Sex in the Middle East.* 1st ed. New York: Palgrave Macmillan, 2010.

Brand, Danie, ed. *Socio-Economic Rights in South Africa.* Pretoria, South Africa: Pretoria University Law Press, 2009.

Browning, Don S., M. Christian Green, and John Witte, Jr. *Sex, Marriage, and Family in World Religions.* New York: Columbia University Press, 2009.

Bugaje, Usman. "Education, Values, Leadership and the Future of Nigeria." Unpublished paper, 2005.

———. "The Islamic Political System and The Political Future of Nigeria," August 3, 1986. http://www.webstar.co.uk/~ubugaje/system4.html

Burlingame, Roger. *Engines of Democracy: Inventions and Society in Mature America.* New York: Ayer, 1976.

Burton, J. "The Origin of the Islamic Penalty of Adultery." *Transactions of Glasgow University Oriental Society* 26 (1978): 12–26.

Caldarola, Carlo, ed. *Religions and Societies: Asia and the Middle East.* Berlin, Germany: Mouton, 1982.

Campo, Juan Eduardo. *The Other Sides of Paradise: Explorations into the Religious Meanings of Domestic Space in Islam.* Columbia, SC: University of South Carolina Press, 1991.

Caner, Ergun, and Emir Fethi Caner. *Unveiling Islam: An Insider's Look at Muslim Life and Beliefs.* Grand Rapids, MI: Kregel Publications, 2009.

Cantemir, Dimitrie. *The History of the Growth and Decay of the Othman Empire.* Translated by N. Tindal. London: 1734.

Carper, Donald L., John A. McKinsey, and Bill W. West. *Understanding the Law.* 5th ed. Cincinatti, OH: Southwestern College Pub, 2007.

Casper, Gerhard. "Rule of Law? Whose Law?" Keynote lecture at the Central European and Euro-Asia Law Initiative (CEELI) Award Ceremony for the American Bar Association, San Francisco, California, 2003.

Chaudhry, Muhammad Sharif. *Human Rights in Islam.* Lahore, Pakistan: All Pakistan Islamic Education Congress, 1993.

Cheema, Shabbir G. *Building Democratic Institutions: Governance Reform in Developing Countries.* Bloomfield, CT: Kumarian Press, 2005.

Chukkul, S. K. "The Penal Code: Origins, Application and Limitations." In *Understanding Shari'a in Nigeria,* edited by A. M. Yakubu, A. M. Kani, M. I. Junaid, 158–66. Ibadan, Nigeria: Spectrum Books, 2001.

Civil Liberties Organization (Nigeria). *Islam and human rights: a human rights education-training manual for Islamic organizations in Nigeria.* Lagos, Nigeria: Civil Liberties Organization, 1999.

Clarke, Kamari Maxine. *Fictions of Justice: The International Criminal Court and the Challenge of Legal Pluralism in Sub-Saharan Africa.* New York: Cambridge University Press, 2009.

Clinton, Robert N., and Richard A Matasar. *Casenote Legal Briefs: Federal Court.* New York: Aspen Publishers, 2003.

Cohen, Ronald Lee, ed. *Justice: Views from the Social Sciences.* New York: Springer, 1986.

Coker, Francis William. "James Harrington 1611–1677." In *Readings in Political Philosophy*, 355–382. New York: Macmillan, 1914.

Convention on the Elimination of Discrimination Against Women. "Convention on the Elimination of All Forms of Discrimination Against Women: Third Report of Canada Covering the Period January 1, 1987 to December 31, 1990." Ottawa, ON: Multiculturalism and Citizenship Canada, 1992.

Cooper, Anderson. "Woman Awaits Stoning Appeal." In *Anderson Cooper 360*, edited by Jeff Koinange. USA: CNN, 2003.

Cornell, Vincent J. *Voices of Islam: Voices of Tradition*. Westport, CT: Praeger Publishers, 2007.

Curtis, Edward E., IV, ed. *The Columbia Sourcebook of Muslims in the United States*. New York: Columbia University Press, 2008.

Dan-Musa, Iro Abubakar. *Party Politics and Personal Struggle in Nigeria*. Abuja, Nigeria: Regent, 2004.

Daniels, Kate, M. A. Abdel Haleem, and Adel Omar Sharif. *Criminal Justice in Islam: Judicial Procedure in the Sharia*. New York: I. B. Tauris, 2003.

Darmaputera, Eka. *Pancasila and the Search for Identity and Modernity in Indonesian Society: A Cultural and Ethical Analysis*. Leiden, Netherlands: Brill, 1988.

Dāwūd, Sunan Abī. *Abū Dādūd Sulaymān ibn al-Ashdath al-Sijistānī: The Third Correct Tradition of the Prophetic Sunna*. Beirut, Lebanon: Dar al-Kotob al-Ilmiyah, 2008.

Deif, Farida. *Perpetual Minors: Human Rights Abuses Stemming from Male Guardianship and Sex Segregation in Saudi Arabia*. New York: Human Rights Watch, 2008.

Doi, Abdur Rahman I. *The Cardinal Principles of Islam (According to the Maliki System)*. Lagos, Nigeria: Islamic Publications Bureau, 1974.

————. *Sharīah: The Islamic Law*. London: Ta-Ha Publishers, 1984.

————. *Sharīah Islamic Law: Revised and Expanded by Clarke Abdassamad*. London: Ta-Ha Publishers, 2008.

————. *The Western Civilization, Islam, and the Muslim Youth*. Cambridge, UK: Muslim Publishing House, 1980.

————. *Women in Sharīah*. London: Ta-Ha Publishers, 1989.

Donders, Yvonne, and Vladimir Volodin, eds. *Human Rights in Education, Science, and Culture: Legal Developments and Challenges*. Hampshire, UK: Ashgate, 2007.

Douglas, Elmer H., ed. *The Mystical Teachings of al-Shadhili: Including His Life, Prayers, Letters, and Followers*. Translated from the Arabic of Ibn al-Sabbagh's Durratal-Asrar wa Tuhfat al-Abrar. Albany NY: State University of New York Press, 1993.

Dowden, Richard. "Africa: Altered States, Ordinary Miracles." *Public Affairs* 1 (2009): 445.

Draz, M. A. *The Moral World of the Quran*. Translated by Danielle Robertson and Rebecca Masterton. London: I. B. Tauris, 2008.

Eagle, William. "Sharia/Comparison." Washington, DC: Global Security, April 26, 2000. http://www.globalsecurity.org/military/library/news/2000/04/000426-islam1.htm

Eaton, Gai. *Islam and the Destiny of Man*. New York: New York Press, 1985.

El Fadl, Khaled Abou. *Speaking in God's Name: Islamic Law, Authority and Women*. Oxford, UK: Oneworld Publications, 2001.

El-Nimr, Raga'. "Women in Islam." In *Feminism and Islam: Legal and Literary Perspectives*, edited by Mai Yamani, 88–101. London: Garment Publishing, 1996.

El-Rouayheb, Khaled. *Before Homosexuality in the Arab-Islamic World, 1500-1800*. Chicago: University of Chicago Press, 2005.

Elias, Taslim Olawale. *The Nigerian Legal System*. London: Routledge and Kegan Paul, 1963.

Emerton, Robyn, Kristine Adams, Andrew Byrnes, and Jane Connors, *International Women's Rights Cases*. Portland, OR: Routledge-Cavendish, 2005.

Engineer, Asghar Ali. *The Rights of Women in Islam*. New Delhi, India: Sterling, 2004.

Esak, Farid. *Quran, Liberation and Pluralism: An Islamic Perspective of England*. Oxford, UK: Oneworld Publications, 1997.

Esposito, John L., ed. *The Oxford History of Islam*. New York: Oxford University Press, 1999.

Esposito, John L., and John O. Voll. *Islam and Democracy*. New York: Oxford University Press, 1996.

Etzioni, Amitai. *Security First: For a Muscular, Moral Foreign Policy*. New Haven, CT: Yale University Press, 2007.

Evans, Malcolm, and Rachel Murray, eds. *The African Charter on Human and Peoples' Rights: The System in Practice 1986–2006*. 2nd ed. Cambridge, UK: Cambridge University Press, 2008.

Eze, Osita C. *Human Rights in Africa: Some Selected Problems*. Lagos, Nigeria: Nigerian Institute of International Affairs & Macmillan, 1976.

Ezzati, A. *A Concise Description of Islamic Law and Legal Opinions*. London: ICAS Press, 2008.

Farooqi, Ausaf. "The Islamic State in the 21 Century." Paper presented during the Fall 2007 lecture series, "Law of Nationbuilding," Chicago-Kent College of Law, October 3, 2007.

Faroqhi, Suraiya. *The Ottoman Empire: A Short History*. Translated by Shelley Frisch. Princeton, NJ: Markus Wiener Publishers, 2009.

Faruqi, I. R. al-. *Social and Natural Sciences*. Islamic Education Series. Jeddah: Hodder and Stoughton, King Abdul-Aziz University, 1981.

Feldman, Noah. *The Fall and Rise of the Islamic State*. Princeton, NJ: Princeton University Press, 2008.

Finckenauer, James O. *The Russian Youth: Law, Deviance, and the Pursuit of Freedom*. New Brunswick, NJ: Transaction Publishers, 1995.

Finnegan, Jim. "Turmoil in the Middle East: Should It Have Been Predicted?" American Century Investments blog, March 8, 2011. http://americancenturyblog.com/2011/03/turmoil-in-the-middle-east-should-it-have-been-predicted/.

Flynn, Vince. *Separation of Power*. New York: Pocket Books, 2001.

Foltz, Richard C. *Animals in Islamic Tradition and Muslim Cultures*. Oxford, UK: One World, 2006.

Franck, Hans Goran, Klas Nyman, and William Schabas. *The Barbaric Punishment: Abolishing the Death Penalty*. New York: Martinus Nijhoff, 2003.

Franco, Paul. *The Political Philosophy of Michael Oakeshott*. New Haven, CT: Yale University Press, 1990.

Friedman, Yaron. *The Nuaayri-Alawis: An Introduction to the Religion, History and Identity*. New York: Brill, 2009.

Friedrich, Carl J. *The Philosophy of Law in Historical Perspective*. 2nd ed. Chicago: University of Chicago Press, 1963.

Frost, Bryan-Paul, and Jeffrey Sikkenga. *History of American Political Thought*. Lanham, MD: Lexington Books, 2003.

Fuller, Lon L. *The Morality of Law: Storrs Lectures on Jurisprudence, Yale Law School, 1963.* New Haven, CT: Yale University Press, 1964.

Gadamer, Hans-Georg. *Truth and Method.* London: Continuum, 1960.

Gambari, Ibrahim A. "Africa and the United Nations in the 21st Century: Challenges and Prospects." Inaugural lecture at The United Nations and Africa's Development in the 21st Century, Africa Centre/United Nations Information Centre Lecture Series, February 7, 2001.

Ghali, M. M. *A Selection of Hadiths of the Prophet.* Cairo, Egypt: New Vision for Translation of Culture, 2008.

Ghamidi, Javed Ahmad. *Oaths and Their Atonement.* Lahore, Pakistan: al-Mawrid, 2005.

Ghanea, Nazila, ed. *Minorities, Peoples, and Self-determination: An Essay in Honor Of Patrick Thornberry.* Leiden, Netherlands: Martinus and Nijhoff, 2004.

Ghunaimi, Mohammad Talaat al-. *The Muslim Conception of International Law and the Western Approach.* The Hague: Martinus Nijhoff, 1968.

———. "Justice and Human Rights in Islam." In *Justice and Human Rights in Islamic Law*, 1–13. Washington, DC: International Law Institute, 1997.

Gish, Steven. *Desmond Tutu: A Biography.* Westport, CT: Greenwood Press, 2004.

Gledhill, Alan. *The Penal Codes of Northern Nigeria and Sudan.* Lagos, Nigeria: African Universities Press, 1963.

Goebel, Julius, Jr. "King's Law and Local Custom in Seventeenth-Century New England." *Columbia Law Review* 31, no. 3 (March 1931): 416–48.

Government of Madras. *The Yearbook of Legal Studies*. Edited by the Department of Legal Studies Law College. Madras, India: Government of Madras, 1960.

Goyette, John, Mark S. Latkovic, and Richard S. Myers, eds. *St. Thomas Aquinas and the Natural Law Tradition: Contemporary Perspectives*. Washington, DC: Catholic University of America Press, 2004.

Gutto, Shadrack. *Equality and Non-Discrimination in South Africa*. South Africa: David Philip, 2002.

Haddad, Yvonne Yazbeck, John L. Esposito, Elizabeth Hiel, and Hibba Abugiderri. *The Islamic Revival since 1988: A Critical Survey and Bibliography*. Westport, CT: Greenwood Press, 1995.

Haghayeghi, Mehrdad. *Islam and Politics in Central Asia*. New York: St. Martin's Press, 1996.

Haleem, Muhammad Abdel, Adel Omar Sherif, and Kate Daniels, eds. *Criminal Justice in Islam: Judicial Procedure in the Sharia*. New York: I. B. Tauris, 2003.

Hall, James Parker, and James De Witt Andrews. *American Law and Procedure*. Vol. 2. Chicago: La Salle Extension University, 1911.

Hallaq, Wael B. *An Introduction to Islamic Law*. Cambridge, UK: Cambridge University Press, 2009.

———. *Shari'a: Theory, Practice, Transformations*. Cambridge, UK: Cambridge University Press, 2009.

Hammond, Scott J., Kevin R. Hardwick, and Howard Leslie Lubert. *Classics of American Political and Constitutional Thought: Origins through the Civil War*. Vol. 1. Indianapolis, IN: Hackett, 2007.

Hanif, N. *Islamic Concept of Crime and Justice: Crime and Justice (Social, Religious and Economic)*. Vol. 2. New Delhi, India: Sarup & Sons, 1999.

Harnischfeger, Johannes. *Democratization and Islamic Law: The Sharia Conflict in Nigeria*. Chicago: University of Chicago Press, 2008.

Harris, Rabia Terri. "Reading the Signs: Unfolding Truth and the Transformation of Authority." In *Windows of Faith: Muslim Women Scholar-Activists in North America*, 172–96. New York: Syracuse University Press, 2000.

Hashimi, Muhammad Ali. *The Ideal Muslim: The True Islamic Personality as Defined by the Qur'an and Sunnah*. Beirut, Lebanon: International Islamic Publishing House, 1997.

Hathout, Maher, Uzma Jamil, Gasser Hathout, and Nayyer Ali. *In Pursuit of Justice: The Jurisprudence of Human Rights in Islam*. Los Angeles, CA: Muslim Public Affairs Council, 2006.

Hayek, Friedrich A. *The Constitution of Liberty*. Chicago: University of Chicago Press, 1960.

———. *The Road to Serfdom: Text and Documents (the Collected Works of F. A. Hayek)*. Edited by Bruce Caldwell. Vol. 2. Chicago: University of Chicago Press, 2007.

Hefner, Robert W., and Patricia Horvatich, eds. *Islam in an Era of Nation-States: Politics and Religious Renewal in Muslim Southeast Asia*. Honolulu, HI: University of Hawai'i Press, 1997.

Heper, Metin, and Nur Bilge Criss. *Historical Dictionary of Turkey*. 3rd ed. Plymouth, UK: Scarecrow Press, 2009.

Heyns, C. *Human Rights Law in Africa*. The Hague, Netherlands: Kluwer Law International, 1996.

Hiskett, Mervyn. *The Development of Islam in West Africa*. New York: Longman, 1994.

Hood, Ralph W., Jr., Peter C. Hill, and W. Paul Williamson. *The Psychology of Religious Fundamentalism*. 1st ed. New York: Guilford Press, 2005.

Hourani, Albert Habib. *A History of the Arab Peoples*. London: Faber, 2002.

Hudson, Wayne, and Azyumardi Azra, eds. *Islam Beyond Conflict: Indonesian Islam and Western Political Theory*. Hampshire, UK: Ashgate, 2008.

Husni, Ronak, and Daniel L. Newman. *Muslim Women in Law and Society: Annotated Translation of al-Ṭāhir al-Haddād's Imra'tunā fi 'l-sharīʿa wa 'l-mujtamaʿ*, with an introduction. New York: Routledge, 2007.

Hussain, Shaikh Shaukat. *Human Rights in Islam*. New Delhi: Kitab Bhavan, 1994.

Hutchison, David. *The Foundations of the Constitution*. Secaucus, NJ: University Books, 1975.

Ibn al-Hajjaj, Imam Abul Hussain Muslim. *Sahîh Muslim*. Translated by Nasiruddin al-Khattab. Houston, TX: Darussalam, 2007.

Ibrahim, Hassan Ahmed. *Sayyid Abd al-Ramān al-Mahdī: A Study of Neo-Mahdīsm in the Sudan*. Boston, MA: Brill, 2004.

Ibrahim, I. A. *A Brief Illustrated Guide to Understanding Islam*. 2nd ed. Houston, TX: Darussalam, 1997.

İlkkaracan, Pinar. *Deconstructing Sexuality in the Middle East: Challenges and Discourses*. Hampshire, UK: Ashgate, 2008.

Imber, Colin, and Norman Calder. *Islamic Jurisprudence in the Classical Era*. New York: Cambridge University Press, 2010.

Inbau, Fred E., James R. Thompson, James B. Zagel, and James, P. Manak. *Criminal Law and Its Administration*. 6th ed. New York: Foundation Press, 1997.

Intan, Benyamin Fleming. *Public Religion and the Pancasila-Based State of Indonesia: An Ethical and Sociological Analysis*. New York: Peter Lang, 2006.

Ipgrave, Michael, and David Marshall, eds. *Humanity: Texts and Contexts; Christian and Muslim Perspectives.* Washington, DC: Georgetown University Press, 2011.

Iqbal, Muhaimin. *General Takaful Practice: Technical Approach to Eliminate Gharar.* Jarkata, Indonesia: Gema Isani Press, 2005.

Ishaq', Ibn. *The Life of Muhammad: A Translation of Ishaq's Sirat Rasul Allah.* Oxford, UK: Oxford University Press, 2004.

Jahangir, Asma, and Hina Jilani. *The Hudood Ordinances: A Divine Sanction.* Lahore, Pakistan: Sang-E-Meel Publications, 2003.

Jega, Attahiru, ed. *Identity Transformation and Identity Politics under Structural Adjustment in Nigeria.* Stockholm, Sweden: Nordic Africa Institute, 2000.

Jenkins, Philip. *The Muslim World: An Overview.* World of Islam. Broomall, PA: Mason Crest Publishers, 2009.

Jones, Jeffrey Richard. *Criminal Procedure Code in the Northern States of Nigeria.* 2nd ed. Zaria, Nigeria: Gaskiya Corporation, 1978.

————. *Some cases on criminal procedure and evidence in the Northern States of Nigeria (1968–1969).* Compiled and annotated by Jones. Zaria, Nigeria: Jones, 1969.

Kaczorowska, Alina. *Public International Law.* New York: Routledge, 2010.

Kadish, Sanford H., ed. *Encyclopedia of Crime and Justice.* New York: Free Press, 1983.

Kamali, Mohammad Hashim. *Freedom, Equality and Justice in Islam.* Kuala Lumpur, Malaysia: Ilmiah Publishers, 2002.

————. *Freedom of Expression in Islam.* Cambridge, UK: Islamic Texts Society, 1997.

————. *Principles of Islamic Jurisprudence*. Cambridge, UK: Islamic Texts Society, 2005.

————. *Shariah Law: An Introduction*. Oxford, UK: Oneworld Publications, 2008.

————. *A Textbook of Hadīth Studies: Authenticity, Compilation, Classification and Criticism of Hadīth*. Leicestershire, UK: Islamic Foundation, 2005.

Kamaruzaman, Kamar Oniah. *Understanding Islam: Contemporary Discourse*. Kuala Lumpur, Malaysia: Saba Islamic Media, 2007.

Kamrava, Mehran. *Islam, Justice and Politics*. London: I. B. Tauris, 2006.

————, ed. *The New Voices of Islam: Rethinking Politics and Modernity—a Reader*. Los Angeles, CA: University of California Press, 2006.

Kardam, Nuket. *Turkey's Engagement with Global Women's Human Rights*. Gender in a Global/Local World. Burlington, VT: Ashgate, 2005.

Karibi-Whyte, A. G. *History and Sources of Nigerian Criminal Law*. Ibadan, Nigeria: Spectrum Law Publishing, 1993.

Keller, Timothy. *Generous Justice: How God's Grace Makes Us Just*. New York: Dutton Adult, 2010.

Khadduri, Majid, and Herbert J. Liebesny, eds. *Law in the Middle East: Origin and Development of Islamic Law*. Clark, NJ: Law Book Exchange, 2008.

Khadduri, Majid, and R. K. Ramazani. *The Islamic Conception of Justice*. Baltimore, MD: Johns Hopkins University Press, 2001.

Khaldun, Ibn, Franz Rosenthal, and N. J. Dawood. *The Muqaddimah: An Introduction to History*. Princeton, NJ: Princeton University Press, 1989.

Khan, Arshad. *Islam, Muslims, and America: Understanding the Basis of Their Conflict*. New York: Algora Publishing, 2003.

Khan, Maimul Ahsan. *Human Rights in the Muslim World: Fundamentalism, Constitutionalism, and International Politics*. Durham, NC: Carolina Academic Press, 2003.

Khan, Muhammad Zafrulla. *Gardens of the Righteous*. London: Curzon Press, 1975.

Khan, Shahnaz. *Zina, Transnational Feminism and the Moral Regulation of Pakistani Women*. Vancouver, BC: University of British Columbia Press, 2007.

Khan, Shujaat. *Family Life Under Islam*. New Delhi, India: Anmol Publications, 2004.

Kidder, Daniel Parish. *The Jewish Nation: Containing an Account of their Manners and Customs, Rites and Worship, Laws and Polity*. New York: Lane & Scott, 1850.

Kirwin, Matthew. "Popular Perceptions of Shari'a Law in Nigeria." *Afro Barometer Briefing Paper*, no. 58 (February 2009): 1–12.

Kohnert, Dirk. "New Nationalism and Development in Africa." *Africa Spectrum* 44, no. 1 (2009): 111–23.

Korieh, Chima Jacob. "Islam and Politics in Nigeria: Historical Perspectives." In *Religion, History, and Politics in Nigeria: Essays in Honor of Ogbu U. Kalu*, edited by Chima Jacob Korieh and G. Ugo Nwokeji, 111–27. Lanham, MD: University Press of America, 2005.

Kravchenko, Svitlana, and John E. Bonine. *Human Rights and the Environment: Cases, Law, and Policy*. Durham, NC: Carolina Academic Press, 2008.

Kukah, Matthew H. *Religion, Politics and Power in Northern Nigeria*. Ibadan, Nigeria: Spectrum Books, 1993.

Kumar, Arvind, ed. *Encyclopedia of Human Rights, Violence and Non-Violence*. New Delhi, India: Anmol Publications, 1998.

————. *Women and Crime*. New Delhi, India: Anmol Publications, 2003.

Kumaravadivelu, B. *Cultural Globalization and Language Education*. 1st ed. New Haven, CT: Yale University Press, 2007.

Kumo, Sulaiman. "Shari'a and the Nigerian Constitution: Issues and Perspective." In *Understanding Shari'a in Nigeria*, edited by A. M. Yakubu, A. M. Kani and M. I. Junaid, 167–80. Ibadan, Nigeria: Spectrum Books, 2001.

Kurzman, Charles, ed. *Modernist Islam, 1840–1940: A Sourcebook*. New York: Oxford University Press, 2002.

Labuschagne, Bart C., and Reinhard W. Sonnenschmidt, eds. *Religion, Politics and Law: Philosophical Reflections on the Sources of Normative Order in Society*. Boston, MA: Leiden, 2009.

Laërtius, Diogenes. *Lives, Teachings, and Sayings of Famous Philosophers*. Translated by R. D. Hicks. Cambridge, MA: Harvard University Press, 1972.

Lampe, Gerald E., ed. *Justice and Human Rights in Islamic Law*. Washington, DC: International Law Institute and Shaybani Society of International Law, 1997, 2010.

Lauterpacht, Elihu, and Christopher J. Greenwood, eds. *International Law Reports*. Vol. 127. New York: Cambridge University Press, 2005.

Layish, Aharon. *Shariah and Customs in Libya Tribal Society: An Annotated Translation of Decision from the Shariah Courts of Ajdabiya and Kufra*. Leiden, Netherlands: Brill, 2005.

Lean, Geoffrey, ed. *Tribute to Barbara Ward: Lady of Global Concern*. Ottawa, ON: World Media Institute, 1987.

Lichtenstrader, Ilse. *Islam and the Modern Age*. New York: Noble Offset Printers, 1958.

Lings, Martin. *Muhammad: His Life Based on the Earliest Sources*. Islamic Texts Society, 1991.

Lippman, Matthew, Sean McConville, and Mordechai Yerushalmi. *Islamic Criminal Law and Procedure: An Introduction*. New York: Greenwood Press, 1988.

Lipton, Edward P. *Religious Freedom in the Near East, Northern Africa and the Former Soviet States*. New York: Nova Science Publishers, 2002.

Llewellyn, Karl N., and E. Adamson Hoebel. *The Cheyenne Way: Conflict and Case Law in Primitive Jurisprudence*. Norman, OK: University of Oklahoma Press, 1953.

Louw, Lirette. "Domestic Effect of the Un Human Rights Treaties in Africa," PhD diss., University of Pretoria, South Africa, 2005.

Lovejoy, Paul E., and Pat Ama Tokunbo Williams, eds. *Displacement and the Politics of Violence in Nigeria*. Leiden, Netherlands: Brill, 1997.

Lubet, Steven. *Modern Trial Advocacy: Analysis and Practice*. 4th ed. Louisville, KY: National Institute for Trial Advocacy, 2009.

Machika, Abbas Abdullahi. *Guide to Advocate* (A Translation of Commentary on Tuhfatul Hukkam) by Qadi Ibn Asin. Zaria, Nigeria: Shankori Educational Publisher, 2008.

Mahmood, Tahir. *Personal Law in Islamic Countries: History, Texts, and Comparative Analysis*. New Delhi, India: Allahabad Law Publishers, 1987.

Maier, Richard A. *Human Sexuality in Perspective*. Chicago: Nelson Hall, 1984.

Mani, Rama. *Beyond Retribution: Seeking Justice in the Shadows of War*. Cambridge, UK: Blackwell Publishers, 2000.

Mansour, Aly Aly. "Hudud Crimes." In *The Islamic Criminal Jurisdiction System*, edited by M. Cherif Bassiouni. New York: Oceana Publications, 1982.

Maravall, Jose Mariá, and Adam Przeworski, eds. *Democracy and the Rule of Law*. New York: Cambridge University Press, 2003.

Marshall, Paul. *The Talibanization of Nigeria: Shariah Law and Religious Freedom*. Washington, DC: Freedom House, 2002.

Maryland Court of Appeals. *Reports of Cases Argued and Determined in the Court of Appeals*. Vol. 84. Frederick, MD: Baughman Bros., 1897.

Masterman, Roger. *The Separation of Powers in the Contemporary Constitution: Judicial Competence and Independence in the United Kingdom*. New York: Cambridge University Press, 2011.

Masters, R. E. L., and Robert Edward Lee, eds. *The Anti-Sex: The Belief in the Natural Inferiority of Women: Studies in Male Frustration and Sexual Conflict*. New York: Julian Press, 1964.

Mathur, Sobhag, and K. M. Rai Mettal, eds. *Spectrum of Nehru's Thought*. New York: Wilso, 1994.

Matson, J. N. "The Common Law Abroad: English and Indigenous Laws in the British Commonwealth." *International and Comparative Law Quarterly* 42, no. 4 (October 1993): 753–79.

Maudoodi, Syed Abul Ala. *Human Rights in Islam*. Leicester, UK: Islamic Publication, 1977.

Mayer, Ann Elizabeth. *Islam and Human Rights: Tradition and Politics*. 4th ed. Boulder, CO: Westview Press, 2007.

Mazrui, Alamin M. and Willy M. Mutunga, eds. *Debating the African Condition: Ali Mazrui and His Critics*. Trenton, NJ: Africa World Press, 2003.

McHugh, Carolyn B. "Separation of Powers." *Utah State Bar Journal* 19 no. 4 (July–August 2006): 1–3.

McMahon, Edward R., and Thomas A. P. Sinclair. *Democratic Institution Performance Research and Policy Perspectives.* Westport, CT: Praeger Publishers, 2002.

McMahon, Rory J. *Practical Handbook for Professional Investigators.* 2nd ed. Boca Raton: CRC Press, 2007.

Meyer, Cheryl L. *The Wandering Uterus: Politics and Reproductive Rights of Women.* New York: New York University Press, 1997.

Mir-Hosseini, Ziba. *Marriage and Trial: Islamic Family Law in Iran and Morocco.* New York: I. B. Tauris, 2000.

Mohamed, Mohamed. "Public anger at the recent stoning of a 13-year-old girl in Somalia shows the growing resentment towards the radical Islamists who have gained control of much of the south and centre of the country," BBC, November 12, 2008, http://news.bbc.co.uk/2/hi/7722701.stm

Montesquieu, Charles-Louis de Secondat. *The Personal and the Political: Three Fables by Montesquieu.* Translated by W. B. Allen. Lanham, MD: University Press of America, 2008.

———. *The Spirit of Laws.* Amherst, NY: Prometheus Books, 2002.

Moors, Annelies. *Women, Property, and Islam: Palestinian Experiences, 1920-1990.* New York: Cambridge University Press, 1996.

Mubarakpuri, Shaykh Safur-Rahman al-, and Ismāīl ibn Umar Ibn Kathīr, Hafī al-Rahmān Mubārakfūrī. *Tafsir ibn Kathir.* Riyadh, Saudi Arabia: Darussalam, 2003.

Mudambi, Ram, Pietro Navarra, and Giuseppe Sobbrio, eds. *Economic Welfare, International Business and Global Institutional Change.* Cheltenham, UK: Edward Elgar, 2003.

Muslehuddin, Mohammad. *Judicial System of Islam: Its Origin and Development.* Lahore, Pakistan: Islamic Publications, 1991.

Muzaffar, Chandra. *Human Rights and the New World Order*. Penang, Malaysia: Just World Trust, 1993.

Mwalimu, Charles. *The Nigerian Legal System*. New York: Peter Lang, 2005.

Nachmani, Amikam. *Europe and Its Muslim Minorities: Aspects of Conflict, Attempts at Accord*. Sussex, UK: Sussex Academic Press, 2010.

Naseer, Hasan Aruri, and Muhammad A. Shuraydi. *Revising Culture, Reinventing Peace: The Influence of Edward W. Said*. New York: Olive Branch Press, 2001.

Nasr, Seyyed Hossein. *Philosophy, Literature, and Fine Arts*. Jeddah, Saudi Arabia: Hodder and Stoughton, King Abdul-Aziz University, 1982.

Nasr, Seyyed Vali Reza. *Mawdudi and the Making of Islamic Revivalism*. New York: Oxford University Press, 1996.

Neal, David. *The Rule of Law in a Penal Colony: Law and Politics in Early New South Wales*. Cambridge, UK: Cambridge University Press, 2002.

Nelson, Harold D., ed. *Nigeria: A Country Study*. Washington, DC: American University, 1982.

Northrup, Cynthia Clark, and Elaine C. Prange Turney, eds. *Encyclopedia of Tariffs and Trade in U.S. History: Debating the Issues; Selected Primary Documents*. Vol. 2. Westport, CT: Greenwood Press, 2003.

O'Kane, John, and Bernd Radtke. *The Concept of Sainthood in Early Islamic Mysticism: Two Works by Al Hakim al-Tirmidhi*. Sufi Series. Concord, MA: Routledge, 1996.

Obilade, Akintunde Olusegun. *The Nigerian Legal System*. Ibadan: Spectrum Books, 2005.

Ojiakor, Ngozi, and Iyke Ojih. *Readings in Nigerian Peoples and Culture*. Enugu, Nigeria: NGIB Publishers, 2006.

Okike, Benedict Ohabughiro. *The Practice of Sharia in Nigeria: A Democratic Secular State.* Imo, Nigeria: Amamihe Publications, 2000.

Olowu, Dejo. *An Integrative Rights-Based Approach to Human Development in Africa.* Pretoria, South Africa: Pretoria University Law Press, 2009.

Omran, Abdel Rahim. *Family Planning in the Legacy of Islam.* New York, NY: Routledge, 2004.

Orens, Geoffrey, ed. *The Muslim World.* New York: H. W. Wilson, 2003.

Orire, Abdulkadir. "Shariah: A Legal System and a Way of Life." In *Understanding Shari'a in Nigeria,* edited by A. M. Yakubu, A. M. Kani and M. I. Junaid, 25–36. Ibadan, Nigeria: Spectrum Books, 2001.

Osman, Mohammed Taib. *Malaysian World-View.* Pasir Panjang, Singapore: Southeast Asian Studies Program, Institute of Southeast Asian Studies, 1986.

Otto, Jan Michiel, ed. *Sharia Incorporated: A Comparative Overview of the Legal Systems of Twelve Muslim Countries in Past and Present.* Amsterdam: Leiden University Press, 2010.

Ouguergouz, Fatsah. *The African Charter on Human and Peoples' Rights: A Comprehensive Agenda for Human Dignity and Sustainable Democracy in Africa.* New York: Aspen Publishers, 2003.

Outhwaite, William. *The Blackwell Dictionary of Modern Social Thought.* Malden, MA: Wiley-Blackwell, 2006.

Owens, Erik C., John D. Carlson, and Eric P. Elshtain, eds. *Religion and the Death Penalty: A Call for Reckoning.* Grand Rapids, MI: Wm. B. Eerdmans, 2004.

Oyebode, Akin. *Law and Nation-Building in Nigeria: Selected Essays.* Lagos, Nigeria: Centre for Political and Administrative Research, 2005.

Palacio, Ana, Caroline Mary Sage, and Michael J. Woolcock. *Law, Equity, and Development.* Washington, DC: The World Bank, 2006.

Pant, Ashok. *It Is Continued.* Lincoln, NE: iUniverse, 2003.

Parekh, Bhikhu C. *Jeremy Bentham: Critical Assessments.* Vol. 1. London: Routledge, 1993.

Patel, Muhammad. *365: A Saying a Day of Hope and Mercy from Prophet Muhammad.* London: Xlibris, 2011.

Patterson, Dennis, ed. *A Companion to Philosphy of Law and Legal Theory.* 2nd ed. Malden, MA: Blackwell Publishers, 2010.

Peters, Rudolph. *Crime and Punishment in Islamic Law: Theory and Practice from the Sixteenth to the Twenty-First Century.* Cambridge, UK: Cambridge University Press, 2005.

————. *The Reintroduction of Islamic Criminal Law in Northern Nigeria: A Study Conducted on Behalf of the European Commission.* Lagos, Nigeria: Spectrum Books, 2001.

Philips, Abu Ameenah Bilal. *The Fundamentals of Tawheed: Islamic Monotheism.* Riyadh, Saudi Arabia: International Islamic Publishing House, 2006.

"'Political Shariah'? Human Rights and Islamic Law in Northern Nigeria." *Human Right Watch Report* 14 (September 21, 2004).

Pollis, Adamantia, and Peter Schwab, eds. *Human Rights: New Perspectives, New Realities.* Boulder, CO: Lynne Rienner Publishers, 2000.

Ponomareff, Constantin V., and Kenneth A. Bryson. *The Curve of the Sacred: An Exploration of Human Spirituality.* Amsterdam: Editions Rodopi BV, 2006.

Pound, Roscoe. *The Separation of Powers.* Indianapolis, IN: National Foundation for Education in American Citizenship, 1945.

Qaradawi, Yusuf al-. *Islam: An Introduction*. Kuala Lumpur, Malaysia: Islamic Book Trust, 2010.

Qasmi, A. H., ed. *International Encyclopedia of Islam*. New Delhi, India: Isha Books, 2006.

Quraishi, Asifa. "Her Honor: An Islamic Critique of the Rape Laws of Pakistan from a Woman-Sensitive Perspective." In *Windows of Faith: Muslim Women Scholar-Activists in North America*, edited by Gisela Webb, 102–35. New York: Syracuse University Press, 2000.

Qushayri, Abu-l-Qasim al-. *The Risalah: Principles of Sufism*. Edited by Laleh Barkhtiar, translated by Rabia Harris. Great Books of the Islamic World, edited by Seyyed Hossein Nasr. Chicago: KAzi Publications, 2001.

Rafiabadi, Hamad Naseem. *Saints and Saviours of Islam*. New Delhi, India: Sarup & Sons, 2005.

Ramadan, Hisham M. *Understanding Islamic Law: From Classical to Contemporary*. Oxford, UK: AltaMira Press, 2006.

Rane, Halim. *Reconstructing Jihad Amid Competing International Norms*. New York: Palgrave Macmillan, 2009.

Ranger, Terence O., ed. *Evangelical Christianity and Democracy in Africa*. New York: Oxford University Press, 2008.

Rauf, Feisal Abdul. *What's Right with Islam: A New Vision for Muslims and the West*. New York: HarperOne, 2004.

Rejwan, Nissim. *The Many Faces of Islam: Perspectives on a Resurgent Civilization*. Gainesville, FL: University Press of Florida, 2000.

Research Society of Pakistan. *Journal of the Research Society of Pakistan* 28 (1991): 25.

Richardson, Sam Scruton, and T. H. Williams. *The Criminal Procedure Code of Northern Nigeria*. London: Sweet & Maxwell, 1963.

Riddell, Peter G., and Tony Street, eds. *Islam: Essays on Scripture, Thought, and Society: A Festschrift in Honour of Anthony H. Johns*. Leiden, Netherlands: Brill, 1997.

Rippin, Andrew. *Muslims: Their Religious Beliefs and Practices*. 3rd ed. New York: Routledge, 2005.

Roald, Anne Sofie. *Women In Islam: The Western Experience*. London: Routledge, 2001.

Rosen, Lawrence. *The Anthropology of Justice: Law as Culture in Islamic Society*. Lewis Henry Morgan Lectures. Cambridge, UK: Cambridge University Press, 1989.

Ross, Susan Deller. *Women's Human Rights: The International and Comparative Law Casebook*. Philadelphia, PA: University of Pennsylvania Press, 2008.

Rushd, Ibn. *The Distinguished Jurist's Primer*. Berkshire, UK: Garnet Publishing, 2000.

Sadiki, Larbi. *The Search for Arab Democracy: Discourses and Counter-Discourses*. New York: Columbia University Press, 2002.

Safi, Louay. *Tensions and Transitions in the Muslim World*. Dallas, TX: University Press of America, 2003.

Saiyidain, K. G. *Islam: The Religion of Peace*. New Delhi: Islam & the Modern Age Society, 1976.

Salahi, Adil. *Muhammad: Man and Prophet; A Complete Study of the Life of the Prophet of Islam*. Leicester, UK: Islamic Foundation, 2002.

Salama, Ma'amoun M. *The Islamic Criminal Jurisdiction System*. Edited by M. Cherif Bassiouni. New York: Oceana Publication, 1982.

Sanusi, Sanusi Lamido. "Fundamentalist Groups and the Nigerian Legal System: Some Reflections," 79–82. London: Women Living Under

Muslim Laws, 2004. http://www.wluml.org/sites/wluml.org/files/import/english/pubs/pdf/wsf/09.pdf

Schabas, William. *The Death Penalty as Cruel Treatment and Torture: Capital Punishment Challenged in the World's Courts*. Boston, MA: Northeastern University Press, 1996.

————, ed. *The International Sourcebook on Capital Punishment*. London: Northeastern University Press, 1997.

Schabas, William A., and Peter Hodgkinson. *Capital Punishment: Strategies for Abolition*. New York: Cambridge University Press, 2004.

Seng, Michael. "In Conflict between Equal Rights for Women and Customary Law: The Botswana Court of Appeal Chooses Equality." *University of Toledo Law Review* 24 (Spring 1993): 543–82.

Senghor, Jeggan Colley, and Nana Poku, eds. *Towards Africa's Renewal*. Hampshire, UK: Ashgate, 2007.

Sevastik, Per, ed. *Legal Assistance to Developing Countries*. 1st ed. The Hague, Netherlands: Kluwer Law International, 1997.

Shah, Niaz A. *Women, the Koran and International Human Rights Law: The Experience of Pakistan*. Leiden, Netherlands: Martinus Nijhoff, 2006.

Shah-Kazemi, Reza. *Justice and Remembrance: Introducing the Spirituality of Imam Ali*. London: I. B. Tauris, 2007.

Sheikh, Muhammad Sultan, and Al-Ma'soomi Al-Khajnadee. *Should a Muslim Follow a Particular Madhhab?* New York: Darussalam, 1998.

Sherburn, Michael A. *Caring for the Caregiver: Eight Truths to Prolong Your Career*. Boston, MA: Jones and Bartlett Publishers, 2006.

Shujaat, Mohammad. *Social Justice in Islam*. New Delhi, India: Anmol Publications, 2004.

Sidahmad, Muhammad Ata Alsid. *The Hudud:The Hudud are the Seven Specific Crimes in Islamic Criminal Law and their Mandatory Punishments.* Petaling Jaya, Malaysia: Muhammad Ata al Sid Sid Ahmad, 1995.

Siddiqui, Ali Liaquat. "The Concept of Justice: Western and Islamic." In *Justice and Human Rights in Islam.* Edited by Gerald E. Lampe. Washington, DC: International Law Institute, 1997.

Sindjoun, Luc, ed. *The Coming African Hour: Dialectics of Opportunities and Constraints.* Pretoria, South Africa: Africa Institute of South Africa, 2010.

Singh, N. K. *Social Justice and Human Rights in Islam.* New Delhi, India: Gyan Publishing, 1998.

Smith, David Whitten, and Elizabeth Geraldine Burr. *Understanding World Religions: A Road Map for Justice and Peace.* Plymouth, UK: Rowman & Littlefield, 2007.

Smith, M. G. *Government in Zazzau 1800–1950.* London: Oxford University Press for the International African Institute, 1960.

Sodiq, Yushau. *An Insider Guide to Islam.* Fort Worth, TX: Trafford, 2010.

Soukhanov, Anne H., and Kaethe Ellis, eds. *Webster's II New Riverside University Dictionary.* Boston, MA: Riverside Publishing, 1976.

Steers, Richard M., and Luciara Nardon. *Managing in the Global Economy.* New York: M. E. Sharpe, 2006.

Stoltenberg, John. *Refusing to Be a Man: Essays on Sex and Justice.* 2nd ed. London: Routledge, 2000.

Stone, Julius. *Human Law and Human Justice.* Stanford, CA: Stanford University Press, 1965.

———. *The Province and Function of Law: Law as Logic, Justice and Social Control.* Cambridge, MA: Harvard University Press, 1950.

Sufian, Sandy, and Mark LeVine, eds. *Reapproaching Borders: New Perspectives on the Study of Israel-Palestine*. Lanham, MD: Rowman & Littlefield, 2007.

Sulami, Mishal Fahm. *The West and Islam: Western Liberal Democracy Versus the System of Shura*. New York: Routledge Curzon, 2003.

Sullivan, Roger J. *Immanuel Kant's Moral Theory*. Cambridge, UK: Cambridge University Press, 1989.

Taylor, Paul M. *Freedom of Religion: United Nations and European Human Rights Law of Practice*. Cambridge, UK: Cambridge University Press, 2005.

Tobi, Niki. *Sources of Nigerian Law*. Lagos, Nigeria: MIJ Professional Publishers, 1996.

Toorawa, Shawkat M., and Roger Allen, eds. *Islam: A Short Guide to The Faith*. Cambridge, UK: Wm. B. Eerdmans, 2011.

Umozurike, U. Oji. *The African Charter on Human and Peoples' Rights*. Cambridge, MA: Martinus Nijhoff, 1997.

Unknown Author. *Hadith of Bukhari*. Vols. 1–4. Forgotten Books, 2008.

Uwakah, Onyebuchi T. *Due Process in Nigeria's Administrative Law System: History, Current Status, and Future*. Lanham, MD: University Press of America, 1997.

Van der Merwe, C. G., and Jacques E. du Plessis, eds. *Introduction to the Law of South Africa*. The Hague, Netherlands: Kluwer Law International, 2004.

Van der Walt, Johan Willem Gous. *Law and Sacrifice: Towards a Post-Apartheid Theory of Law*. London: Birbeck Law Press, 2005.

Vatikiotis, Michael R. J. *Political Change in Southeast Asia: Trimming the Banyan Tree*. New York: Routledge, 1996.

Vikør, Knut S. *Between God and the Sultan: A History of Islamic Law*. New York: Oxford University Press, 2005.

Vogel, Frank E. *Islamic Law and Legal System: Studies of Saudi Arabia*. Leiden, Netherlands: Brill, 2000.

Waliggo, John Mary. *Struggle for Equality: Women and Empowerment in Uganda*. Eldoret, Kenya: Amecea Gaba Publications, 2002.

Wallace, Harvey. *Africa Today*. Denver, CO: Africa Today Associates, 1998.

Wallace, Harvey, and Cliff Roberson. *Principles of Criminal Law*. 4th ed. Boston, MA: Allyn & Bacon, 2007.

Weimann, Gunnar J. *Islamic Criminal Law in Northern Nigeria: Politics, Religion, Judicial Practice*. Amsterdam: Amsterdam University Press, 2010.

Werner, Alice. *The Natives of British Central Africa*. New York: Negro Universities Press, 1969.

White, Theodore H. *The Making of the President 1972*. Reissue ed. New York: Harper Perennial, 2010.

Whitman, James Q. *The Origins of Reasonable Doubt: Theological Roots of the Criminal Trial*. New Haven, CT: Yale University Press, 2008.

Widner, Jennifer A. *Building the Rule of Law: Francis Nyalali and the Road to Judicial Independence in Africa*. New York: W. W. Nortion & Company, 2001.

Williams, Bernard, Graham Langtree, Lynda Jean Clarke, and Susan Amanda Kennick. *One World Many Issues*. Cheltenham, UK: Nelson Thornes, 2001.

Williams, F., and S. Miles. *Hausaland Divided: Colonialism and Independence in Nigeria and Niger*. London: Cornell University Press, 1994.

Williams, Rowan. "Civil and Religious Law: A Religious Perspective." Foundation lecture at the Royal Courts of Justice, London, February 7, 2008.

Witte, John, Jr. *God's Joust, God's Justice: Law and Religion in the Western Tradition*. Cambridge, UK: Wm. B. Eerdmans, 2006.

Witte, John, Jr., and Johan D. van der Vyver, eds. *Religious Human Rights in Global Perspective: Religious Perspectives*. Cambridge, MA: Kluwer Law International, 1996.

Woerlee, G. M. *The Unholy Legacy of Abraham*. Leicester, UK: Matador, 2008.

Wren, J. Thomas. *Inventing Leadership: The Challenge of Democracy*. Cheltenham, UK: Edward Elgar, 2007.

Yadudu, Auwalu Hamisu. "Islamic Law and Reform Discourse in Nigeria: A Comparative Study and Another View." Phd diss., Harvard Law School, 1985.

———. "*Shari'a in a Multi-Religious Society: The Case of Nigeria.*" In *Understanding Shari'a in Nigeria*, edited by A. M. Yakubu, A. M. Kani and M. I. Junaid, 145–55. Ibadan, Nigeria: Spectrum Books, 2001.

Yakubu, A.M., A.M. Kani, and M.I. Junaid, eds. *Understanding Shari'a in Nigeria*. Ibadan, Nigeria: Spectrum Books, 2001.

Yamani, Mai, ed. *Feminism and Islam: Legal and Literary Perspectives*. London: Ithaca Press, 1996.

Younos, Farid. *Gender Equality in Islam*. Bloomington, IN: Authorhouse, 2002.

Yust, Karen-Marie, ed. *Nourishing Child and Adolescent Spirituality: Perspectives from the World's Religious Traditions*. Oxford, UK: Rowman & Littlefield, 2005.

Zafar, Emmanuel. *Law and Practice of Islamic Hudoods.* Lahore, Pakistan: Khyber Law Publishers, 2005.

The Zakat Handbook: A Practical Guide for Muslims in the West. Chicago: The Zakat Foundation of America, 2008.

Zalman, Greta. "Confessions." In *Cases and Materials on the Law of Criminal Procedure in the Northern States of Nigeria.* Zaria, Nigeria: Ahmadu Bello University, 1969.

Zalman, Marvin. *Cases and Materials on the Law of Criminal Procedure in the Northern States of Nigeria.* Zaria, Nigeria: Ahmadu Bello University, 1969.

Index

A

Abdullah bin Amr, 121

Abiodun v. A. G. Federation, 189

Abiola, Alhaji Moshood, 16–17

Abu Hanîfah, 169

Abu Hurairah, 121

ACPRA. *See* African Charter on
Human and Peoples' Rights
(Ratification and Enforcement)
Act

Actus non-facit reum nisi mens sit
rea, 152

Adam, 99–100, 254

Adamu, Idris, 99

Adultery

    laws in Turkey, 52

    penalty of death for, 51

    proof of, 96

Africa, 79

African Charter, 196

African Charter on Human
and Peoples' Rights (Banjul
Charter), 194

African Charter on Human and
Peoples' Rights (Ratification and
Enforcement) Act (ACPRA)

    Abiodun v. A. G. Federation and,
    189

    Article 2, 104, 105

    Article 3, 104

    Article 26, 104

    I. G. P. v. ANPP, 190

    Ration 9, 190

African Commission on Human
and Peoples' Rights, 105,
194–195